Concrete Block Construction

3rd edition

Robert Putnam

With Collaboration of
John Burnett

American Technical Society  Chicago 60637

COPYRIGHT © 1951, 1957, 1973
BY AMERICAN TECHNICAL SOCIETY

Library of Congress Catalog Number: 73-75302

ISBN 0-8269-0507-2

First Edition

1st Printing 1951
2nd Printing 1952
3rd Printing 1953
4th Printing 1955

Second Edition

5th Printing 1957
6th Printing 1959
7th Printing 1961
8th Printing 1964
9th Printing 1966
10th Printing 1970

Third Edition

11th Printing 1973

No portion of this publication may be reproduced by any process such as photocopying, recording, storage in a retrieval system or transmitted by any means without permission of the publisher.

PRINTED IN THE UNITED STATES OF AMERICA

Preface to the Third Edition

The Third Edition of *Concrete Block Construction* is designed to provide a comprehensive guideline for the building tradesman. The concrete masonry fundamentals it presents are important not only for the conventional applications to building construction, but also for the applications of concrete masonry to closely related trades. For the pre-apprentice or apprentice, this new edition offers clear-cut instruction in the fundamentals of concrete block construction. For upgrading and retraining of foremen and construction supervisors, it offers a diversity of coverage with detailed up-to-date information.

The new edition discusses the modern methods of manufacturing which assure products of uniform size and quality. Also: the development of the system of modular coordination of building components, which has simplified and standardized design and planning problems in the building industry, is covered in the new edition.

Accident prevention in the building industry cannot be over-emphasized. For this reason, a new chapter on general safety as well as safety practices in relation to the handling of masonry tools and materials is included.

New chapters have been added to discuss in detail the materials and practices involved in mixing mortar and concrete. The standards and specifications discussed have been carefully researched and checked to conform to the latest standards.

A new chapter has also been added to provide an introduction to prefabricated masonry panel construction which is rapidly developing in the field.

Appendix A offers a review of practical mathematics useful to the mason. Modern communications and reciprocal trade agreements between different nations have created problems because of the lack of a universal standard of weights and measures. For this reason, *Appendix A* includes tables for the conversion of English to metric and metric to English systems of weights and measures.

This book provides an understandable and thorough guideline in trade structure, safety, tools, materials and construction practices for students, apprentices and instructors as well as for journeymen and supervisors in the building trades.

Appreciation is expressed to the National Concrete Masonry Association for their thoughtful advice on the text.

THE PUBLISHERS

Contents

Chapter
- **1** Structure of the Trade, 1
- **2** Safety and Tools, 13
- **3** Mortar: Basic Materials and Mixing, 36
- **4** Concrete: Basic Materials and Mixing, 51
- **5** Concrete Formwork, 70
- **6** Footings: Design and Construction, 95
- **7** Foundations: Design and Construction, 115
- **8** Concrete Block Masonry, 133
- **9** Panel Construction, 196

Appendix
- **A** Math for the Mason, 202
- **B** Constructions with Concrete Block, 214
- Index, 223

Structure of the Trade

Chapter **1**

Of all the various types of masonry units, concrete blocks are by far the most widely used in modern building construction. Almost every new building will employ concrete blocks in some capacity. Walls may be constructed entirely of concrete blocks, or blocks may be used in conjunction with brick masonry, wood or steel framing, or concrete. The advantages of using concrete blocks in construction are numerous. The units are large, lightweight, strong, and inexpensive. They also have excellent sound and temperature insulating properties. It is essential, therefore, that the professional mason have a thorough knowledge of the properties and uses of concrete block.

Structure of the Trade

The masonry trades are structured into various levels of craftsmen: apprentice, journeyman, foreman, superintendent.

Apprenticeship or learning usually lasts three years. From man's earliest history apprentices in the various crafts were indentured (a contract binding one person to work for another for a given length of time to learn a trade) to a master craftsman (a contractor) for a number of years to learn the trade.

In the past, in many cases, the

apprentice's father had to pay the master a fee to get him to teach his son the trade. From the medieval days down through most of the 19th century, the apprentice would live with the master and would get room and board plus some clothing. However, he was a virtual slave to the master, subject to his every wish. Both old and new certificates of apprentice indentures are reproduced on pages 4 and 5.

Note that today the apprentices are protected by Federal, State, and the Local J.A.C. (Joint Apprenticeship Committee) in regard to hours of work, wages, and conditions of employment, and there is no control over the apprentices outside of working hours. Also, apprentices are now selected from applicants who meet the standards of the local J.A.C. In most cases the apprentice is indentured to the J.A.C. and they assign him to a contractor. If the contractor runs out of work, the J.A.C. will place him with another contractor. This permits the J.A.C. to control the training and handle the federal and veteran's paperwork.

The *journeyman* or experienced craftsman is one who has completed an apprenticeship in the trade. He is now a free agent and can work for any contractor he pleases. He may travel from place to place, going where the work is to be found.

The *foreman* is a journeyman who has been placed in the job of supervising a group of men. He is given this job because of his ability as a craftsman and his knowledge of how to supervise other craftsmen.

The *superintendent* is usually a foreman who has been promoted to this important position. He is in charge of all the work in the field for his contractor and supervises the work of the foreman. Some large contractors have a *general superintendent* to oversee the *job superintendents*.

In the construction industry the *foreman* and *superintendent* keep their union membership. Many of the smaller contractors are permitted to retain their union cards in some unions.

Large contractors will employ an *estimator* who works in their offices to estimate the cost of the jobs the contractor wants to bid on. Working from blueprints and specifications, he performs a quantity take off; that is, measures areas to be constructed of masonry and determines the amount of materials required. He must be skilled in mathematics, blueprint reading, trade practices and the cost of labor and materials.

The last person in this team of workers, supervisors and estimator is the *contractor*. He must be knowledgeable in all phases of the business. He must know all the regulations governing the construction industry plus how to provide the money for payrolls and materials.

Structure of the Trade

On-the-Job Contracting Practices

It is common in the trade for a man to work his way up the ladder of responsibility from apprentice to contractor staying at each level until he is proficient and conditions, plus drive, enable him to move ahead. The majority of the contractors in the various skilled trades have worked their way up this ladder. They are craftsmen as well as businessmen.

When a craftsman has worked his way up the ladder of experience and aspires to become a contractor, he must prepare himself for operating under a whole new set of rules and conditions. As a contractor he will be risking his own money on the gamble that his knowledge and experience in estimating work, handling men and keeping up with the paperwork that is required today will pay a profit.

With these factors understood, the new contractor stands ready to bid against his fellow contractors on the work that is available. When there is a good supply of work ready to be bid and the new contractor has a crew of men that he knows can produce the work required, he will have a good chance of success. By starting small and bidding only on work that is fully understood, there is a chance to make money and progress to bigger and better jobs. Contracting is a rewarding endeavor for those who are suited for it by ability, temperament and aggressiveness to stick it out through good and bad times.

Therefore, to be successful the new contractor should consider the following rules, conditions, laws and facts which he will have to know and work with.

1. Develop a good knowledge of estimating material and labor costs to do a given job. Remember that no two jobs are ever alike. Conditions of weather, availability of men, changing costs for materials and labor, plus the differences in architects and general contractors can together or individually change the cost of doing a given job.

2. The contractor must know the laws and regulations he must follow, use and invoke at times to protect himself and his work force. These include the lien laws (used to protect against loss due to failure of the owner or general contractor to pay his bills), local permits and inspections as called for, the collection and payment of federal, state and local taxes on the men employed, sales taxes, use taxes, property and inventory taxes on office and storage yard.

Also there are a number of different types of insurances that must be carried. These include compensa-

Concrete Block Construction

𝕿𝖍𝖎𝖘 𝕴𝖓𝖉𝖊𝖓𝖙𝖚𝖗𝖊 witnesseth, That

Jacob Peterson, with the consent of his mother, Mary Ann Griffith, hath put himself, and by these presents, and for other good causes, doth voluntarily and by his own free will and accord, put himself apprentice to Hiram Miller to learn the art, trade, and mystery of a House Carpenter and, after the manner of an apprentice, to serve the said Hiram Miller from the day of the date hereof, for and during, and to the full end and term of Three Years Ten Months and Fifteen Days next ensuing. During all which time the said apprentice doth covenant and promise, that he will serve his master faithfully, keep his secrets, and obey his lawful commands—that he will do him no damage himself, nor see it done by others, without giving him notice thereof—that he will not waste his goods, nor lend them unlawfully—that he will not play at cards, dice, or any other unlawful game, whereby his master may be injured—that he will neither buy nor sell, with his own goods nor the goods of others, without license from his master—and that he will not absent himself day nor night from his master's service, without his leave—nor haunt ale-houses, taverns, nor play-houses; but in all things behave as a faithful apprentice ought to do, during the said term. And the said master, on his part, doth covenant and promise, that he will use the utmost of his endeavors to teach or cause to be taught or instructed, the said apprentice in the art, trade or mystery of a House Carpenter and that he will procure and provide for him sufficient meat, drink & lodging fitting for an apprentice during the said term—and that he will give him Forty dollars per Year payable Quarterly in lieu of Clothing and two Quarters Night Schooling—And for the true performance of all and singular the covenants and agreements aforesaid, the said parties bind themselves each unto the other, firmly, by these presents.

In witness whereof, the said parties have interchangeably set their hands and seals hereunto. Dated the Twentieth day of July, Anno Domini 1844.

THE ABOVE IS AN EXACT TRANSCRIPT OF ORIGINAL INDENTURE WRITTEN IN THE YEAR 1844

Structure of the Trade

BRICKLAYERS AND STONE MASONS APPRENTICE AGREEMENT

THIS AGREEMENT Made this _____ day of _____, 19___, between _____, herein referred to as the "Apprentice", and (if a minor) _____, herein referred to as the "Guardian", and the BRICKLAYERS LOCAL 21 OF ILLINOIS APPRENTICESHIP AND TRAINING PROGRAM, a common law trust created by an agreement dated November 23, 1965, and administered by a Board of Trustees, herein called the "BOARD OF TRUSTEES."

WITNESSETH:

1. THE APPRENTICE AGREES:

    (a) To work under the assignments and direction of the Board of Trustees for a period of 3 years as defined under the Rules and Regulations and Standards as promulgated by the Board of Trustees;

    (b) To accept assignments by the Board of Trustees to such contractor or contractors as the Board of Trustees may from time to time select;

    (c) To accept the wages, hours and working conditions established by the collective bargaining agreements between the UNITED ORDER OF AMERICAN BRICKLAYERS AND STONE MASONS' UNION NO. 21, herein called the "Union," and the BUILDERS' ASSOCIATION OF CHICAGO, and the ASSOCIATED MASONRY CONTRACTORS OF GREATER CHICAGO, in force from time to time during the period of this agreement, as the wages he shall receive from, and the working conditions under which he will be employed by such contractor or contractors;

    (d) While attending the trade school established by the Board of Trustees, he will abide by the Rules and Regulations and Standards adopted by the Board of Trustees and any amendments thereto adopted during the period of this agreement;

    (e) Upon the signing of this agreement and in accordance with the requirements of the collective bargaining agreements, to join the Union; and

    (f) To accept, and be governed by, the decisions of the Coordinator as to his work assignments throughout the period of apprenticeship, subject only to the Apprentice's right of appeal herein provided for.

2. The Apprentice FURTHER AGREES that, if he fails to comply faithfully with all rules and regulations governing his attendance at the trade school established by the Board of Trustees, and all terms and conditions imposed on his on-the-job training by the collective bargaining agreements, he shall be subject to such reasonable penalties as may be imposed by the Coordinator.

3. The Apprentice FURTHER AGREES that the first three months of employment following the signing of this agreement shall be a probationary period; that during this period this agreement may be cancelled by either party without the formality of a hearing; that at the end of each six-month period of employment he will take such examination as may be prescribed by the Coordinator, and that if he does not successfully pass any one of such examinations, his indenture may be cancelled or his probationary period extended. The Apprentice shall have the right to appeal any ruling of the Coordinator to the Board of Trustees.

4. The Apprentice FURTHER AGREES that the Board of Trustees may cancel the apprenticeship agreement and remove the Apprentice from the Apprenticeship Program for cause. Such removal by the Board of Trustees shall cancel his classification of Apprentice and his opportunity to complete his training.

5. THE BOARD OF TRUSTEES AGREES:

    (a) During the period of this agreement it will use every reasonable effort to place the Apprentice with contractors for on-the-job training so that the Apprentice will be employed as continuously as possible and receive training in all phases of the trade specified in the Rules and Regulations and Standards governing the Apprenticeship and Training Program in force from time to time during the period of this agreement. The Board of Trustees does not guarantee full time employment to the Apprentice, if the Board is unable to find contractors ready to accept the Apprentice for on-the-job training.

    (b) Upon successful completion of the apprenticeship term fixed by this agreement, to cause to be issued to the Apprentice a certificate showing him to be a qualified journeyman bricklayer.

6. BOTH PARTIES AGREE that if any differences arise between the Apprentice and the contractor by whom he is employed concerning matters of apprenticeship, they shall be adjusted by the Coordinator, subject to review by the Board of Trustees. If, at any time, the Apprentice feels himself aggrieved by any decision of the Coordinator affecting his apprenticeship, he may appeal to the Board of Trustees for a review of the Coordinator's decision. Such appeal shall be in writing and filed within a reasonable time after the decision. It need not be in any particular form, but shall state clearly the reason for the Apprentice's dissatisfaction with the decision of the Coordinator.

7. This agreement may be cancelled by mutual consent of the parties hereto.

IN WITNESS WHEREOF, the parties hereto have signed this instrument the date and year first above written.

_____
(Signature of Apprentice)

_____
(Parent or Guardian)

BRICKLAYERS LOCAL 21 OF ILLINOIS
APPRENTICESHIP AND TRAINING PROGRAM

By_____
(Apprentice Coordinator)

ATTEST: For the United Order of American Bricklayers and Stone Masons, Local 21 of Illinois of the Bricklayers, Masons and Plasterers' Interntional Union of America.

_____ _____
(President)   (Secretary-Treasurer)

Registered by _____
(Name of registration agency)

Date_____ By_____
(Signature and title of authorized official)

tion, unemployment, accident, property damage, fire, theft, car and truck insurances, business loss, etc. Each one of these items costs quite a bit of money and must be included in the cost of doing business. Too many beginning contractors fail to consider these costs in their bidding of a job and end up having to take it out of the profit (if any) on the job—which is really taking these costs out of their own wages.

3. Most construction will involve tradesmen other than masons: such as carpenters, painters, electricians, plumbers, etc. Each trade, of course, has its own union and working rules. A masonry contractor must be fully aware of the rules of other trade unions and abide by them in order to successfully complete a job.

4. As the contractor advances in work he will find that each architect, general contractor and owner that he works for will have different conditions and rules governing the jobs they design and build. It is therefore very important to study and understand these variations so that the cost of working under these conditions can be added into the bid for the job. The plans and specifications must be gone over carefully to pick out each condition, rule and method set down in both items.

Anything that is not clear should be questioned in writing to the architect before the bid is sent in. No verbal agreement should ever be accepted or given. Everything should be in writing and signed by the architect or the general contractor. Written and signed work orders should be issued for any changes, additions or deletions in the work.

It is the responsibility of each contractor on a job to check the blueprints, specifications, and job site for omissions or errors in his particular field and call them to the attention of the architect. The architect, in turn, will provide the contractor with written or drawn corrections. If the contractor makes any errors in preparation for his work and attempts to overcome them on his own, he assumes responsibility for any resulting flaw or failure in his own work.

All changes in work to be done on the job site should be given in writing as work orders by the architect and general contractor. Temporary lighting, power, cleanup and removal of rubbish, use of scaffolds, use of hoist for lifting material and equipment to various floors, availability of work area in reasonable time to get the work done, storage of material at the job site and on various floors, use of water and many other items must all be agreed on by job conferences between the architect, general contractor and the masonry contractor. The other trades should be consulted on the cost of their services for anything that they will be asked to provide to the contractor.

5. The masonry contractor must

Structure of the Trade

also have available for his men the required equipment which will enable them to do the job in the best and shortest time possible. Poor equipment or trying to do the job with insufficient equipment is a good way to lose money. Scaffolding is a good example of this rule; if the job is short of scaffolding, then there will be a lot of unnecessary moving of scaffolds, resulting in high labor costs.

Not having the masonry materials in the required amounts and in the right place at the right time will increase the labor cost due to high-priced skilled men waiting for material to arrive or to be moved.

6. Labor relations and cost accounting tied in with job financing all combine to make or break a contractor. The contractor must be aware of his labor and overall operating costs under varying conditions. He must be able to keep accurate cost accounts or have an accountant do it for him. Labor costs can vary considerably depending on how many men are available on the labor market and what the contractor's reputation is as a person to work for. As an overall statement, poor cost accounting is one of the most common causes of a contractor's failure.

7. The beginning contractor must also remember that on most commercial jobs, the general contractor retains ten percent of the total contract cost as a protection for him to make sure the masonry contractor will repair any defects or other problems for a period of one year. This means that if the contractor does a number of jobs in a year each one will have this ten percent withheld for one year. This will tie up a lot of his working capital and he may have to borrow additional money to stay in business. The cost of this borrowed money must be included in the cost of the job to enable the contractor to stay in business.

Joint Apprenticeship Committee and Apprenticeship Standards

The building industry has, in cooperation with the U.S. Department of Labor, Bureau of Apprenticeship and Training, set up National Standards of Apprenticeship. These standards define what the term *apprentice* in the trade shall mean. The standards set forth age limits, educational requirements, length of apprenticeship, ratio of apprentices to journeymen, hours of work and wages.

The Joint Apprenticeship Com-

Concrete Block Construction

mittee, commonly known as the J.A.C., is composed of equal representation from labor and management, with consultants from the Bureau of Apprenticeship and the State or local Board of Education attending to act as advisors without a vote.

The J.A.C. has the delegated power to set the local standards consistent with the basic requirements established by the National Committee. The apprentice, when he signs the indenture agreement, agrees to live up to all its provisions and in turn is protected by its rules and regulations.

The J.A.C. also establishes the curriculum for the related classroom work plus supervising the on-the-job training the apprentice receives. When an apprentice completes his training, the J.A.C. notifies the Bureau of Apprenticeship, and this agency issues a completion certificate which is recognized throughout the United States and Canada as proof of reaching journeyman status. See page 8.

Blueprints and Specifications

In addition to practical training with tools and materials, the masonry apprentice will devote much time learning to read and understand blueprints and specifications. This knowledge is essential to the journeyman as well as the foreman and contractor because it is the only way he will know the architectural requirements of a structure. Blueprints or working drawings are the architect's means of communicating instructions for the erection of a structure. They show the location, dimensions, and necessary materials for building the structure.

Specifications are a written set of instructions as to kinds of material, quality of workmanship, etc., that accompany a complete set of working drawings for a structure.

Specifications amplify and supplement the set of working drawings. They also give much of the information that cannot adequately be presented on each sheet of the set of drawings. Specifications also include information such as the legal responsibilities, methods of purchasing equipment, and the insurance requirements on the building.

The blueprints and the specifications function together as a whole. What is in either is considered to be in both. All items which are necessary for the completion of the struc-

Concrete Block Construction

```
FHA Form 2005                U.S. DEPARTMENT OF HOUSING AND URBAN DEVELOPMENT        Form Approved
VA Form 26-1852                          FEDERAL HOUSING ADMINISTRATION               Budget Bureau No. 63-R0055
Rev. 3/68                    For accurate register of carbon copies, form
                             may be separated along above fold. Staple
    Plan 329 (includes 2 car garage)
                             completed sheets together in original order.
    ☐ Proposed Construction          DESCRIPTION OF MATERIALS      No. _____
                                                                        (To be inserted by FHA or VA)
    ☐ Under Construction

Property address _____ City _____ State _____

Mortgagor or Sponsor _____          _____
                            (Name)                              (Address)
Contractor or Builder _____          _____
                            (Name)                              (Address)
```

INSTRUCTIONS

1. For additional information on how this form is to be submitted, number of copies, etc., see the instructions applicable to the FHA Application for Mortgage Insurance or VA Request for Determination of Reasonable Value, as the case may be.
2. Describe all materials and equipment to be used, whether or not shown on the drawings, by marking an X in each appropriate check-box and entering the information called for in each space. If space is inadequate, enter "See misc." and describe under item 27 or on an attached sheet.
3. Work not specifically described or shown will not be considered unless required, then the minimum acceptable will be assumed. Work exceeding minimum requirements cannot be considered unless specifically described.
4. Include no alternates, "or equal" phrases, or contradictory items. (Consideration of a request for acceptance of substitute materials or equipment is not thereby precluded.)
5. Include signatures required at the end of this form.
6. The construction shall be completed in compliance with the related drawings and specifications, as amended during processing. The specifications include this Description of Materials and the applicable Minimum Property Standards.

1. EXCAVATION:
Bearing soil, type __Sand and Gravel__

2. FOUNDATIONS:
Footings: concrete mix __2500 #__ ; strength psi _____ Reinforcing _____
Foundation wall: material __Poured Conc. 8"__ Reinforcing _____
Interior foundation wall: material _____ Party foundation wall _____
Columns: material and sizes __3" adj. Post__ Piers: material and reinforcing _____
Girders: material and sizes __1 Beam 7" at 15.3 #__ Sills: material _____
Basement entrance areaway _____ Window areaways _____
Waterproofing __Tar__ Footing drains _____
Termite protection __Shield at Brick__
Basementless space: ground cover _____ ; insulation _____ ; foundation vents _____
Special foundations _____
Additional information: _____

3. CHIMNEYS:
Material __Face Brick__ Prefabricated (make and size) _____
Flue lining: material __Vitrified Clay__ Heater flue size __8 x 12__ Fireplace flue size __12 x 12__
Vents (material and size): gas or oil heater __5" G.I.__ ; water heater __3" G.I.__
Additional information: _____

4. FIREPLACES: OPTIONAL
Type: ☒ solid fuel; ☐ gas-burning; ☐ circulator (make and size) _____ Ash dump and clean-out __10__
Fireplace: facing __Brick__ ; lining __Fire Brick__ ; hearth __Ceramic__ ; mantel __None__
Additional information: _____

5. EXTERIOR WALLS:
Wood frame: wood grade, and species __Cedar #2__ ☒ Corner bracing. Building paper or felt __15# Felt__
Sheathing __Asphalt impregnated Fiberboard__ ; thickness __1/2"__ ; width __4 x 8__ ; ☒ solid; ☐ spaced __8"__ o.c.; ☐ diagonal;
Siding __Aluminum__ ; grade _____ ; type _____ ; size _____ ; exposure _____ ; fastening __Nailed__
Shingles _____ ; grade _____ ; type _____ ; size _____ ; exposure _____ ; fastening __Per Mfg.__
Stucco _____ ; thickness _____ "; Lath _____ ; weight _____ lb.
Masonry veneer __Face Brick $60/M__ Sills __Lime Stone__ Lintels _____ Base flashing _____
Masonry: ☐ solid ☐ faced ☐ stuccoed; total wall thickness _____ "; facing thickness _____ "; facing material _____
Backup material _____ ; thickness _____ "; bonding _____
Door sills _____ Window sills _____ Lintels _____ Base flashing _____
Interior surfaces: dampproofing _____ coats of _____ ; furring _____
Additional information: _____
Exterior painting: material __Exterior lead and oil__ ; number of coats __3__
Gable wall construction: ☐ same as main walls; ☐ other construction __Aluminum siding in gable__

6. FLOOR FRAMING: 2 x 10 - 16" o.c.
Joists: wood, grade, and species __#2 Fir__ ; other _____ ; bridging __1 x 3__ ; anchors _____
Concrete slab: ☒ basement floor; ☐ first floor; ☐ ground supported; ☐ self-supporting; mix __5 sk.__ ; thickness __3"__
reinforcing _____ ; insulation _____ ; membrane _____
Fill under slab: material __Sand__ ; thickness __4__ ". Additional information: _____

7. SUBFLOORING: (Describe underflooring for special floors under item 21.)
Material: grade and species __1/2" plyscore__ ; size __4 x 8__ ; type __Plyscore__
Laid: ☒ first floor; ☐ second floor; ☐ attic _____ sq. ft.; ☐ diagonal; ☐ right angles. Additional information: __Solid__

Fig. 1-1. The beginning of a typical specifications sheet.

Structure of the Trade

ture, even though not mentioned in one or the other, are considered to be included. If the specifications and the working drawings are in conflict, normally the specifications take precedence. The specifications are binding on all parties, including the sub-contractors.

Fig. 1-1 shows part of a typical specifications sheet used by the Veteran's Administration and the Federal Housing Authority.

The Construction Specifications Institute (CSI) Format

Advances in technology and methods of processing data have often made the reading of specifications cumbersome and confusing. The Construction Specifications Institute in Washington, D.C., has made an attempt to remedy this situation with the publication of the *CSI Format*. The *Format's* value lies in its potential for unifying and universalizing the specifications. It offers a logical framework as well as a standard for the many persons who must read the specifications. The *Format* is comprised of four major groupings:

Bidding Requirements
Contract Forms
General Conditions
Specifications (Technical)

Within this last grouping of *Specifications*, 16 permanent *divisions* are found. These divisions are constant in sequence and short in name. "Divisions" do not name units of work but rather relationships of units of work. The units of work are the "sections" within the divisions.

These divisions were established by considering construction relationships: materials, trades, functions and locations of specified work. The 16 divisions of Specifications in the *Format* are:

Division 1—General Requirements
Division 2—Site Work
Division 3—Concrete
Division 4—Masonry
Division 5—Metals
Division 6—Wood and Plastics
Division 7—Thermal and Moisture Protection
Division 8—Doors and Windows
Division 9—Finishes
Division 10—Specialties
Division 11—Equipment
Division 12—Furnishings
Division 13—Special Construction
Division 14—Conveying Systems
Division 15—Mechanical
Division 16—Electrical

Concrete Block Construction

Checking On Your Knowledge

The following questions give you the opportunity to check up on yourself. If you have read the chapter carefully, you should be able to answer the questions. If you have any difficulty, read the chapter over once more so that you have the information well in mind before you go on with your reading.

DO YOU KNOW

1. What is the difference between brick masonry and cement masonry?
2. How many years does the typical term of apprenticeship last?
3. What is the J.A.C.?
4. Who sets up national standards of apprenticeship?
5. What is an indenture agreement?
6. What happens if the specifications and working drawings are in conflict?
7. What is the CSI format?
8. How the 16 parts of the CSI Specifications are related?

Safety and Tools

Chapter 2

Before beginning actual work on a building, the mason should carefully consider the safety measures necessary to protect himself and his fellow workers against accidents. Every building mechanic should be aware of the particular hazards of his own trade as well as those of associated trades. The accident rate is comparatively high in the building industry. Accidents often result in partial or total disability and are sometimes fatal. In addition to these serious accidents there is the possibility of sustaining innumerable minor cuts and bruises that are not only painful but temporarily handicap the workman. To reduce this accident rate to a minimum, the mason must become safety conscious; he must learn to think of the safety of his fellow workers as well as his own. Every man on the job must know how to prevent accidents, and must have a keen sense of responsibility toward his fellow workmen.

Safety education today has become an important phase of every training program. Under the 1970 Federal *Occupational Safety and Health Act* (OSHA), the employer is required to furnish a place of employment free of known hazards likely to cause death or injury. The *employer* has the specific duty of complying with safety and health standards as set forth under the 1970 act. At the same time, *employees* also have the duty to comply with these standards.

Of first importance in a "Safety First" campaign is the education of the worker. This education must become a part of his daily training

Concrete Block Construction

National Safety Council

National Safety Council

as he learns the technical and manipulative skills of his job. Generally, a person becomes injured because of his own carelessness or the carelessness of some other person. To prevent accidents and injuries, observe all safety regulations, use all safety devices and guards when working with machines, and learn to control your work and actions so as to avoid danger. Training for safety is every bit as important as learning to be a skillful craftsman and should be a part of the worker's education.

In the performance of his work, the mason handles materials, manipulates hand tools, and operates machines which if improperly handled or used may result in serious injury. If an injury should occur, seek first aid no matter how slight the injury. Blood poisoning may result from an insignificant scratch. It is advisable to take a first aid course at the first opportunity.

General Safety on the Job

Safety is a combination of knowledge and awareness: *knowledge* and *skill* in the use and care of your tools and *awareness* on the job of the particular hazards and safety procedures involved. Tool skills may be learned; awareness, however, depends on attitude. An attitude of care and concern while on the job will help prevent injuries not only to yourself, but also to your fellow workers. Always be alert while on the job and follow recommended safety procedures. If in doubt, ask questions.

1. Wrestling, throwing objects, and other forms of horseplay should be avoided. Serious injuries may be the result.

2. Provide a place for everything, and keep everything in its place.

3. Keep the arms and body as

Safety and Tools

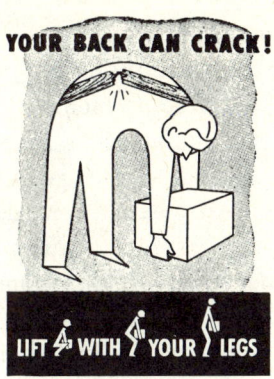

National Safety Council

nearly straight as possible when lifting heavy objects. Place your feet close to the object. Bend your knees, squat, and keep your back as straight as possible. Lift with the legs—not with the back. If the object is too heavy or too bulky, get help.

4. Never place articles on window sills, stepladders, or other high places where they may fall and cause injuries. Check scaffolds and ladders for articles before they are moved.

5. Oil, water, and other slippery substances left on the floor may cause a serious accident.

6. Keep all work spaces clear of tools and material. Things left scattered on the floor may cause stumbling and result in serious injury from a fall.

7. Notify your immediate superior of any known violations of safety rules or of conditions you think may be dangerous.

8. Replace faulty tools and equipment.

9. Immediately report all accidents, no matter how slight, to your superior, and report for first aid treatment.

10. Don't take chances.

National Safety Council

First Aid

A mason's equipment is not complete without a few essential first-aid supplies. These supplies should include at least antiseptics, bandages, and first aid for burns. Such provisions will help to prevent infection after minor skin injuries, bruises, and burns. Provision should be made also to avoid excessive loss of blood, heat exhaustion, and eye injuries. A minimum supply of first-aid provisions should include the following materials:

Antiseptic. A small bottle with applicator, plastic squeeze bottle, or aerosol spray can of a reliable antiseptic.

Bandages. A package of sterile

sealed three or four-inch compresses; a small roll of 1-inch gauze; a five-yard roll of ½ inch adhesive tape; and a package of adhesive bandages of assorted sizes.

Heat Exhaustion. One bottle of 50 sodium chloride (common table salt) tablets. There are two kinds of sodium chloride tablets — the plain and the enteric coated. The enteric coated do not dissolve until they reach the intestines. This prevents stomach disturbances.

Eye Protection. Every tool kit should contain a good pair of goggles for eye protection when drilling or cutting stone or concrete.

Instruction. The physical well-being of the mason is of equal or greater importance than his skill or knowledge of the trade. The mason must be physically fit in order to do his work properly. He must not only keep himself physically fit but he must be safety conscious also in order to protect himself and his fellow workers against accidents and the consequent loss of time on the job. Although the mason may be safety conscious and take every precaution possible to prevent accidents, nevertheless, he should be able to administer simple first aid to an injured worker when accidents occur. A reliable instruction book on first aid should have a place in his tool kit. The *American Red Cross First Aid Book* is recommended.

Accidents are all too frequent in the construction industry, yet the severity of these accidents is not so great as in many other industries. Large construction organizations have their safety engineers, doctors, nurses, and hospital facilities. However, the small organizations, unfortunately, cannot provide these aids. Therefore, the mason in the small organization must be his own safety engineer and be prepared to administer first aid to an injured worker. It is of prime importance then that every mechanic become safety conscious, thinking in terms of safety for himself and others while performing every operation in the process of erecting a building. Since safety instruction becomes most effective when given as the situation or need arises, such instruction is given throughout this book in connection with the various construction operations.

It is not within the scope of this text to deal with first aid, hence this information must be obtained from another source such as the textbook issued by the American Red Cross. However, a few suggestions are given here.

1. The mason should develop safety consciousness, since "an ounce of prevention is worth a pound of cure".

2. He should protect his eyes with goggles when working near flying objects.

Safety and Tools

National Safety Council

3. Slight cuts, bruises, or skin breaks should be treated immediately with an antiseptic and protected with a bandage to prevent infection. *Note:* Never put adhesive tape directly on the wound.

4. Cover burns immediately with a sterile bandage. No medication or cleanser should be administered except by qualified medical personnel.

5. To avoid heat exhaustion, a construction worker should drink plenty of water and take salt tablets to replace the salt lost from the body through perspiration.

6. Before moving an injured worker, always examine him for broken bones. This precaution may prevent compound fractures.

7. In case of serious injuries, always call or see a doctor as quickly as possible.

Clothing

Safety, comfort, and convenience are the watchwords for selecting clothing to be worn on any construction job. The mason should avoid clothing with unnecessary protrusions such as loose cuffs, loops, flaps, etc., which may catch on tools, materials or scaffolding. If the mason is working with any sort of caustic material, he must be careful not to expose his skin to it. Long sleeves with snug fitting cuffs, rubber gloves, and safety glasses are recommended.

Good, sturdy, leather shoes with hard toe-caps should be worn to protect the feet from falling objects and from dampness. Never wear soft-soled shoes as you might step on a nail which would puncture the soft sole and enter the foot.

The hard hat is a must on many construction jobs. Any building, except in the house field, requires the protection of an approved metal or plastic hard hat. There is the constant danger of some workman dropping a tool or piece of material from one of the floors above or from a scaffold. A hard hat should be worn if there is any danger of falling materials or if there is a crane being used. Wear safety goggles and a dust mask when the work requires it.

Tools and Equipment

The greatest care must be taken in handling tools and equipment. Careless handling is very likely to cause serious accidents. Remember that trowels may have sharp edges. Be especially careful with them when working near others. Do not leave

Concrete Block Construction

trowels and other hand tools where you or another worker might trip over or fall upon them. Also, never go off and leave them on scaffolding, walls, superstructure, etc., because they may fall or be knocked off and injure someone below.

Most jobs will employ mechanical equipment. Motors, gears, and other moving parts are always hazardous unless treated correctly and with care. Fig. 2-1 shows a modern mixer with the motor and gears enclosed in a protective housing. This housing should be removed *only* for servicing —never while the machine is in operation. The guard over the filler opening should be closed whenever the machine is running, except when loading. When loading, hands must be kept away from the mixer blades.

Power saws are also very dangerous when handled carelessly and must be treated with great respect. Fig. 2-2 illustrates the safe use of a power saw.

One very important rule is "know your machine". Machinery must be operated by someone who is thoroughly familiar with it. Always fol-

Fig. 2-1. A mechanical mixer must provide protection from moving parts. (Gilson Bros. Co.)

Safety and Tools

Fig. 2-2. Safety glasses should be worn when operating a power saw.

low the manufacturer's instructions or suggestions.

Electricity

Electricity is the power supply for much of the mechanical equipment used on construction jobs today. Temporary lighting wires are found strung throughout the jobs during construction. Electricity is a very dangerous power. There is nothing to show that the power is flowing through the wires except when a light is burning or a motor is turning. The electricity is there whether it is used or not. Great care must be taken not to touch any bare wire, or to create any condition where the current can flow through your body to a ground. Wet scaffolds, metal lath ceilings and wet ground are dangerous, as the wetness or mass of metal improves the grounding condition, permitting a greater flow of current to pass through the body. This causes severe burns and possible death.

Never attempt to touch a person who has live current flowing through him or you too may be killed. Try to remove the wire or equipment creating the problem by pushing or lifting it off using a dry piece of wood. Shut off the electricity immediately, if possible; this is the safest method.

National Safety Council

Check all wires and equipment for bare spots, poor connections and for proper grounding before using them. Keep wire up off the ground and never operate electrical equipment in wet locations without the proper grounding conditions or instantaneous overload-shutoff devices.

Make sure all equipment has three-wire, grounded-type cords, using adequate size wire to carry the required load. Undersized wire may cause a fire due to overheating or may cause a motor burnout when operating under a heavy load.

Never connect electrical equipment to a power source unless the switch is in an OFF position. When work is completed, shut off the power. Report defective power tools and remove from the job site.

Chemicals

The modern mason in the course of his work, may come into contact with chemicals. Some of them when used without the proper precautions can cause serious burns or loss of sight. Never use any material without first determining what dangers it may present and how to use it safely. Read all the manufacturer's directions and check with previous users to find out what problems may be encountered.

Wear rubber gloves and safety glasses plus the proper body covering to prevent chemicals from coming into direct contact with the skin. Keep a pail of clean water available to wash off any chemicals that might accidentally come in contact with the skin.

Scaffolds

Since a great deal of the mason's work is done on scaffolding of various kinds, there is an ever present possibility of a serious injury — to yourself and others. The three main hazards while working on or under scaffolds are falling, dropping tools or material, and faulty scaffolding. Always watch your step, keep your balance, and handle your equipment carefully.

Scaffolds must be built to support the load they are to carry. According to the National Safety Council, they should be designed to support at least four times the anticipated load of men and materials. This is necessary for safety because sometimes unexpected additional loads are placed upon the scaffold.

It is essential that those who erect scaffolding be familiar with the requirements of the safety codes or statutes of his own state as well as the national standards. The *Standard Safety Code for Building Construction* gives detailed requirements for the materials to be used and the manner of erection of scaffolds.

The mason uses four basic types of scaffolds and each of these types can be constructed of either wood or metal and sometimes a combination of the two materials. The basic types are as follows:

1. *Trestle scaffolds:* planks laid across trestles make safe scaffolds up to 10 feet high.
2. *Built-up scaffolds:* either wooden pole scaffolds or steel sectional scaffolds.
3. *Rolling scaffolds:* scaffolds on wheels that permit them to be moved.

4. *Hanging scaffolds:* suspended scaffolds supported by cables or metal straps. (Some large scaffolds in high ceiling areas are hung from cables to beams above to keep the floor area clear.)

A *swing stage scaffold* is also used at times for some exterior work, but it is not as common as the others. A swing stage scaffold, such as the one shown in Fig. 2-3, is supported from above, using ropes and pulleys which permit it to be raised or lowered as needed. This type of scaffold is difficult to use, but is sometimes necessary for veneer and other exterior work.

For *wooden scaffolds*, all supports and planks must be of sound lumber, free of large knots, cracks or split ends. All uprights must be cross-braced; ledgers and bearer planks must not be spaced more than 8 feet apart for use with 2″ x 10″ planks. New lumber standards will now reduce this plank to 1½″ x 9½″ net size. Allowances will have to be made for this by reducing ledger spacing.

On all scaffold platforms, the planks must be laid tight together to keep the materials from dropping

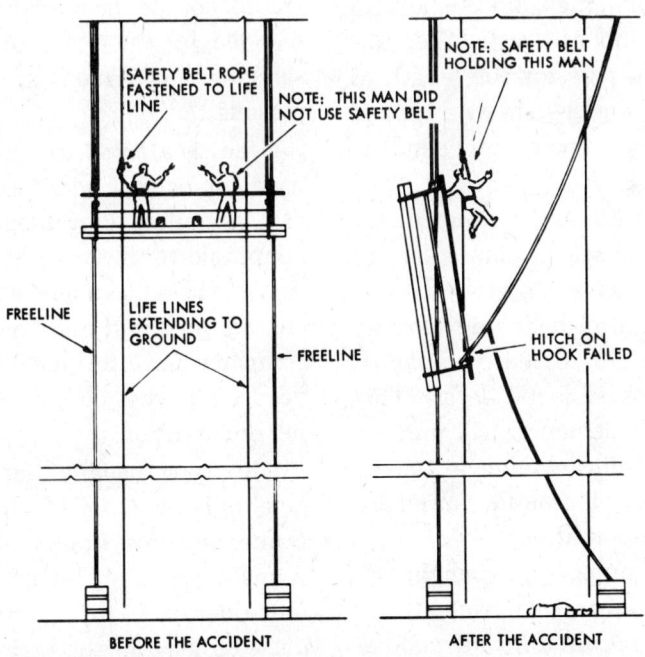

Fig. 2-3. Swing stage scaffold safety devices. (National Safety Council.)

on the workers below. Plank ends should extend at least 6 inches but not more than one foot beyond the bearer planks so they will not slip off. On steel scaffolds planks should have cleats nailed across their ends underneath so they cannot slide off the metal cross bars.

Scaffolds for masonry must be at least four feet wide so as to permit a safe passage between the mortar board and the building.

Guard rails and toe boards should be used on all scaffolds over one stage in height. Not more than 4 to 5 inches of open space should be allowed between the scaffold and the walls.

Tie the scaffold to the building at every other staging from the bottom to the top and at every other upright scaffold pole for the length of the scaffold. Fig. 2-4 shows a typical wooden double pole, independent scaffold.

Scaffolds built on the ground must have the poles set on planks laid in solid contact with the ground so as to provide a firm unsinking footing. Nail the upright to these planks so they will not slide off later. This method of construction will prevent the scaffold from falling over due to sinking into wet ground caused by rain or other conditions.

To safely support the weight of the planks, men and materials, 4″ x 4″ poles are required for all wooden mason scaffolds over one stage in height. Poles of 4″ x 6″ are recommended for the first 32 feet of scaffolds exceeding 32 feet in height.

Most contractors stock only certain basic scaffold material in their storage yards. It is cheaper to use a 4″ x 4″ pole for a simple scaffold when you have it on hand anyway. It is useable for all scaffolds and because of its size can be nailed repeatedly without splitting.

Wooden scaffolds should not exceed 40 feet in height. Anything above this height should be built of steel for fire safety and strength.

State and National Safety Regulations vary considerably for scaffolding. Local laws must be followed. Fig. 2-5, for example, shows heavy trade, double pole scaffold recommended by the State of California safety orders. This is acceptable for masons.

Steel scaffolds are now widely used for overall adaptability. They can be built to any height and are adaptable to all types of job conditions. These scaffolds can be purchased or rented and the supplying companies give technical services on needs and types best suited for each job or condition.

The type usually used for low heights is made up of prefabricated frames and cross braces. See Fig. 2-6. A factor of safety of not less than four times the load is required. Care must be used in the erection of the scaffold so that it rests on a firm base

Safety and Tools

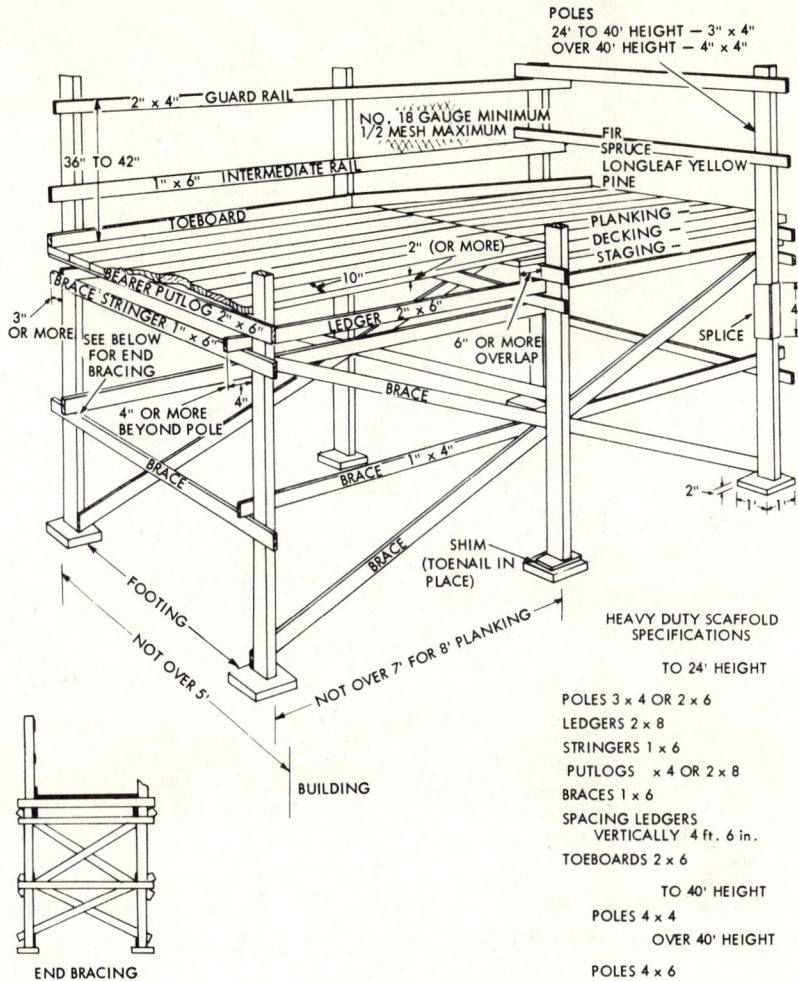

Fig. 2-4. Typical double pole wood scaffold, showing safe construction for a single stage height. Multiple stage scaffolds require 4" x 4" poles and 2" x 8" bearer planks. (National Safety Council)

and is kept plumb and level as it is assembled. It must be inspected daily. Care must be taken to keep the frames from injury or from rusting so that they do not lose part of their design strength. Safety rules for metal scaffolding, recommended by the Steel Scaffolding and Shoring Institute, are shown on page 26.

Rolling scaffolds should have large strong wheels provided with locking devices. Never move a rolling scaffold while men are on the scaffold. Always clean the floor ahead of

23

Concrete Block Construction

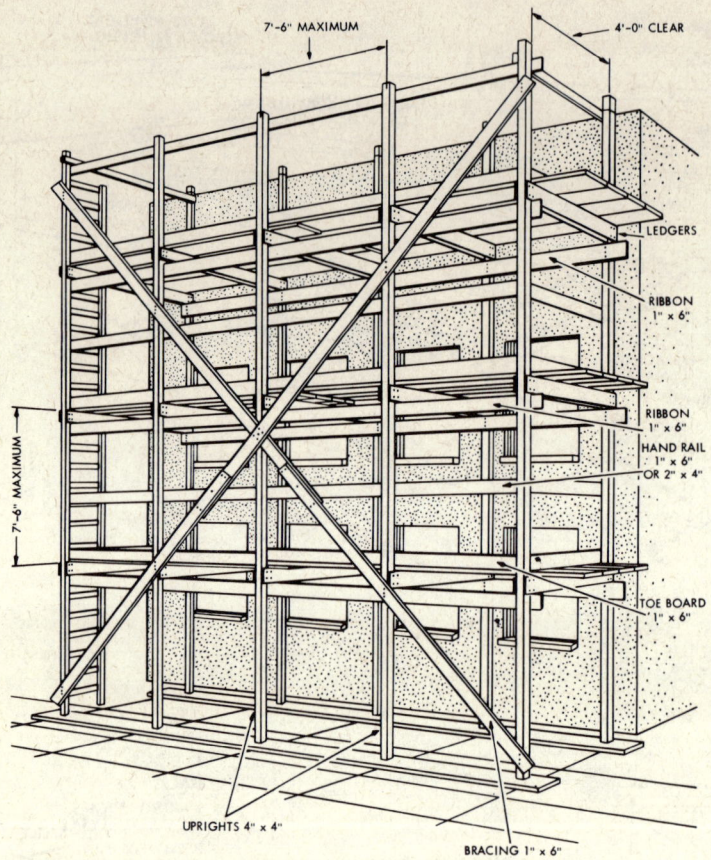

Fig. 2-5. A heavy trade, double pole scaffold must meet state code requirements. (State of California, "Construction Safety Orders")

the move to be made so that the wheels will not be blocked by an obstruction which might cause the scaffold to tip over. All planks on rolling scaffolds should be securely fastened down so they cannot slide off while the scaffolds are moved.

Hanging and *swing stage scaffolds* depend upon the cables or block and tackle to support them. Never use frayed cable or cable clamps that are worn out. Inspect all these items before using the scaffold; your life depends upon it. Old ropes and worn blocks are perhaps the greatest danger in using swing stage scaffolds. Insist on good equipment, make sure the supports are securely fastened and tied off so they cannot slip or work loose.

Safety and Tools

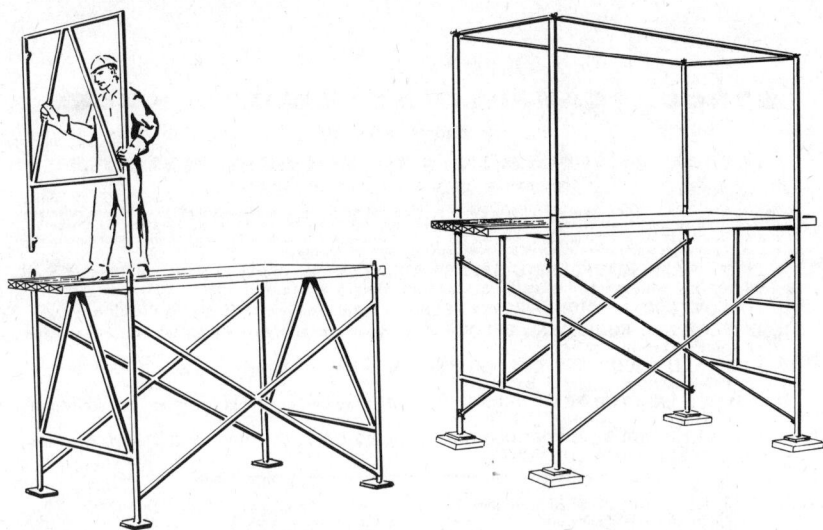

Fig. 2-6. Prefabricated metal frames and diagonal braces are assembled quickly to provide safe scaffolds.

When the mason has to work on a swing stage scaffold, it must be tied to the building at each end so as not to swing away from the building.

Safety belts fastened to life lines should be used at all times. See Fig. 2-3. Use only safety approved equipment with the proper guard rails installed. Never overload the scaffold; keep it under its rated load capacity at all times.

Building Enclosure

With year-round construction now an established practice, the enclosure of buildings to permit both interior and exterior work to continue even in freezing weather often creates a dangerous condition for the worker. Temporary heaters, if they are not properly vented, may give off obnoxious or deadly fumes. Salamanders, gas or gasoline heaters are very dangerous, as the carbon monoxide gases given off are odorless but lethal.

The mason usually works on scaffolds and may be up near a ceiling; therefore he will get the full force of these gases first because the gas is lighter than air and will rise to the ceiling. All temporary heaters must be constructed with positive venting of the combustion chamber, and the resulting gases must be piped to the outside. The vent pipes must be of the proper size and have gastight points. "You only live once—don't make your life a short one."

Concrete Block Construction

STEEL SCAFFOLDING SAFETY RULES
as Recommended by
STEEL SCAFFOLDING AND SHORING INSTITUTE
(SEE SEPARATE SHORING SAFETY RULES)

Following are some common sense rules designed to promote safety in the use of steel scaffolding. These rules are illustrative and suggestive only, and are intended to deal only with some of the many practices and conditions encountered in the use of scaffolding. The rules do not purport to be all-inclusive or to supplant or replace other additional safety and precautionary measures to cover usual or unusual conditions.

I. **POST THESE SCAFFOLDING SAFETY RULES** in a conspicuous place and be sure that all persons who erect, dismantle or use scaffolding are aware of them.

II. **FOLLOW LOCAL CODES, ORDINANCES** and regulations pertaining to scaffolding.

III. **INSPECT ALL EQUIPMENT BEFORE USING** — Never use any equipment that is damaged or deteriorated in any way.

IV. **KEEP ALL EQUIPMENT IN GOOD REPAIR.** Avoid using rusted equipment — the strength of rusted equipment is not known.

V. **INSPECT ERECTED SCAFFOLDS REGULARLY** to be sure that they are maintained in safe condition.

VI. **CONSULT YOUR SCAFFOLDING SUPPLIER WHEN IN DOUBT** — scaffolding is his business, **NEVER TAKE CHANCES.**

A. **PROVIDE ADEQUATE SILLS** for scaffold posts and use base plates.

B. **USE ADJUSTING SCREWS** instead of blocking to adjust to uneven grade conditions.

C. **PLUMB AND LEVEL ALL SCAFFOLDS** as the erection proceeds. Do not force braces to fit — level the scaffold until proper fit can be made easily.

D. **FASTEN ALL BRACES SECURELY.**

E. **DO NOT CLIMB CROSS BRACES.**

F. **ON WALL SCAFFOLDS PLACE AND MAINTAIN ANCHORS** securely between structure and scaffold at least every 30' of length and 25' of height.

G. **FREE STANDING SCAFFOLD TOWERS MUST BE RESTRAINED FROM TIPPING** by guying or other means.

H. **EQUIP ALL PLANKED OR STAGED AREAS** with proper guard rails, and add toeboards when required.

I. **POWER LINES NEAR SCAFFOLDS** are dangerous—use caution and consult the power service company for advice.

J. **DO NOT USE** ladders or makeshift devices on top of scaffolds to increase the height.

K. **DO NOT OVERLOAD SCAFFOLDS.**

L. **PLANKING:**
1. Use only lumber that is properly inspected and graded as scaffold plank.
2. Planking shall have at least 12" of overlap and extend 6" beyond center of support, or be cleated at both ends to prevent sliding off supports.
3. Do not allow unsupported ends of plank to extend an unsafe distance beyond supports.
4. Secure plank to scaffold when necessary.

M. **FOR ROLLING SCAFFOLD THE FOLLOWING ADDITIONAL RULES APPLY:**
1. **DO NOT RIDE ROLLING SCAFFOLDS.**
2. **REMOVE ALL MATERIAL AND EQUIPMENT** from platform before moving scaffold.
3. **CASTER BRAKES MUST BE APPLIED** at all times when scaffolds are not being moved.
4. **DO NOT ATTEMPT TO MOVE A ROLLING SCAFFOLD WITHOUT SUFFICIENT HELP** — watch out for holes in floor and overhead obstructions.
5. **DO NOT EXTEND ADJUSTING SCREWS ON ROLLING SCAFFOLDS MORE THAN 12".**
6. **USE HORIZONTAL DIAGONAL BRACING** near the bottom, top and at intermediate levels of 30'.
7. **DO NOT USE BRACKETS ON ROLLING SCAFFOLDS** without consideration of overturning effect.
8. **THE WORKING PLATFORM HEIGHT OF A ROLLING SCAFFOLD** must not exceed four times the smallest base dimension unless guyed or otherwise stabilized.

N. For "PUTLOGS" and "TRUSSES" the following additional rules apply:
1. **DO NOT CANTILEVER OR EXTEND PUTLOGS/TRUSSES** as side brackets without thorough consideration for loads to be applied.
2. **PUTLOGS/TRUSSES SHOULD EXTEND AT LEAST 6"** beyond point of support.
3. **PLACE PROPER BRACING BETWEEN PUTLOGS/TRUSSES** when the span of putlog/truss is more than 12'.

Safety and Tools

Fig. 2-7. Building enclosures must be properly ventilated.

Concrete Block Construction

Fig. 2-7 shows a typical building enclosure.

Housekeeping

Good housekeeping is not just another extra chore for the workman. It is an important element in accident prevention and efficiency on the job. Good housekeeping begins with planning ahead. Storage areas should be planned for ease of access to materials but not in the way of traffic and construction. Materials should be neatly stockpiled. Access areas and walkways should be kept clear of loose materials and tools. Containers for trash and pits or bins for waste materials should be provided and conscientiously used.

It is the responsibility of each and every man on the job to maintain his area in good working order. A neat and orderly work area is a reflection of a proper attitude toward safety by all concerned.

Tools for Masonry

Learning the proper use and care of tools is an essential part of apprenticeship in any trade. The tools for masonry are highly specialized in that there is usually only one type of tool that is suitable for each step in masonry construction, and also, that these tools are used *only* in the masonry trades. A piece of finished masonry construction may be considered a "hand-tooled" product. For this reason, the mason may take particular pride in the individuality of his profession. Buy quality tools, take care of them and they will become part of your trade—an indispensable part.

Compared with most other building trades, the mason carries relatively few hand tools to the job. The mason's basic personal tool kit which he will be expected to bring to the job consists of assorted trowels and jointers, a plumb rule (level), brick hammer and brick set, steel square, line, retractable steel tape, and folding rule.

The mason carries certain tools in his toolbox. Others are supplied by the contractor. This division of ownership of the tools has been worked out over a period of years with the interest of all in mind.

The small hand tools are the property of the journeyman mason. He carries them from job to job. The larger tools are placed on the job by the contractor. The mason, however, is responsible for the care of tools furnished him by the contractor for as long as they remain in his possession.

The most important things to consider in selecting personal tools are strength of material, design, and comfort. Some types of tools, such as trowels and jointers, will vary from different manufacturers in size, shape, and weight. The first consideration should be to obtain the tool made of the best possible materials. This not only assures long life but also makes for speed and efficiency on the job. The sizes or shapes will be determined by the nature of the job and personal preference. As the mason gains more experience, he will develop an individual "feel" for particular sizes, shapes, and weights of tools. In other words, whichever tool "feels" the best is probably the best tool for the job.

Trowels

Trowels are the most important and most used tools in block masonry, and great care should be taken in selecting them. As with all tools, the mechanic should buy the best that he can afford. Better trowels are hand ground to the proper shape, taper and balance out of one-piece forgings of high grade steel alloys. Stamped, welded trowels are cheaper, but will readily warp, wear down, and break. The mason will be money ahead in the long run by buying trowels that will give long and dependable service.

Trowels are available in lengths from about 9″ to 14″ and widths from about 4½″ to 7″ and may be either wide heeled or round heeled. Again, the type of job and personal preference will determine what sizes, shapes and lift to buy. Fig. 2-8 shows some typical masons' trowels.

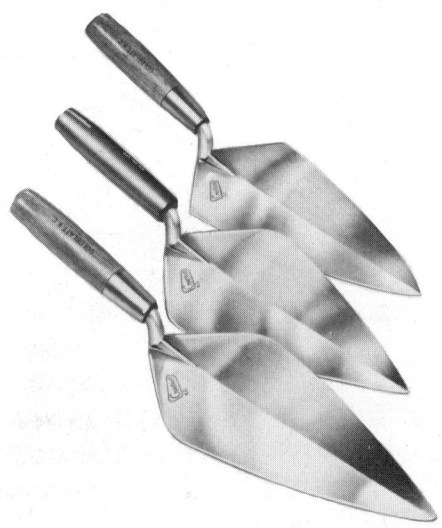

Fig. 2-8. Mason's trowels. Note the different heel shapes, ranging from sharp (top) to rounded (bottom). (Goldblatt Tool Co.)

Jointers

A jointer (also called joint tool or finishing tool) is used to "finish" the mortar joints between the units in a masonry structure. Finishing the joint smooths and compresses the face of the joint, giving a pleasing appearance and, as will be discussed later, assures watertightness of the joint. Jointers are usually either cast

Concrete Block Construction

or forged metal rods, or stamped split tubes with the ends rounded or angled to provide a particular shape of convex joint. For long horizontal joints, a joint runner (sometimes called a "sled" runner) is recommended. Fig. 2-9 shows some typical jointers. Fig. 2-10 shows the joint or sled runner being used in laying concrete block.

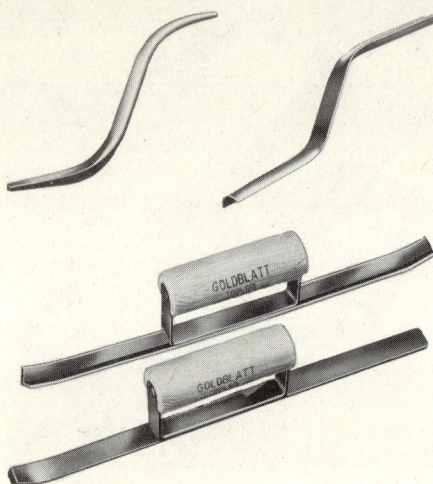

Fig. 2-9. Jointers. Regular jointers (top) are used to finish mortar joints in most masonry work. Longer jointers, called sled runners (bottom) are used to finish long horizontal joints. (Goldblatt Tool Co.)

Fig. 2-10. Sled runner being used in concrete block construction. (Goldblatt Tool Co.)

Safety and Tools

Levels

Professional masonry is not possible without the combination level and plumb rule commonly called *level*. (Fig. 2-11) It is used constantly to check the wall as it goes up to assure that it is absolutely true vertically (plumb) and that each course of block is level horizontally. The mason knows that the level and trowel "go hand in hand" as he will often have one in one hand and one in the other. Levels suitable for masonry are available in lengths from 42″ to 48″. (The mason may keep a shorter level, 14″ to 24″, for smaller work or inside spaces.) A good level has two bubble gages in the center for leveling and two at either end for plumbing. This allows the mason to pick up the level from any position and immediately apply and read it.

Steel Square

A steel square (Fig. 2-12) is used by masons when *laying up* (constructing) corners to assure a true 90 degree corner. It is also used to set the corner bricks or blocks in the dry layout of the first course in a masonry structure. The steel square is the same tool as the carpenter's framing square.

Line

The mason's line is important in keeping each course of brick or block level and the wall true and *out-of-wind* (free of hollows or bulges) as the units are being laid up between the leads (corners). The line is usually a strong cord of nylon or similar material. It is available in different sizes and colors, and in lengths up to 1000 feet. Fig. 2-13 shows a line in use. Note that it is stretched in such

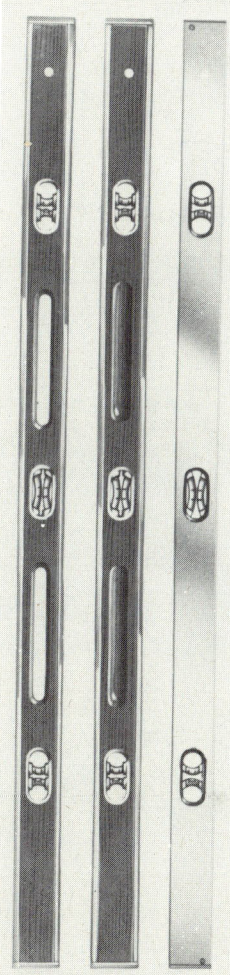

Fig. 2-11. Levels (plumb rules) are available in either wood or metal. (Goldblatt Tool Co.)

Concrete Block Construction

a way as to provide a level guideline for the top edge of the brick or block in each course. The line is held in place by corner blocks (Fig. 2-14).

If the corner must be kept clear for plumbing and truing (for instance, if one mason is laying up the corners while another is completing the courses) line pins or cut nails may be used to stretch the line.

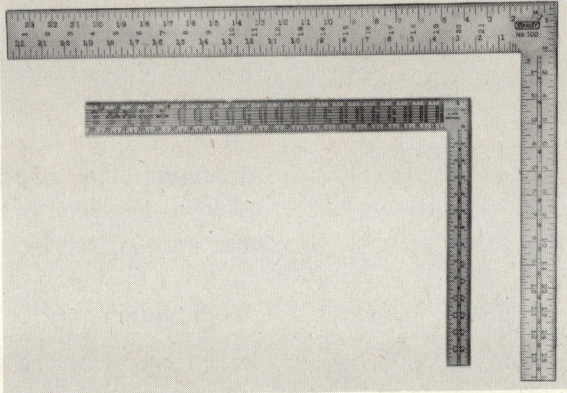

Fig. 2-12. Steel squares.

Fig. 2-13. Mason's line is used to align the top edge of each course.

Safety and Tools

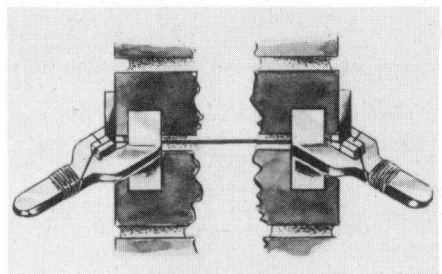

Fig. 2-14. Corner blocks are used to hold the line securely in place. (Goldblatt Tool Co.)

Rules

For measuring and layout, the mason will have two kinds of rules: a retractable steel tape, usually ten to twelve feet long, and a six foot folding rule with a six inch sliding rule on the first section for inside measuring. Fig. 2-15 illustrates the two commonly used rules. These types of rules are also available with special scales and markings for masonry.

Tool Bag

The mason usually carries his personal tools in a tool bag. The 18″ canvas bag is the most popular and will usually contain the following items: large trowel, pointing trowel, round and V jointer, mason's line, corner blocks, line pins, cut nails, folding rule, steel tape, and short plumb rule. The long plumb rule may be carried in the leather straps on the outside of the tool bag.

In addition to the tools just described, the mason will usually carry such items as chalk, pencils, and knives in his tool kit.

Power Tools and Equipment

Besides his own hand tools, there will be other larger tools and equipment available to the mason. Most of the heavy time-consuming operations such as transporting, lifting and mixing which were formerly

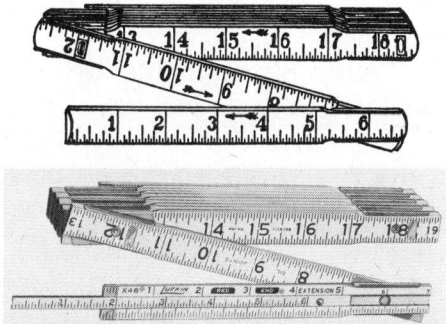 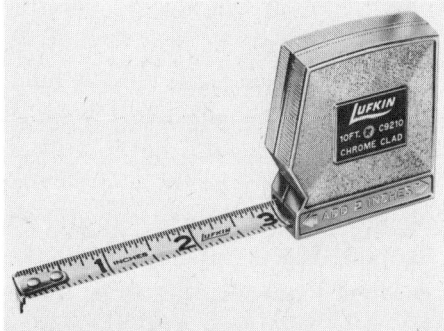

Fig. 2-15. Folding rule and tape.

33

Concrete Block Construction

Fig. 2-16. Gasoline engine powered mortar mixer.

done by hand are now done by mechanical means. Although the mason himself will not be operating this equipment, he will benefit directly from it and should be familiar with it. He should know what it does, how it does it, what its capacities and limitations are in order that he and others may use it to full advantage. Fig. 2-16 shows a modern gasoline engine driven mortar mixer. Note the safety devices: the engine and gears are enclosed; the mixing drum is completely covered by a safety guard. The only time this guard is opened is when the machine is being loaded.

Electric masonry saws are used when a large number of brick, block or glazed tile must be cut to a special size. As with all machinery, these tools should be operated only by experienced and cautious persons. Fig. 2-2 shows a table-mounted masonry saw being used to cut a concrete block.

Safety and Tools

Checking On Your Knowledge

The following questions give you the opportunity to check up on yourself. If you have read the chapter carefully, you should be able to answer the questions.

If you have any difficulty, read the chapter over once more so that you have the information well in mind before you go on with your reading.

DO YOU KNOW

1. What is necessary to do a safe, competent job?
2. How to lift a heavy object?
3. What to do if safety violations are discovered on the job?
4. The safe use of a scaffold?
5. What kind of clothing a mason should wear?
6. Three types of protective equipment a mason may use?
7. When the motor housing on a mechanical mixer may be removed?
8. Three things to check for before using power tools?
9. What to do when you are through using a power tool?
10. Why good housekeeping is important.
11. What should be the first consideration in buying a tool?
12. What is the most important and most used tool in masonry?
13. Why the plumb rule is necessary in masonry?
14. How to assure a true 90 degree corner in masonry work?

Chapter 3

Mortar: Basic Materials and Mixing

Any masonry structure, such as a wall, a foundation, a fireplace, although made up of bricks, stone or concrete blocks, is a solid, one-piece unit. This is because the individual units are bonded together by a strong, durable material called *mortar*. This chapter will cover the materials used in making mortar, the various types of mortars, their properties and where they are used, and the different methods of mixing and delivery.

Mortar Materials

Mortar for unit masonry may be defined as a compound of cementitious materials and sand with sufficient water to reduce the mixture to a workable consistency. The cementitious materials are cement and hydrated lime. The cement is the main binding agent and supplies most of the strength of the mortar. The most common type of cement is portland cement. In fact, over 95 percent of all the cement manufactured in the United States is portland cement. See Fig. 3-1.

Portland Cement

In 1824, Joseph Aspdin, a plasterer and bricklayer of Leeds, England, was experimenting to produce a mortar that would harden under water. He achieved this by burning limestone and clay together in his

Mortar: Basic Materials and Mixing

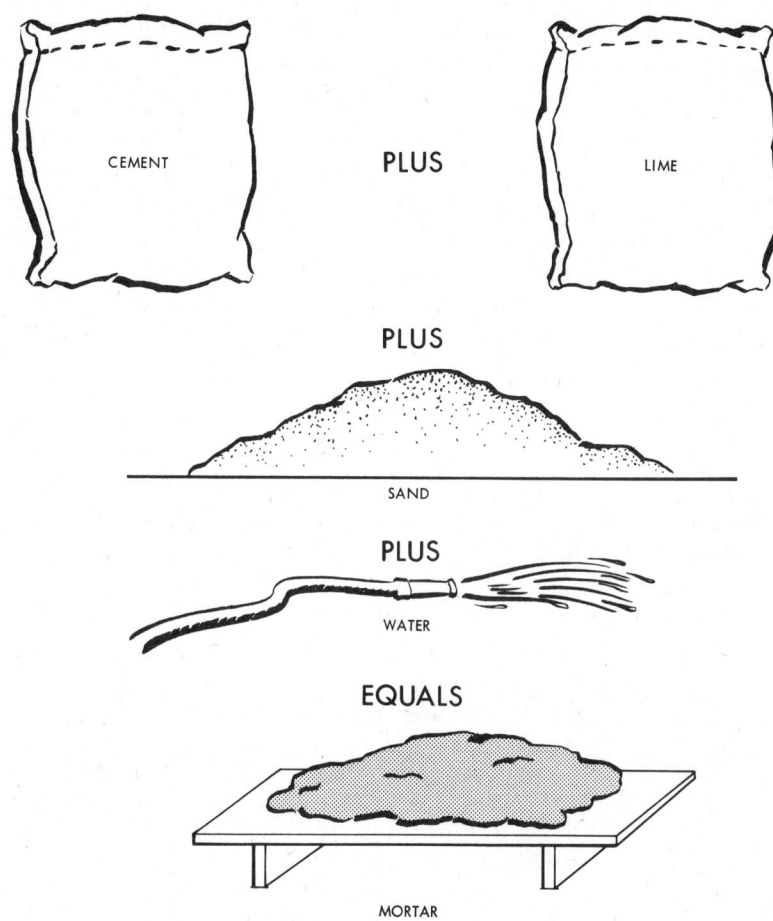

Fig. 3-1. The ingredients of mortar.

kitchen stove. The gray powder was called portland cement because of its resemblance to stone quarried on the Isle of Portland.

Since its invention, portland cement has replaced almost all other cements, both natural and artificial. This is due to low cost and superiority. Portland cement has become a standardized product of high quality and uniformity, regardless of where it is made. It is manufactured all over the United States and Canada and in most other countries.

Modern cements are manufactured in the same basic manner that Joseph Aspdin used. Some form of lime, which may be obtained from

Concrete Block Construction

limestone, marble, chalk, slag, oyster shells or coral; is mixed with certain kinds of clay; this is ground and then calcined at temperatures around 2,700°F. The ingredients lime, silica, aluminum oxide, and iron oxide combine chemically and form lumps or clinkers. The clinkers are pulverized and a small amount of gypsum is added to control the setting properties. Fig. 3-2 illustrates the process of manufacturing portland cement.

This cement is a combination of calcium silicates and aluminates. Water starts a complex reaction yielding crystalline substances in an amorphous gel which sets as a hard mass.

Cement hardens as a result of hydration of the materials in it. While setting takes place in a short time, the cement requires several days for the hydration to become complete. As a result, cement continues to increase in hardness for about a month and in some cases for years.

Portland cements are quite uniform commercial products and when the term *cement* is used without qualification, portland is usually the type to which reference is made. To

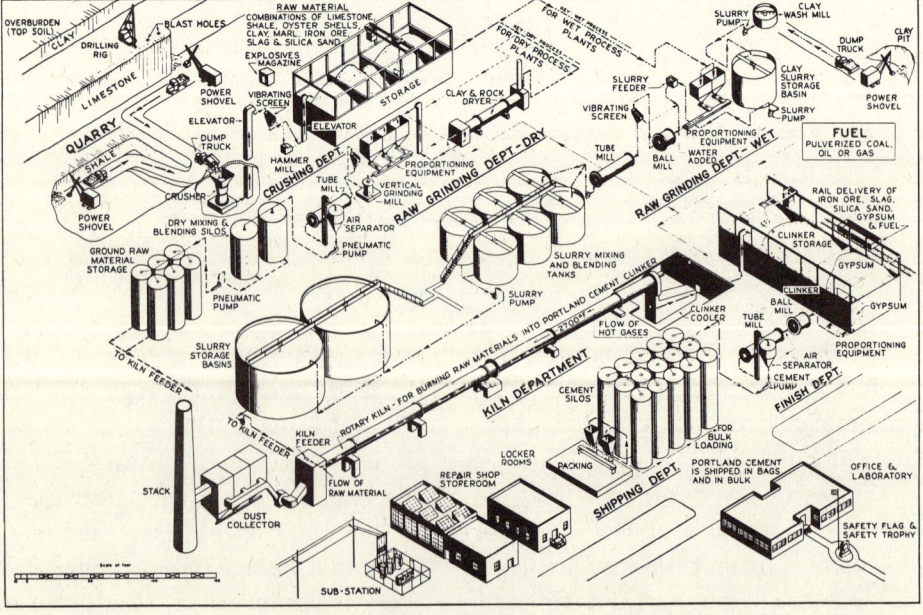

Fig. 3-2. A typical portland cement manufacturing plant.

Mortar: Basic Materials and Mixing

avoid misunderstandings, it should always be called portland cement.

The specifications of the American Society for Testing and Materials (ASTM) cover five types of portland cement and establish requirements relative to the physical properties and chemical composition for each type. Cement of any one of these types is satisfactory for use in mortars, but Types I and III are those generally used in mortar. The other types are used mainly in concrete. *Type I* is a general purpose cement. It is the one the mason will use under most conditions. *Type III* is "high early strength" cement. Although it takes as long as Type I to set, Type III achieves its full strength much sooner. It is sometimes specified for cold weather masonry because it requires shorter protection time.

Air-Entraining Cement. This product contains small quantities of a chemical which increases the amount of air held by the mortar or concrete made from the cement. The additional air usually improves the workability of the mortar and concrete and increases the resistance to freezing and thawing. The strength, however, is usually less than that obtained with the average untreated cement. Such cements are not required for average construction but may be specified for special jobs where the specific use requirements would best be met by a material of these characteristics. Air-entraining portland cements are designated *Type I-A* and *Type III-A*, and may be used interchangeably with Types I and III.

Lime

While cement provides the strength of mortar, if it were used by itself in the mortar, the mixture would be stiff and unworkable. For this reason, lime is introduced into the mixture as a plasticizing agent. Plasticity means the degree of smoothness and workability of the mixture. Lime also increases the water retentivity (water-holding capacity) of the mortar. This decreases the tendency of the mortar to lose water, called bleeding, and reduces separation or segregation of the sand.

Lime, calcium oxide (CaO) or hydrated calcium oxide. ($Ca(OH)_2$) is one of the most common minerals in the world. It is very active chemically and combines easily with other elements. In some forms it is extremely caustic and in all forms it is highly alkaline. While the mineral lime is present in many combinations, only the combination with carbon dioxide which forms limestone (calcium carbonate, $CaCO_3$) is important as a source of lime.

Lime for mortar or other use is obtained by quarrying limestone, which is a rock made up mostly of calcium carbonate. In order to change limestone into a lime suitable

Concrete Block Construction

Fig. 3-3. Dolomitic lime plant and quarry. (Ohio Lime Co.)

Fig. 3-4. Rotary kilns in which lime is burned. (Marblehead Lime Co.)

for mortar it is crushed, screened, selected, washed, and graded. Fig. 3-3 shows how lime is removed from an open pit quarry. The selected stone is then placed in kilns where it is heated up to 2,500°F. This process drives off the moisture and also removes certain gasses from the stone, especially carbon dioxide. This is a calcining process similar to that used for gypsum. It is also referred to as *lime burning*. Fig. 3-4 shows rotary kilns in which lime is burned.

The product of the calcining or burning is *quicklime*, chemically calcium oxide (CaO). Calcining lime is a process that is nearly as old as the use of fire. It is likely that it was discovered by ancient man when he built a fire on limestone rock.

Quicklime is a very caustic material. When it comes in contact with water a violent reaction occurs that is hot enough to boil the water. It can also cause severe burns on the skin. In the past quicklime was the material the mason received on the job and he had to use it to make mortar. The first step in using quicklime is to slake or hydrate it. This is done by adding enough water to it so that the oxide becomes a hydroxide ($Ca(OH)_2$). During the slaking process the caustic quicklime becomes very hot and is hazardous to work with.

Today the lime manufacturers slake the lime as part of the process of producing lime for mortar. The slaking is done in large tanks where water is added to convert the quicklime to *hydrated lime* without saturating it with water. The hydrated lime is a dry powder with just enough water added to supply the chemical reaction. Hydration is usually a continuous process and is done in equipment similar to that used in calcining. After the hydrating process the lime is pulverized and bagged.

The ASTM designates lime for clay masonry as *Type S*.

Sand

Sand is the aggregate component of mortar. It is commercially available almost anywhere and is quite inexpensive, but it is still just as important in mortar as the cementitious materials. For good strong mortar, the sand must be clean and well graded.

Cleanness. Sand purchased from a reputable commercial supplier will almost always be well washed and ready to use. However, a mason or contractor will sometimes have to obtain sand from a questionable source. If there is any possibility that the sand may contain impurities, it should be tested. The two chief impurities that make sand unfit for use in mortar are silt and organic matter. There are simple tests to determine the presence and amount of each in a given batch of sand. Fig. 3-5 shows the test for silt content. Simply put two inches of

Concrete Block Construction

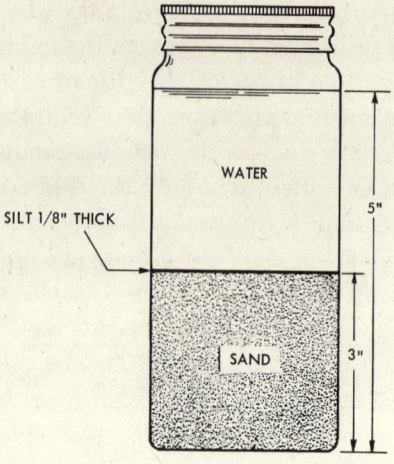

Fig. 3-5. Test for silt content in sand.

the sand to be used in a clear glass jar. An ordinary quart mason jar will work perfectly for this test. Then fill the jar partly full with clean water and shake vigorously. Let it stand for an hour. The sand will settle to the bottom leaving any silt in the sample lying on top of the sand. If the silt layer measures more than 1/8 of an inch, the sand is unfit for use in mortar and must be washed before using.

Organic matter in sand will cause a weak and non-durable mortar. If the amount of organic matter is not known, the *colorimetric test* will easily determine it. First, make a three percent solution of sodium hydroxide by dissolving one ounce of sodium hydroxide (available at any drug store) in one quart of distilled water. (*CAUTION:* Sodium hydroxide is highly caustic and can cause serious burns and ruin clothing so take great care while handling it.) Next, fill a pint jar that is graduated in ounces to the 4½ ounce mark with a dry sample of the sand. Then add the sodium hydroxide solution to the seven ounce mark. Replace the lid tightly and shake the mixture thoroughly. Then let it stand 24 hours. At the end of this time, the color of the liquid will indicate the amount of organic matter in the sand. If the liquid is clear, the sand is free of organic matter. If it is slightly straw-colored, there is a slight amount of organic matter but not enough to be seriously objectionable. Any darker color indicates too much organic matter and the sand should not be used. See Fig. 3-6.

Fig. 3-6. Colorimetric test for organic matter in aggregate.

Mortar: Basic Materials and Mixing

Grading. Grading means the difference in size of sand particles. A well graded sand contains particles of several different sizes. See Figure 3-7.

Sand must be well graded as to particle size if a satisfactory mortar is to be obtained. Owing to the great differences in the sands of various localities, the standard specifications permit a rather wide range in sizes but a better graded sand, if available, will yield a more workable and better mortar in almost every respect.

The ASTM requirements for grading represent the extreme limits and it is specified that "the gradation of the material from any one source shall be reasonably uniform and shall not be permitted to vary over the extreme range" and that it "shall be so graded that neither the proportion finer than a No. 16 sieve and coarser than a No. 30 sieve nor the proportion finer than a No. 30 sieve and coarser than a No. 50 sieve exceeds 50 per cent." For purposes of comparison, Table 3-1 gives the ASTM specification ranges of sieve analyses together with the analysis of an average commercial sand and that of one of more nearly ideal grading.

In a good mortar, all the sand particles are completely coated with cementitious material (paste) and hence a sand containing a high proportion of fine particles may require much more paste than either a properly graded material or one made up chiefly of larger particles. However, sufficient fine material should be

Fig. 3-7. A well graded sample of sand; mixed (above) and separated (below).

Concrete Block Construction

TABLE 3-1 SIEVE ANALYSES FOR MORTAR SAND

SIEVE NUMBER	PERCENTAGES PASSING EACH SIEVE		
	A.S.T.M. SPECIFICATIONS	COMMERCIAL	MORE NEARLY IDEAL
4	100	100	100
8	95-100	98	97
16	60-100	88	84
30	35-70	64	50
50	15-35	26	27
100	0-16	5	6

present to separate the larger particles and to fill the spaces (voids) between them, thus yielding an easily workable mortar. When all the sand particles are coated and lubricated with the paste of cementitious material, the smaller particles act more or less as ball bearings, thus permitting the particles of aggregates to roll over each other and producing a plastic workable mortar which will serve as a continuous uniform bedding for the block or other structural units.

Water

The water used in mortar should be clean and practically free from acids, alkalis, salts, and organic matter. As a general rule, water that is used for drinking (potable) will be suitable for making mortar.

Admixtures

Standard mortar consists of only four ingredients: cement, lime, sand, and water. Any other material added to the basic mortar is called an admixture. The most common admixtures are accelerants and retardants. An accelerant is an agent which speeds up the curing time of mortar. This type of admixture is sometimes specified when the working conditions are very cold and there is the danger of mortar freezing before it is completely set. Calcium chloride is the admixture usually specified for this purpose. Calcium chloride present in a mortar will corrode metal. Therefore, its use in reinforced masonry is discouraged by most building codes. Studies have shown that calcium chloride in excess of two percent of the total volume of mortar will eventually weaken it. Building codes and specifications on the allowable amount of calcium chloride vary from zero to two percent. For cold weather work (temperatures below 40°F.) most codes recommend warming the materials, the use of heating devices and Type III (high early strength) cement instead of admixtures.

Retardants are admixtures which slow down the curing time of mortar. They may be specified when the conditions are very hot and dry, causing the mortar to set too rapidly and never attain its strength. Again, most codes discourage the use of retardants where other means of retarding, such as insulation, may be used.

Mortar Colors

Mortar may be colored in order to match or contrast with the color of the masonry units. There are several commercial coloring additives available on the market. These are usually pure mineral or metallic oxides that are colorfast and resistant to acids and alkalis. When they are used properly they do not affect the composition and workability of the mortar. The reputable manufacturer will have exact specifications for mixing printed on the container. As with any additive to the basic mortar mix, these specifications must be followed exactly.

Specifications for the amount of coloring additives to use vary, but the amount should not exceed 15 percent of the weight of the cement.

Carbon black may be used to darken mortar in amounts up to 3 percent of the weight of the cement.

Mortar Properties and Types

The American Society for Testing and Materials has classified different formulas for mortar into *types* according to proportions, properties and usage. Where the mortar is to be used, such as in interior or exterior walls, foundations, or columns and pilasters, will call for certain *properties* which, in turn, are created by the proportions of the materials in the mortar mix. Properties are the characteristics that determine which type of mortar is to be used for a specific job. These properties are strength, durability, workability, and water retentivity. Although each type of mortar has all these qualities, the degrees of each will vary from type to type. The mason must remember that all mortar, according to the conditions to which it will be exposed, must be prepared and applied toward the goals of permanence and watertightness.

Strength and Durability

The terms *strength* and *durability* should not be confused. Strength means the amount of stress (tension and compression) that the mortar is able to withstand. Durability means the degree of resistance to external elements, such as weather and chemicals, and to aging. The two do not go hand in hand. In fact, it will be seen that a very high strength mortar, because of its composition, will lose a small amount of durability. On the other hand, a mortar proportioned for high durability will have to sacrifice a small amount of strength.

Workability

Workability means the ease or difficulty with which the mortar works under the trowel. As with all properties, workability is determined by the proportion of materials. Workability is increased by including more of the plasticizing agent, lime, or by reducing the amount of sand. Again, to increase workability, some strength and durability may have to be sacrificed. It must be emphasized that *all* good mortars are strong, durable, and workable. There is no one type that is best for all conditions. The mason must be able to analyze the purpose and conditions of each job and know which type of mortar is best suited for it.

Water Retentivity

Water retentivity is the property of mortar which prevents the rapid loss of water to masonry units of high suction and prevents "bleeding" when the mortar is in contact with relatively impervious units. In both cases the result is incomplete curing which causes the mortar joint to be weak and permeable to moisture. High water retentivity also improves the workability of mortar.

Lime has the property of water retentivity; therefore, mortars with high lime content will have high water retentivity. This property is quite important where the working or weather conditions are very hot and dry, causing a high rate of evaporation.

Mortar Types

Most building codes and specifications call for ASTM mortar *Types M, S, N,* or *O.* Table 3-2 shows the proportion for each type.

Note that the formulas allow for variations of proportions within the types but that the volume of sand never exceeds three times the combined volume of cement and lime. Any more sand would make for a weaker and less workable mortar. Typical mortar formulas are: M—1 part cement, ¼ part lime, 3 parts sand; S—1 part cement, ½ part lime, 4½ parts sand; N—1 part cement, 1 part lime, 6 parts sand; O—1 part cement, 2 parts lime, 9 parts sand.

Type M. Note in Table 3-2 the high cement to lime proportion. This makes for a very strong mortar. Type M would be specified where high compressive stress occurs, such as in heavy load bearing walls. The rel-

Mortar: Basic Materials and Mixing

TABLE 3-2 PROPORTIONS OF MORTAR TYPES

TYPE	MATERIAL (parts by volume)			
	PORTLAND CEMENT	HYDRATED LIME		SAND
		MIN.	MAX.	
M	1		1/4	Not less than 2 1/4 and not more than 3 times the sum of the total volume of cement and lime
S	1	1/4	1/2	
N	1	1/2	1 1/4	
O	1	1 1/4	1 1/2	

atively high proportion of cement makes this type more prone to expansion and contraction, thus slightly less durable than Type S. For this reason, it is usually specified for exterior construction in moderate climates and for interiors. Type M mortar is also specified for below grade structures in contact with earth such as foundations and retaining walls.

Type S. This is a very good general-purpose mortar. It has good workability and strength and excellent durability. It is specified for above grade exteriors exposed to severe weathering. It is also used in interiors and in all load-bearing structures unless only Type M is specified. Types M and S are usually interchangeable.

Type N. Excellent workability is the characteristic of this mortar because of its high lime content. Although it does not have the strength of Types M or S, it may still be used in bearing walls above grade if the stress is not too great. It is widely used in veneers, partitions and some exterior walls where climatic conditions are negligible.

Type O. Type O is extremely plastic and workable but has relatively low strength. Some codes do not allow this type of mortar at all while others allow it for non-bearing partitions.

Table 3-3 shows a typical building code for allowable compressive stresses which indicates the comparative strengths of the different types of mortar.

Concrete Block Construction

TABLE 3-3 ALLOWABLE COMPRESSIVE STRESSES IN UNREINFORCED UNIT MASONRY

CONSTRUCTION	COMPRESSIVE STRENGTH OF UNITS IN PSI	ALLOWABLE COMPRESSIVE STRESSES OVER GROSS CROSS-SECTIONAL AREA IN PSI			
		TYPE M MORTAR	TYPE S MORTAR	TYPE N MORTAR	TYPE O MORTAR
Solid Masonry of solid brick	8000 plus 4500 to 8000 2500 to 4500 1500 to 2500	400 250 175 125	350 225 160 115	300 200 140 100	250 150 110 75

Mortar Measurements

The proportions for mortar types described above are based on *volume* measurements, and mortar materials are packaged and delivered accordingly. Portland cement is packaged and delivered in bags containing 1 cubic foot, which weighs 94 pounds. Hydrated lime is packaged in 50 pound bags which contain approximately 1 cubic foot. Sand is delivered by the cubic foot or cubic yard. So a 1:1:6 mortar would call for one bag of cement, one bag of lime and six cubic feet of sand for six cubic feet of mortar.

Mortar Mixing

Mortar for masonry is usually mixed on the job site in portable mechanical mixers of the type described in Chapter 2. On some very small jobs, it may be mixed by hand in a mortar box using a mortar hoe especially designed for this purpose. See Fig. 3-8.

For hand mixing, put one half the desired quantity of sand in a clean box. Over it spread the specified quantity of hydrated lime and portland cement. Then add the remaining half of the sand. This "sandwich" operation permits a more thorough mixing with less effort. While dry, turn the mixture twice with a hoe and then pull it to one end of the

Mortar: Basic Materials and Mixing

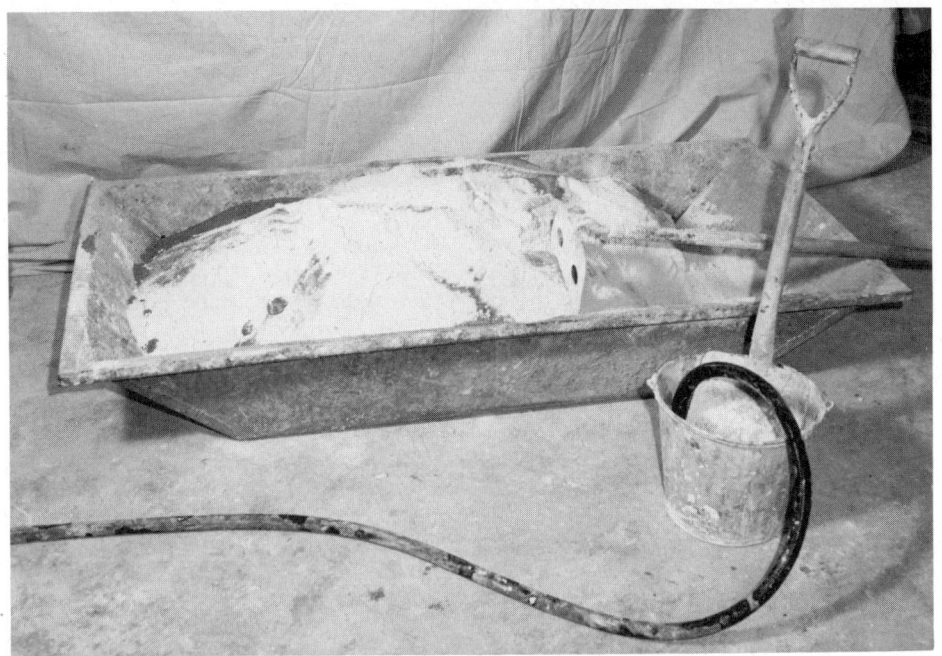

Fig. 3-8. Mixing box and hoe.

box. Add water and cut the dry mixture back into it. Continue to add water until the desired consistency is obtained.

For machine mixing first add a small amount of water to the drum. This will prevent the mixture from balling or caking up on the machine paddles. Next add one third the required amount of sand and then all the required amounts of lime and cement. As the paddles are turning, add sand and water until the desired consistency is obtained. After all the ingredients are in the drum, continue mixing for at least three more minutes. The drum must be completely emptied before the next batch is begun. The manufacturer's recommendations for maximum load should never be exceeded.

Portable mechanical mixers have several advantages over hand mixing. They assure a uniform mixture, are very speedy, and are easily operated by one man. See Fig. 2-16.

Concrete Block Construction

Checking On Your Knowledge

The following questions give you the opportunity to check up on yourself. If you have read the chapter carefully, you should be able to answer the questions. If you have any difficulty, read the chapter over once more so that you have the information well in mind before you go on with your reading.

DO YOU KNOW

1. What quantities of lime, cement, and sand are used in Type M mortar?
2. What the primary components of mortar are?
3. What the names are for the most commonly used cementitious materials?
4. What is meant by the term "bleeding"?
5. The names of four general types of mortar.
6. What benefits to mortars are experienced when air-entraining cements are used?
7. How natural cements are produced?
8. What would happen to mortar made only of cementitious materials?
9. Why it is that when sand composed of very fine particles is used in mortar, *more* cementitious materials are necessary?
10. What special treatment should be given to sand which contains clay?
11. How much sand can be safely used in a mortar?

Concrete: Basic Materials and Mixing

Chapter **4**

Most building construction using concrete block will also involve solid concrete work. For instance, concrete block walls usually rest directly on solid concrete footings or foundations. Also, block masonry and concrete work may be proceeding at the same time. Although he will not usually be directly involved in mixing or placing concrete, it is essential that the mason be familiar with the nature of concrete and how it is used.

Concrete is one of the most interesting building materials in use today. Because of its capability of being molded or formed to almost any size or shape and its outstanding strength and durability characteristics, it is probably the most versatile building material of all. This chapter will cover the components of concrete, the characteristics of the different types of concrete, and the mixing of concrete.

The materials used to make concrete are portland cement, water, and aggregate. Water added to cement reacts with the cement to form what is called a *cement paste*. As it is mixed, the paste forms a coating on all particles and pieces of the aggregate. When the mixture has been placed as, for example, for a sidewalk or structural part, a chemical reaction takes place in the cement paste which causes it to harden. This hardening process binds all of the aggregate together, forming a permanent and dense mass which is known as concrete.

Fig. 4-1 shows a piece of concrete which has been sawed in half.

Concrete Block Construction

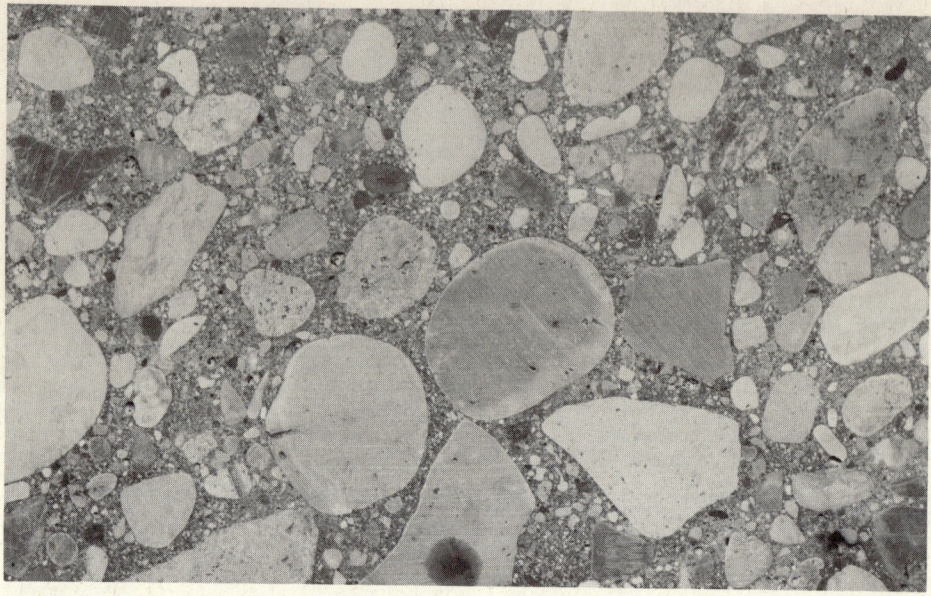

Fig. 4-1. A piece of concrete which has been sawed in two to show how the fine and coarse aggregates combine to form a solid mass.

Aggregates

The sand and crushed stone or gravel used in concrete are known as aggregates; sand is further classified as *fine aggregate* and the crushed stone or gravel as *coarse aggregate*. The fine aggregate is of varying sizes so that the smaller particles tend to fill the spaces (voids) between the larger particles. For the same reason, the coarse aggregate also is composed of varying sizes. When the fine and coarse aggregates are mixed together, the fine aggregate tends to fill the small voids between the smaller pieces of the coarse aggregate. This results in a dense, solid mass.

Fine aggregates consist of natural or manufactured sand with particle sizes up to about ¼ inch. (Note that this is about the same as mortar sand described in Chapter 3.)

Coarse aggregates are those with particle sizes greater than ¼ inch. The maximum size specifications for coarse aggregates will vary according to the purpose for which a given batch of concrete is intended. For instance, a floor requiring a smooth finished surface and bearing

Concrete: Basic Materials and Mixing

only light loads may require as little as ⅜ inch maximum size particles, whereas a heavy duty foundation may call for up to 2½ inch particles. Even larger particles may be specified for such massive structures as dams or bridge abutments.

The aggregates for concrete must also be clean. Aggregates obtained from a reliable dealer will almost always be clean and graded. However, if the contractor must dig his own from natural sand or gravel beds, he should test samples for impurities. The two main impurities that might be present are silt and organic matter. The tests for the presence of these impurities as described for mortar sand in Chapter 3 may be applied to concrete aggregates as well.

Fine Aggregate (Sand)

The term fine aggregate, or sand, applies to any finely divided material of rock or mineral origin, the particles of which have a diameter ranging from $\frac{1}{20}$ to 2 mm., which will not injuriously affect the cement, and which is not subject to disintegration or decay. Sand is almost the only material which is sufficiently cheap and which will fulfill these requirements, although stone screenings (the granulated or pulverized material resulting from stone crushing) and powdered slag have been used as substitutes.

Quartz sand is the most durable and unchangeable. Sands which consist largely of grains of feldspar, mica, etc., which will decompose upon prolonged exposure, are less desirable than quartz.

Grading. Grading means the particle distribution in a batch of aggregate. The most satisfactory sand is a mixture of coarse and fine grains, with coarse grains predominating. It makes a denser, stronger concrete than does fine-grained sand when both sands are mixed with the same quantity of cement. In other words, very fine sand may be used alone but it makes a weaker concrete. In a given quantity of very fine sand, there are more grains or particles than in the same quantity of coarse sand. More water is required to mix mortar or concrete using very fine sand. The water forms a film and separates the fine grains, thus producing a larger volume of concrete but with less density and strength.

A well-graded sand has particles ranging in size from very fine up to those which will pass through a screen having meshes ¼" square. As previously explained, the larger particles should predominate in quantity. Fig. 4-2 shows a good sand for making concrete. Note that the particles are of various sizes and that the larger sizes predominate. Well-graded sand not only makes stronger concrete but allows a more economical use of cement paste in

Concrete Block Construction

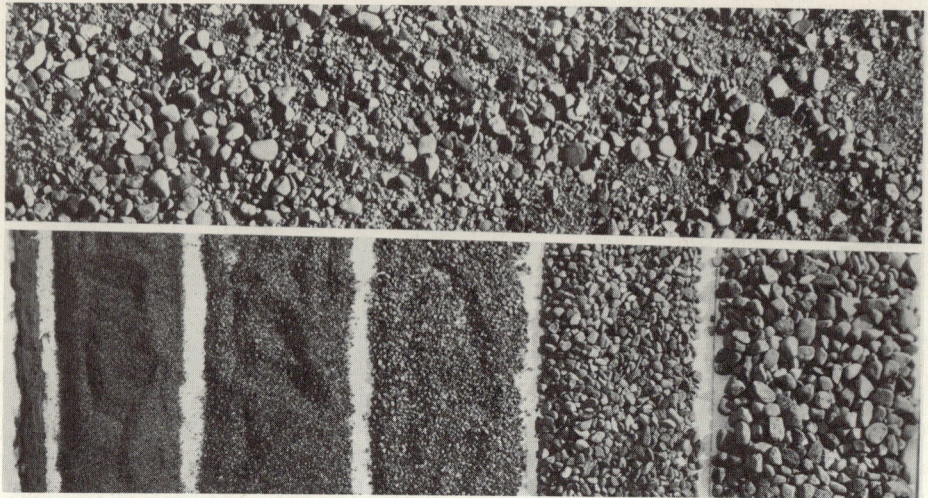

Fig. 4-2. Fine aggregate for concrete. Top: Good concrete sand. Bottom: The same sand which has been screened to show the different particle sizes.

filling the voids and binding the aggregate together.

The particles of sand may be either round or angular. The idea that sand should be sharp (angular) has been disproved by tests which show that there are fewer voids in round than angular sand. There is really little difference in the strengths of concrete made using sharp and round sand except that round sand helps to produce a denser mix. On the other hand, cement paste adheres to the angular sand somewhat better than to the smooth surfaced round sand particles, so either type of sand can be used successfully. The shape of the particles is not nearly so important as their soundness and their being properly graded from fine up to ¼ inch.

Coarse Aggregates

Coarse aggregates for making regular concrete may consist of crushed stone or gravel taken from gravel pits which are found in many parts of the country.

Crushed Stone. Trap rock is the hardest and most durable stone that can be crushed and used for making concrete. This stone is dark, heavy, close-grained, and of igneous origin. Granite makes good crushed stone for concrete, and generally it is less expensive than trap rock. Hard limestone also may be crushed and used to advantage in concrete making, but it is not as strong as granite or trap rock and is affected by fire. Only the hardest grades of sandstone can be used for making concrete.

Concrete: Basic Materials and Mixing

Grading Crushed Stone. In general, stone is crushed in sizes ranging from ¼″ to 2½ inches. When the stone is crushed, some of it will become much smaller than the ¼″ minimum usually considered the smallest usable size. This should be discarded or used as sand. After crushing, the stone should be screened and the different sizes kept separate or mixed together to fit the needs of various concrete mixes. The pieces should be square or triangular in shape. Flat, elongated, or thin pieces should never be used.

In concrete which is to be used for ordinary structural parts such as floors, foundations, footings, etc., the sizes of crushed stone used as coarse aggregate should be a mixture varying from ¼″ to 1¼″, or from ¼″ to 1½ inches. The smaller size is best for thin structural items. Mixtures of even smaller sized crushed stone should be used for concrete which is subject to severe wear.

For reinforced concrete members which are small and have steel bars spaced close together, crushed stone should be graded to include a mixture of pieces varying from ¼″ to ¾″ in size. This size aggregate should also be used for fireproofing structural steel. Where concrete members are larger and the steel not so close together, the crushed stone mixture may vary from ¼″ to 1¼ inches.

For concrete items which are massive, the crushed stone mixture may vary from ¼″ or ½″ up to 2½ inches. Massive items include retaining walls, extra thick foundations, etc.

Gravel. The term *gravel* refers to stone as it occurs naturally in gravel banks. Generally, gravel is small pieces of stone which are somewhat rounded in shape. It makes good coarse aggregate because it is hard and close textured. Often in the past it has been the practice to use the sand and gravel directly from gravel banks for coarse and fine aggregate. This practice should be avoided because in most cases too much sand is present and the pieces of stone are not properly graded. In addition, bank-run material may contain too high a percentage of silt or organic matter. If, however, bank gravel is used, it should be washed. After washing, it should be retested to see that it is suitable for use.

Grading Gravel. When gravel is used as a coarse aggregate, the sizes of individual pebbles making up the various mixes should be approximately the same as outlined for crushed stone.

If, for example, a mixture of gravel ranging from ¼″ to 1½″ in size is required, it is not necessary that exactly equal amounts of the various sizes be used. However, the best grading, and therefore the best

Concrete Block Construction

Fig. 4-3. Coarse aggregate for concrete. Top: Good concrete gravel. Bottom: The same gravel which has been screened to show the different particle sizes.

concrete, results when the various sizes are fairly well divided as to the quantity of each. Fig. 4-3 shows good concrete gravel and the variety of sizes. It will be seen that the various sizes of pebbles are nearly, but not exactly, equal in amount.

To secure a suitable mixture of gravel for concrete, it is advisable to screen the gravel as it comes from the bank and then mix the various sizes somewhat as suggested by Fig. 4-3. Good concrete just does not happen. Instead, care must be exercised in the selection of the aggregate. The use of improper aggregate always results in poor concrete and unsatisfactory structural work.

Blast Furnace Slag. Blast furnace slags are composed chiefly of silica, alumina, magnesium, and lime. Any blast furnace slag can be used as coarse aggregate if it weighs a minimum of 70 pounds per cubic foot. Such aggregate, like crushed stone or gravel, should be well graded.

Rubble. The aggregate for rubble concrete is similar to regular concrete except that from 20 to 65 percent of the mass of the concrete is taken up by the large stones. The use of large stones in massive concrete, such as drains, is economical

Concrete: Basic Materials and Mixing

and satisfactory if no voids are left between them in the concrete.

Lightweight Aggregates

Lightweight aggregate for concrete is a commercially manufactured product available under several brand names. It is made by burning certain minerals or blast furnace slag at very high temperature in rotary kilns, causing the minerals to expand, producing a hard, sound aggregate. Concrete made with this type of aggregate called *lightweight concrete* has similar properties of strength and endurance to that made with natural aggregate but is much more expensive. Its main use is in such prefabricated units as large wall panels, especially in tall buildings, where lightness is a definite advantage.

Water

Generally, if water is suitable for drinking (potable), it will be satisfactory for making concrete. Again, silt and organic matter are the two main deleterious materials that may be present in mixing water. Normally, any harmful amount of silt will be visible to the naked eye. If water containing silt must be used, it should be stored in settling basins before use.

Cement

The history and manufacturing process of portland cement were presented in Chapter 3. The American Society for Testing and Materials (ASTM) provides for five types of portland cement: Types I, II, III, IV, and V. Each type has particular properties which suits it for specific purposes.

Type I is a general purpose cement. It may be used in almost any location and in every type of concrete structure where the special properties of the other types are not required. It is also the most economical of all the types.

Type II is a modification of Type I. It has much the same properties as Type I except that it is slightly more resistant to sulfate attack. Sulfates present in groundwater will cause concrete exposed to it to deteriorate. This is a problem only in some of the western states. Type II is usually specified in these areas for below-grade structures such as footings, foundations, basement walls, drainage structures, etc., which are exposed to soil contaminating sulfates.

Sulfate attack is also common in industrial areas due to sulfur dioxide air pollution. Rain water precipitates the sulfur dioxide as a weak sulfuric acid which will attack concrete.

Type II also generates heat at a slightly lower rate than Type I. This property is especially important when concrete is placed during hot weather and the concrete may begin to set too rapidly for proper workability.

Type III is called *high-early strength* cement. This is because it gains its full strength at a much faster rate than the other types. Because of this property, forms may be removed and the structure put in use earlier.

Type IV is a very specialized cement in that it develops its strength at a much slower rate than the other types. Because of this, the rate of heat generation is also much lower. Therefore, Type IV is used almost exclusively in massive structures such as large gravity dams where the rate of temperature rise during setting is a critical factor.

Type V is also a very specialized cement. Its special property is high sulfate resistance. Its use is specified only for concrete exposed to severe sulfate attack.

Cement Distribution. Most cement for job site mixing is packed in paper sacks which hold one cubic foot or 94 pounds. Cement for ready mix concrete plants, which provide most of the concrete used today, is delivered in bulk form and sold by the ton.

Cement Storage. Cement is easily damaged by water and will readily absorb moisture from the atmosphere unless carefully protected. Therefore, prior to use, it should be kept in a dry place.

Damaged Cement. Cement which is allowed to absorb moisture will form into lumps. If these lumps cannot be pulverized by lightly striking them with a shovel, the cement is not fit for use.

Proportioning Concrete Mixtures

The primary objectives in selecting proportions of ingredients for concrete are to achieve a mix that is workable when ready to place; that will, when hardened, have the degrees of strength and durability required for the purpose of the structure, and will be as economical

Concrete: Basic Materials and Mixing

as possible while still retaining the desired properties. No one of these properties is more or less important than the other. In fact, they are so interrelated that the apprentice mason may at first be confused by the several different reasons for varying amounts of materials for particular purposes. However, with continued practice and experience, he will come to understand why and how a mix is proportioned a certain way for a certain job.

Water-Cement Ratio. Cement mixed with water makes up the *cement paste* which binds the aggregate particles into a strong solid mass. The quality of the cement paste is the most important factor in assuring the desired properties of the hardened concrete. A higher proportion of water to cement will afford a more workable mixture, whereas a mixture with less water and more cement will be stronger when hardened. Thus, a basic rule for proportioning concrete is to use as small amount of water in proportion to cement as possible, so long as the mixture remains workable. Workability is difficult to measure, but an experienced mason can readily judge it. Proportioning concrete mixtures, therefore, is an art as well as a science. Specifications for water-cement ratios are given as decimal fractions. For instance, a mixture calling for a 0.45 water-cement ratio means that the mix will consist of 45 percent water and 55 percent cement by *pounds*. In other words, 100 pounds of cement paste using this ratio would consist of 45 pounds of water to 55 pounds of cement. *(Note:* one pound of water is equivalent to one pint liquid measure.) This method is used on large jobs where a slight variance in proportions would multiply the variance and cause large batches to deviate considerably from the prescribed formula. On smaller jobs, the water-cement ratio is given as gallons of water per bag of cement.

Aggregate Proportions. The selection of proper aggregates for the mixture is an important economic factor. The cement is by far the most expensive ingredient in concrete so it is advisable to minimize the cement-water requirement by using as stiff a mixture as possible and by using well graded aggregate. Remember that the aggregate particles must be completely coated with cement paste in order to assure a tightly bonded, strong, durable, and watertight structure. Considerably less paste is required to coat one large particle than to coat several small ones occupying the same amount of space. Thus, for economy as well as for strength, the coarse aggregate should contain the largest size allowable according to specifications. Remember, however, that the smaller particles and the fine

Concrete Block Construction

 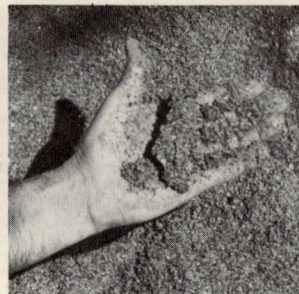 

Fig. 4-4. Left: If sand falls apart it is damp. Middle: If sand forms a ball it is wet. Right: If sand sparkles and wets the hand it is very wet.

aggregate fill in the "voids" between the larger particles, improving workability, solidity, and strength. So, as always, the aggregate should be well graded from fine to coarse.

Moisture Content in Sand. Fine aggregate (sand) will always contain a certain amount of water at the time of mixing. This will necessarily affect the amount of water to add in mixing, so it is necessary for the mason to judge the approximate amount of water in the sand he is going to use. For the purpose of proportioning, sand may be classified as *damp, wet,* or *very wet.*

A simple method for determining the amount of moisture is by squeezing a handful of the sand to be used. See Fig. 4-4. Table 4-1 gives corrected proportions for water-cement ratios when the sand is damp, wet, or very wet.

Bulking in Sand. Sand will increase greatly in volume as it is handled, particularly if it is very moist. This is called *bulking*. This tendency makes it very difficult to judge the volume accurately. For this reason, sand should be measured by weight rather than volume whenever possible.

TABLE 4—1

IF MIX CALLS FOR:	Use these amounts of mixing water, in gallons, when sand is:		
	DAMP	WET	VERY WET
6 gal. per sack of cement	5 1/2	5	4 1/4
7 gal. per sack of cement	6 1/4	5 1/2	4 3/4

Concrete: Basic Materials and Mixing

Slump. The *consistency*, or degree of stiffness or fluidity, of concrete when it has been mixed and ready to place is called *slump*. Slump is measured in inches. High slump concretes are fluid while low slump concretes are stiff. Slump is determined mainly by the water-cement ratio. A high water-cement ratio causes high slump and, conversely, low water-cement ratios will lower the slump. In most cases, lower slumps within allowable ranges for various types of structures will make for better concrete.

The field test for slump is shown in Fig. 4-5. The sheet metal cone measures 8 inches in diameter at the bottom and 4 inches at the top and is 12 inches high. It is placed on a clean dry surface and filled approximately 1/3 full with the trial mixture. The concrete is then rodded 25 times with a metal rod. Then another 1/3 of concrete is added and rodded 25 times. The rod should extend all the way through the second 1/3 and just into the bottom 1/3. Next, the cone is completely filled, the top is raked off level, and the rodding repeated as above. Then the cone is removed by lifting it straight up, leaving the fresh concrete. The slump is now measured by placing the rod across the top of the cone and extended over the concrete sample. Then, with a rule, measure the distance between the top of the concrete sample and the bottom edge of the rod. This distance is the slump rating of the entire batch.

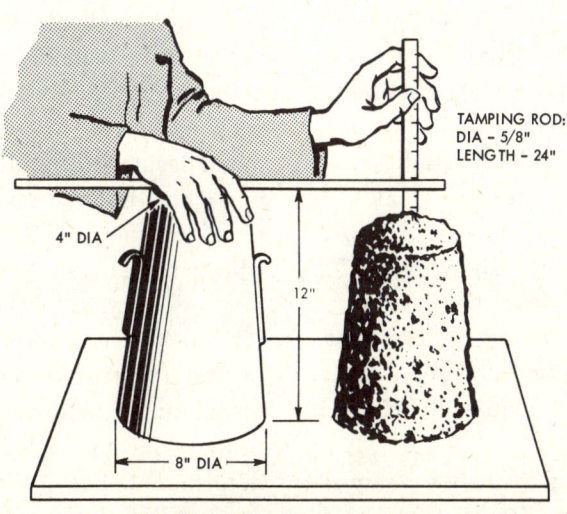

Fig. 4-5. Slump test for concrete.

Concrete Block Construction

Trial Proportions

Not many years ago, it was customary to specify the proportions (quantities of cement, sand, and crushed stone or gravel) for regular concrete mixes by such designations as 1:2:4, 1:3:5, etc. The 1:2:4 designation, for example, meant 1 part cement, 2 parts sand, and 4 parts crushed rock or gravel. This method of specification fails to assure satisfactory results for the following reasons.

1. It does not specify the quantity of mixing water which is so essential in making strong and watertight concrete.

2. It does not consider the grading of the aggregates.

3. It does not allow for variation in volume resulting from the tendency toward bulking of moist sands.

Present-day methods of specifying regular concrete mixes are made by paying careful attention to the amounts of water, the moisture content of the sand, and the amounts of aggregates used in the mix.

Recommended trial qualities of concrete and amounts of the ingredients for each, for various classes of work, are shown in Table 4-2. This table can be used as a guide to proportioning concrete materials according to the total amount of water required with each sack of cement.

Determining Suitable Proportions. Suppose, for example, it is necessary to determine the proper mix (proportioning of all ingredients, including damp sand and water) for building a water tank. For this job, the concrete must be watertight and be able to stand severe exposure to weather.

Table 4-2 shows that for a job of this kind, a 6-gallon paste should be used. But, for a trial batch, using one cubic foot (one sack) of cement, $2\frac{1}{4}$ cubic feet of sand, and 3 cubic feet of crushed stone or gravel, only $5\frac{1}{2}$ gallons of water can be added when mixing the ingredients, because (as previously explained) two cubic feet of damp sand will contain $2 \times \frac{1}{4}$, or $\frac{1}{2}$ gallon of moisture. This $\frac{1}{2}$ gallon plus the $5\frac{1}{2}$ gallons makes up the total of 6 gallons required per sack of cement.

Assuming a mechanical mixer is to be used, first place the correct amount of water in the mixer. Add one sack of cement, $2\frac{1}{4}$ cubic feet of sand, and 3 cubic feet of crushed rock or gravel, and run the mixer for at least two minutes. By noting how the resulting mix handles and places, it can be determined readily whether changes in the proportions are necessary to fit the needs of the job. If the concrete is a smooth, plastic, workable mass that will place and finish well, the correct proportions for the job have been determined. Fig. 4-6 shows at (A), a mix which lacks sufficient mortar,

Concrete: Basic Materials and Mixing

TABLE 4-2 RECOMMENDED PROPORTIONS OF WATER TO CEMENT AND SUGGESTED TRIAL MIXES

KIND OF WORK	Add U.S. Gals. Of Water To Each Sack of Cement If Sand Is			Suggested Mixture For Trial Batch		
	Very Wet	Wet	Damp	Cement Sacks	Sand Cu. Ft.	Crushed Rock or Gravel Cu. Ft.

FIVE GALLON PASTE FOR CONCRETE SUBJECTED TO SEVERE WEAR, WEATHER OR WEAK ACID AND ALKALI SOLUTIONS

KIND OF WORK	Very Wet	Wet	Damp	Cement Sacks	Sand Cu. Ft.	Crushed Rock or Gravel Cu. Ft.
Colored or plain topping for heavy wearing surfaces and all two-course work for pavements, tennis courts, floors, etc..........	\[Maximum size aggregate 3/8 inch\] 4 1/4	Average sand 4 1/2	4 3/4	1	1	1 1/2
One-course industrial, floors and all concrete in contact with weak acid or alkali solutions..................	\[Maximum size aggregate 3/4 inch\] 3 3/4	4	4 1/2	1	1 3/4	2

SIX GALLON PASTE FOR CONCRETE TO BE WATERTIGHT OR SUBJECTED TO MODERATE WEAR AND WEATHER

KIND OF WORK	Very Wet	Wet	Damp	Cement Sacks	Sand Cu. Ft.	Crushed Rock or Gravel Cu. Ft.
Watertight floors such as industrial plant, basement etc........ Watertight foundations............... Concrete subjected to moderate wear or frost action such as driveways, walks, tennis courts, garage floors, etc................. All watertight concrete for swimming and wading pools, bird baths, fish ponds, septic tanks, storage tanks, etc.................. All base course work such as floors, walks, drives, etc............... Steps, chimney caps, blocks, concrete masonry, fireplaces, etc..... All reinforced concrete structural beams, columns, lintels, slabs, residence floors, etc............	\[Maximum size aggregate 1 1/2 inches\] 4 1/4	Average sand 5	5 1/2	1	2 1/4	3

SEVEN GALLON PASTE FOR CONCRETE NOT SUBJECTED TO WEAR, WEATHER OR WATER

KIND OF WORK	Very Wet	Wet	Damp	Cement Sacks	Sand Cu. Ft.	Crushed Rock or Gravel Cu. Ft.
Foundations, walls footings, mass concrete, etc., not subjected to weather, water pressure or other exposure	4 3/4	Average sand 5 1/2	6 1/4	1	2 3/4	4

Concrete Block Construction

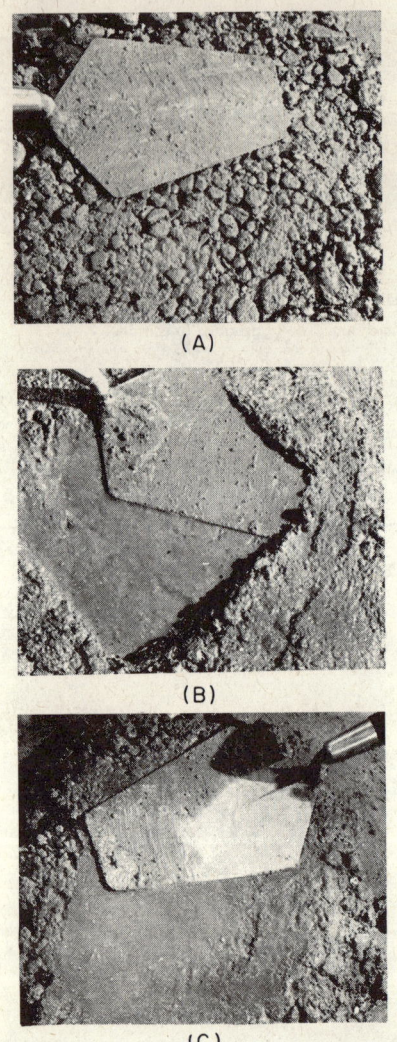

Fig. 4-6. Top: Concrete mixture which lacks sufficient mortar. Middle: Concrete mixture having excess cement and sand. Bottom: Concrete mixture having correct proportions.

at (B), a mix having excess cement and sand, and at (C) a mix with good proportions. While the mix shown at (C), in Fig. 4-6, is good, it will not satisfy every condition.

For example, it may be too stiff for use in making some concrete objects where the mix must surround reinforcing or run into narrow forms, etc. Thus, the particular job at hand, to some extent, governs the condition of mixes.

Correcting Trial Mixture. If the trial mix is not workable under the conditions of the job, the amounts of aggregate used in the concrete must be changed. *However, the amount of water should not, under any circumstances, be changed.* The trial batch of 1 part cement, 2¼ parts sand, and 3 parts coarse aggregate may, for example, be too stiff or too wet or may lack smoothness and workability.

When the trial proportion gives a mixture that is too wet, add small amounts of sand and coarse aggregate in the proportion of 2¼ parts of sand and 3 parts coarse aggregate until the correct workability is obtained.

If it is necessary to use more sand than is shown in the proportions given in Table 4-2, for instance, an extra ½ cubic foot—it is important to deduct the moisture carried by this additional sand.

If the concrete is too stiff and appears crumbly, succeeding batches can be mixed with less aggregate.

Under ordinary conditions, a concrete mix should be *mushy* but not *soupy*. The mushy mix will hold together while a soupy mix may sepa-

Concrete: Basic Materials and Mixing

rate in handling, with the larger pieces of aggregate sinking in the mass.

In some cases, concrete specifications still call for concrete as a 1:2:4 mix. There may be danger in following such a specification exactly, as explained in the following.

Suppose that a 1:2:4 mix is specified and that the sand available for use is average in regard to moisture. First of all, unless the approximate amount of moisture in the sand is determined, the cement paste will be diluted. In addition, sand of average moisture content is bulked at least 20 percent because the moisture forms a film around each sand particle and thus forces the various particles farther apart. If such bulked sand is used in a 1:2:4 mix, the resulting concrete will be 20 percent short on sand and will detract from the strength and density of the concrete. To overcome this shortage, a mix of $1:2\frac{1}{4}:3$, as recommended in Table 4-2, or $1:2\frac{1}{2}:3\frac{1}{2}$ should be used. This might result possibly in some oversanding, but that condition would be much better than undersanding. As seen, there is a strong possibility for discrepancy between the specification and the actual mix. For this reason, this type of specification should be avoided.

Air Entrainment

One of the most important advances in concrete construction has been the development of air entrainment. Air-entrained concrete contains extremely small air bubbles throughout the cement-water paste. The bubbles are so small that there may be as many as 3000 billion in one cubic yard of concrete.

Although developed and used primarily for its high resistance to freeze-thaw damage, air entrained concrete has been found to have other desirable properties as well. As compared to concrete using regular cement, air entrained concrete is more workable, thus requiring less water and sand, is more watertight, and is highly resistant to chemicals such as sulfates and the various salts used as de-icers on city streets and sidewalks. It is logical, therefore, that air entraining cement or an entraining admixture is specified in concrete formulas for sidewalks, driveways, etc., in areas having severe winters and various salts are used as de-icers. Garage floors in these areas should also be made of air entrained concrete, as vehicles coming in from salted streets and highways will drip enough salty moisture to cause rapid deterioration.

Concrete Block Construction

Air entraining portland cements are available in types I-A, II-A, and III-A, which correspond with the specifications for regular Types I, II, and III as described earlier in this chapter. There are also air entraining admixtures available under several brand names. These admixtures will give satisfactory results if the manufacturer's directions on the container are followed.

Admixtures

Admixtures are any materials added to the portland cement-water-aggregate mixture in order to improve or add specific properties such as accelerating or retarding setting time, air entrainment, water repellents, etc. Most specifications or codes discourage the use of admixtures for accelerating or retarding when alternatives, such as modified curing methods, are available. However, the use of air entraining admixtures are advised where air entraining portland cement is not used.

Calcium chloride is sometimes used to accelerate the setting time of fresh concrete in freezing weather. This practice should be avoided if at all possible, as calcium chloride in any appreciable quantity will weaken the concrete. Most building codes, if not actually forbidding the use of calcium chloride, limit the allowable quantity to 2 percent of the total mixture. Recommended alternatives are the using of Type III (high early strength) portland cement, or the warming of materials before mixing or the using of heating devices during curing. Calcium chloride is *never* to be used as an anti-freeze, as the quantity required to be effective is enough to completely ruin the concrete. Calcium chloride also corrodes metal and is prohibited in prestressed concrete.

Ready Mixed Concrete

Most concrete construction jobs use ready mixed concrete. The main reasons for this are that ready mix precludes the time and space involved in storing and handling the raw materials, the labor involved in on-the-job mixing, and the clean-up of waste materials. Purchasers may also be assured of receiving any quantity of concrete of uniform quality at exactly the time it is needed.

Ready mixed concrete is usually prepared in one of two ways: central

Concrete: Basic Materials and Mixing

Fig. 4-7. A typical ready mix truck.

mixed or transit mixed. Central mixing is the complete mixing of the concrete in a central batch plant. The concrete is then loaded into special trucks of the type shown in Fig. 4-7 for delivery to the job site. The concrete is in rotating drums which keep it plastic and workable until time to place.

If a job requires only one truckload or less, the concrete may be transit mixed. In this method, the raw materials, cement, aggregate and water, are placed directly into the drum which revolves and mixes the concrete on the way to the job site.

Job Site Mixing

On some small jobs where ready mix is not available or impractical, concrete may be mixed on the job. Portable mechanical mixers are usually employed in these situations. See Fig. 4-8. These mixers are available with capacities ranging from a few cubic feet up to several cubic yards. The operator must be familiar with the manufacturer's specifications for maximum load and mixing speed. These should *never* be exceeded.

Fig. 4-8. A typical small portable concrete mixer.

The procedure for loading and mixing is as follows. First, the materials are measured according to the specifications. Then, about 10 percent of the amount of water to be used is poured into the drum. The drum is then set in motion, and the cement and aggregate are added gradually along with more water.

The water should be added at such a rate that when all of the cement and aggregate are in the drum, about 90 percent of the specified amount of water has been added. The mixing time is measured from the time all the solid materials are in the drum. Most specifications call for at least one minute of mixing time for mixers of up to 1 cubic yard capacity with an increase of 15 seconds for each additional cubic yard.

After the minimum mixing time has elapsed, the mixture should be tested for stiffness, or slump. If it appears to be too stiff to be workable, additional water may be added up to the maximum amount allowed in the specifications. As the amount of water in the mixture is critical in regard to the ultimate strength of the hardened concrete, the specified amount should never be exceeded. If the mix remains extra stiff, some workability must be sacrificed for the sake of strength.

Hand Mixing

Although hand mixing of concrete is seldom required, the mason should know the correct way of doing it. First, the dry cement and aggregate are mixed thoroughly on a clean, dry, waterproof surface. Then the dry materials are mounded and a depression is made in the middle. Water is gradually added to the depression as the dry material is turned in toward the middle with a shovel. Continue mixing until all the ingredients are thoroughly combined and the aggregate is completely coated with paste.

Concrete: Basic Materials and Mixing

Checking On Your Knowledge

The following questions give you the opportunity to check up on yourself. If you have read the chapter carefully, you should be able to answer the questions. If you have any difficulty, read the chapter over once more so that you have the information well in mind before you go on with your reading.

DO YOU KNOW

1. What the three basic materials in making concrete are?
2. The two classifications of aggregate and their sizes?
3. What is meant by grading of aggregate?
4. What lightweight aggregate is and where it is used?
5. The five types of portland cement and the differences between them?
6. What is meant by a 0.45 water-cement ratio?
7. Why the aggregate proportion in a concrete mix is an important economic factor?
8. How to determine the amount of moisture in sand?
9. What is meant by *bulking* in sand?
10. What is meant by *slump*?
11. The three main factors in modern methods for specifying concrete mixes?
12. How to determine the correct amount of water for a concrete mix?
13. What one of the most important developments in concrete construction is?
14. What admixtures are?
15. Why the use of calcium chloride should be avoided?
16. Why ready mix is so widely used?

Chapter 5: Concrete Formwork

As well as understanding the nature of concrete itself, the mason should also be aware of the various steps and methods in preparing for placing concrete since, as mentioned earlier the concrete block walls must rest directly on the finished footings and foundations. Also, should the journeyman become a foreman, superintendent, or contractor, it is essential that he be familiar with all phases of construction and understand the relationship of the work of the mason and that of the other trades.

This chapter will cover the construction of general formwork, including footings, foundations and walls, and will cover the all-important relationship of the mason and carpenter in the construction and use of formwork. Foundations with slab-at-grade construction are also covered.

The care required in the construction of the footings and foundations of homes cannot be over emphasized. If the footing is not laid correctly on firm earth, cracks will develop in the foundation wall, and it will be very difficult to make the foundation waterproof. If the foundation is not square, if the dimensions are not accurate, and if the top is not exactly according to grade requirements, adjustments must be made in the structure of the building that will affect many aspects of the work to be done later.

The actual forming is done differently in various areas of the country. In rural areas or where only one building is to be built, forms are made of boards and 2″ × 4″ members. After the forms are stripped, the lumber is used for rough flooring, sheathing, and structural purposes. Contractors building a number of

Concrete Formwork

houses have forms made in modular 4 × 8 foot panels (or other sizes) using 2 × 4 inch frames and sheathing or plywood for face material. These forms are used over again many times. Many contractors use manufactured form panels which are designed for durability and to provide fast, efficient erection. In larger cities, forms may be rented or purchased from companies that make a specialty of concrete products and building forms.

Concrete as a Material

It is important that the carpenter have an understanding of concrete as a material, because he must build forms strong enough to hold it in place until it sets. When forms fail, the time spent in erecting them is lost and much material is expended. On the other hand, labor and forming material can be wasted if the forms are made strong beyond sensible safe limits. The method and equipment used to place the concrete also has a bearing on how the forms should be designed.

Loads on a foundation wall are generally considered as hydraulic loadings that result in lateral pressure. In other words, the concrete acts as though it were in a liquid state, pushing sideways against the forms.

Basic Formwork

The broad surfaces of the forms are generally plywood sheets. These are held the desired distance apart and prevented from spreading further by devices known as ties. Vertical members serve to stiffen the sheathing and horizontal members known as wales (or walers) hold them in line. The ties generally are fastened through some form of holder which transfers the pressure to the wales. Generally the ties, walers and vertical members are spaced uniformly in both the horizontal and vertical direction because they are designed to take the maximum load at all levels in the form. It is important that the builder appreciate the fact that forms must stand a great deal of pressure. The ties do the work of retaining the concrete and spacing the forms to give the required wall thickness. The vertical members and the wales stiffen the forms. Bracing serves the main purpose of keeping the forms in correct position.

Excavation for Basement

In firm soil, shallow excavations up to 5 feet in depth require a clearance of 18 inches outside the building lines for erecting and removing forms. For deeper excavations, 2 feet or more must be allowed for working space between the building lines and the excavation.

To arrive at the depth of the excavation, the builder should study the vertical section view taken

Concrete Block Construction

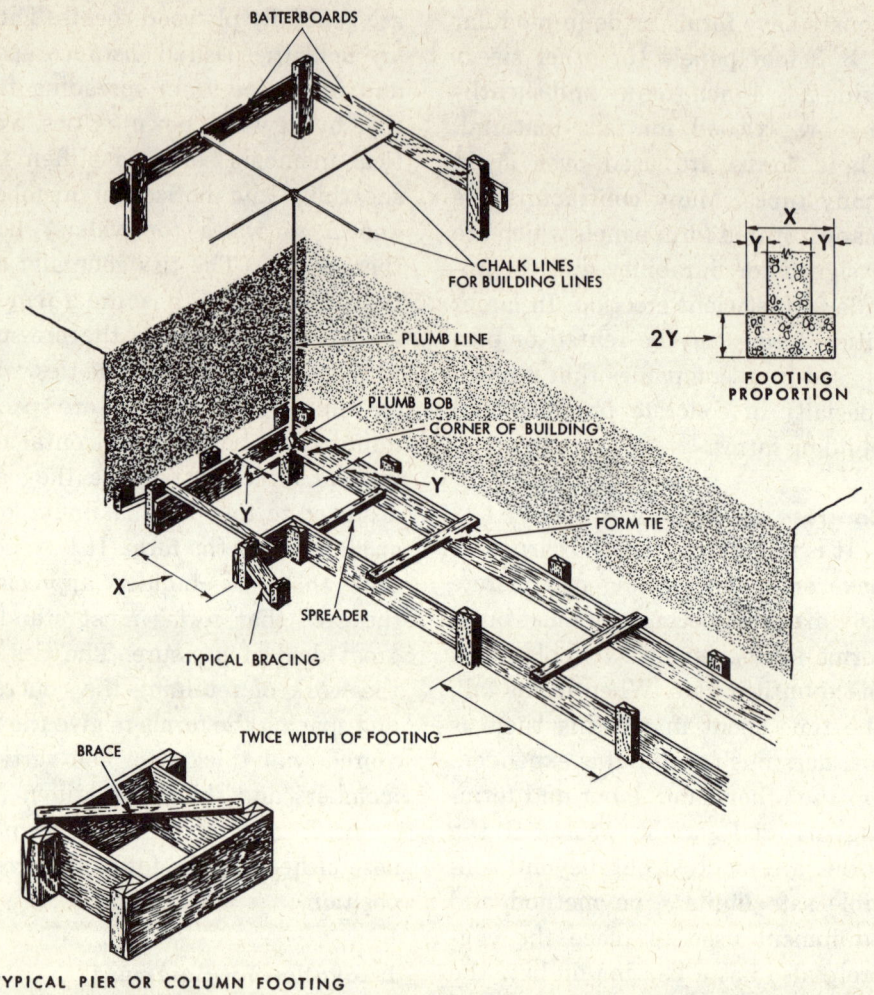

Fig. 5-1. Forming for foundation and pier or column footings.

through the house and calculate the dimensions from the top of the foundation grade to the bottom of the footing. The distance the foundation will project above the finished grade will be marked on the section view.

There must be a minimum exposure of concrete of 8 inches from grade to the lowest wood member as one means of protection from termites. It is also important that surface water be drawn away from the house and,

Concrete Formwork

therefore, it becomes necessary that the grade be sloped away in all directions. The excavation should be made so the earth is not disturbed in the bottom of the areas where the footings are to be placed.

The work of excavating should not be done until all stakes have been checked to see that the building is located correctly from the lot lines and has correct dimensions.

Forms for Footing

After all excavations have been made to the correct depths, forms for the footings are laid out and erected. The footings must be straight and level and must rest on undisturbed earth so that the load of the building may be transferred to the ground in a uniform manner. There must be no settling later.

Fig. 5-1 shows a typical method of forming for footings.

"T" Type Footing. A "T" type footing such as shown in Fig. 5-2 provides a starter wall for the foundation and gives the forms a shoulder to rest on. It is used when the foundation is low. Several operations and much time is saved in forming the foundation wall later. The location and the thickness of the foundation wall will not have to be determined. There is no problem in pulling the forms together at the bottom and adjusting them for irregularities in the footing. The manner of making the "T" type footing is shown in Fig. 5-2 and Fig. 5-3.

Some builders in different parts of the country use keys. After the footing has been poured and the concrete has been struck off flush, a key made up of a piece of 2" × 4" with edges tapered or 2" × 2" is pressed into the top surface before it has set. The key serves as a tie between

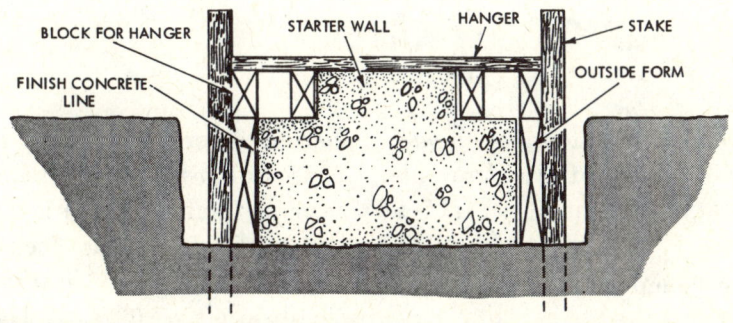

Fig. 5-2. "T" type forms are made by suspending wall form boards accurately above the footing forms.

73

Concrete Block Construction

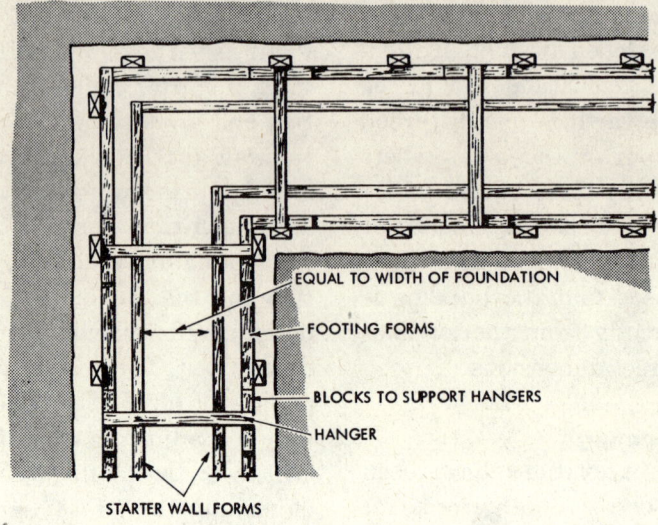

Fig. 5-3. View from above shows how the starter wall forms are spaced.

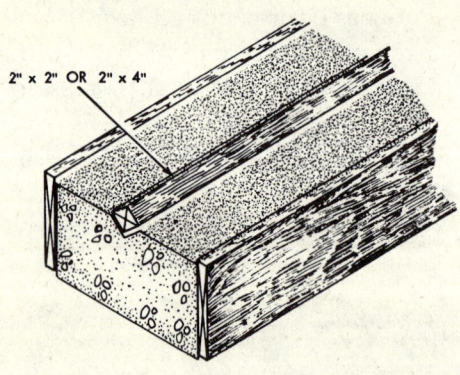

Fig. 5-4. A key is made by pressing a piece of wood into the footing before the concrete sets.

the footing and the foundation wall which will be placed later preventing lateral movement. See Fig. 5-4.

Concrete Foundation Forming Systems

There are several different types of forming systems because of a number of different problems and because of individual preferences. One type of forming, which is still used today though it has been largely replaced, is called "built-up" or "built-in-place" forming. The materials used are 2" × 4" vertical members and 1" × 6" boards. After the

Concrete Formwork

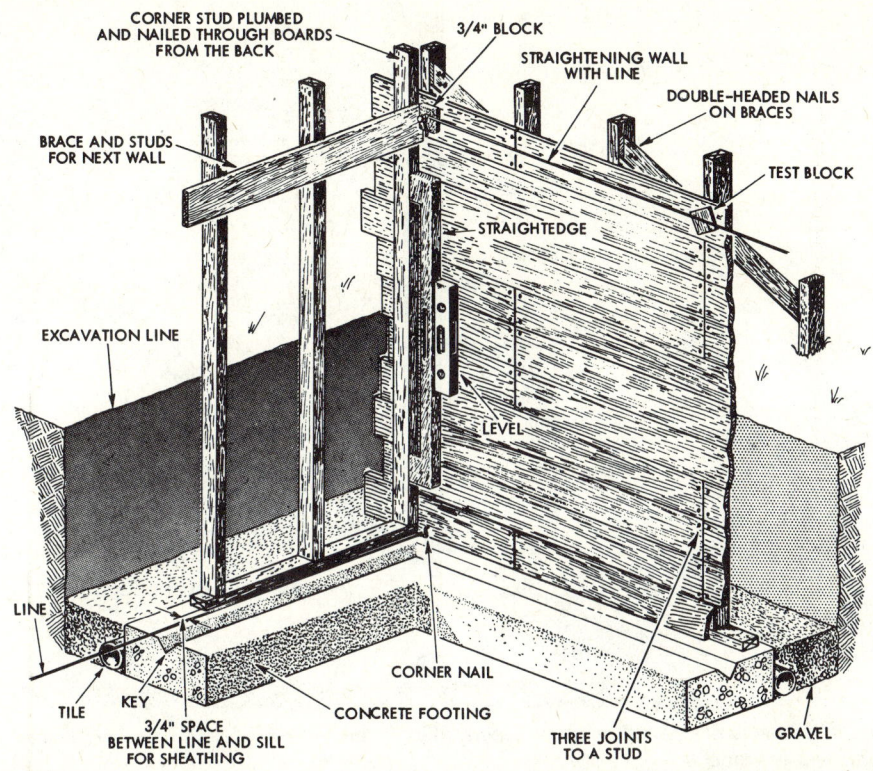

Fig. 5-5. Built-in-place forming is used when the builder wishes to use the form material in the structure of the house.

forms are stripped, the materials used to build the forms are utilized in the building of the house. See Figs. 5-5 and 5-6.

Boards are also used when the form is to be torn apart and the wood used in building the structure. Green lumber should be avoided because exposure to air and sun causes it to shrink. Shrinkage opens joints and allows part of the wet concrete to leak out leaving a concentration of the aggregate. On the other hand, if the wood is too dry it will soak up water from the concrete and will swell. This may bring about distortion in the forms. It is good practice to hose down the forms the day before the concrete is to be placed and to continue hosing up to the time of placing.

Forms for basement foundations

Concrete Block Construction

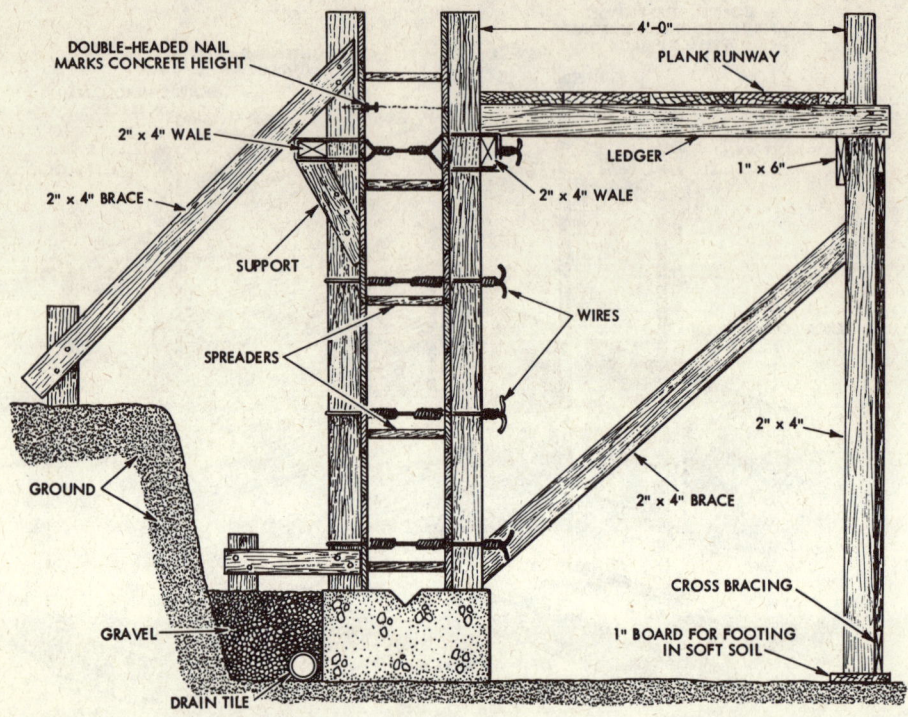

Fig. 5-6. A sectional view through formwork which is built-in-place. Notice the wire ties, wood spreaders and bracing.

are usually made of 4′ × 8′ plywood panels on frames made of 2″ × 4″s. Templates or jigs are not necessary for these forms, because the sheets of plywood have exact dimensions and have perfectly square corners. The frames are assembled to fit the plywood sheet. The plywood is made for this particular purpose in ⅝ and ¾ inch thicknesses. Plywood panels are by far the fastest and most economical panels to fabricate. They last longer and give a far better finish to the wall than sheathing, leaving a wall surface which is quite smooth. These panels may be obtained with a plastic surface that is waterproof, abrasion resistant, and easy to clean. Forms with plywood faces can be reused many times. Patented forms with metal frames provide edge protection for the plywood panels. The panels may be replaced when damaged or worn.

Ordinary plywood panels are given a coat of oil so that they will separate from the wall without difficulty. The oil coating also permits

Concrete Formwork

them to be cleaned easily. If the walls are to be painted or plastered, however, the oil in the concrete may prevent the finish from bonding. Some other agent may be used, such as a lacquer.

Much of the concrete forming today is done using panel forms made by the builder. Some builders make the forms on the job site, while others build them elsewhere and transport them from job to job. They are made as large as can be conveniently carried and put in place. For low walls, the forms are made by nailing a number of 1 inch boards to evenly spaced 2 × 4 inch uprights. When the forms are stripped, the material may be reused in building the house.

The forms used for houses with basements are modular 4 × 8 foot panels (or other convenient sizes) made with frames of 2 × 4 inch members having intermediate stiffeners and faced with pieces of ¾ inch plywood. Several types of ties are used. Wire ties and band iron are still used but have been largely replaced by snap ties and various patented devices. See Fig. 5-7 for an example of this type of forming.

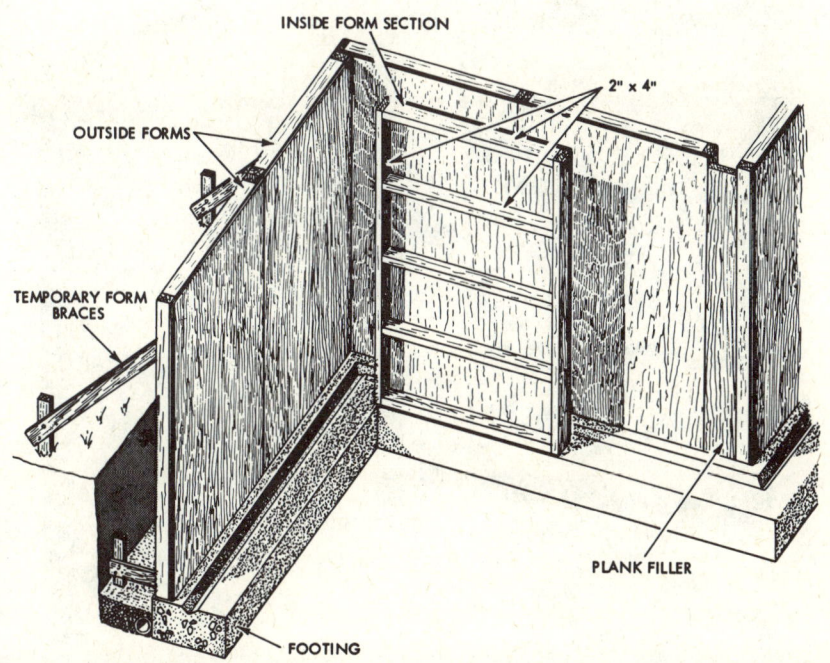

Fig. 5-7. Panels with fillers of various sizes can be adapted to most forming problems and may be re-used many times.

Concrete Block Construction

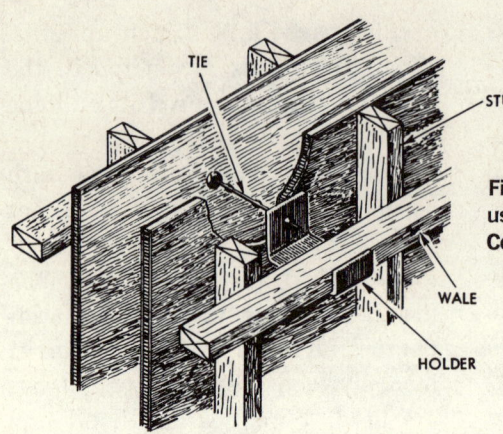

Fig. 5-8. Patented form ties and holders are used to hold wales against studs. (Allenform Corporation)

Fig. 5-9. Some manufactured panels have steel frames and plywood faces. Patented corners and form ties are used to speed up assembly. (Universal Form Clamp Co.)

Concrete Formwork

A number of manufacturers have developed several ingenious forming systems to replace, or to supplement, forms built on the site. Some are quite simple, using sheets of plywood and special ties and clamps. Wood wales stiffen the plywood sheets and keep them in line. See Fig. 5-8. Other forming systems use panel units with steel frames and plywood faces. They come in several sizes and require a variety of tying devices to meet special forming problems. See Fig. 5-9. The patented forms have several advantages, the most important of which are that they can be erected quickly by fewer men, they can be reused a great many times, and they are very durable. The companies that manufacture forms rent or sell them to builders. Some provide a service whereby they analyze the forming problems, prepare working drawings, and submit complete material lists. When a builder has much work that must be frequently repeated, it pays him to purchase a set of manufactured forms.

Form Ties. A form tie is a device that passes through both sides of a form, retaining them against the lateral pressure of the concrete. One type of tie that has been used for many years is the wire tie. See Fig. 5-10.

Snap ties are very popular and are used by many builders. The forms are kept the proper distance apart by means of washers which are fixed to the tie. Two places about an inch inside of each washer are weakened by flattening. These are the points where the tie will be broken off after the forms are removed. See Fig. 5-11.

Building Forms for Low Walls

Forms for low walls are generally

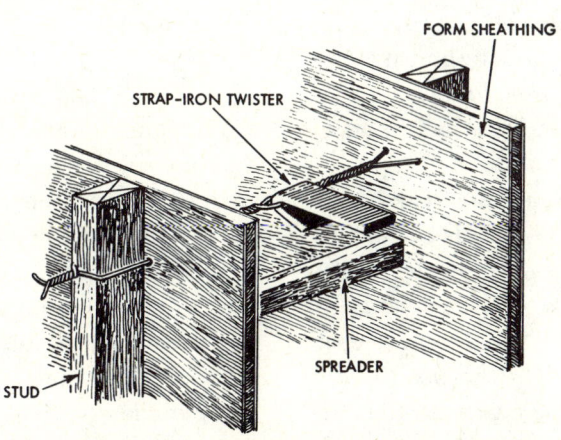

Fig. 5-10. Wire ties are twisted until the studs draw the sheathing tight against the spreaders.

Concrete Block Construction

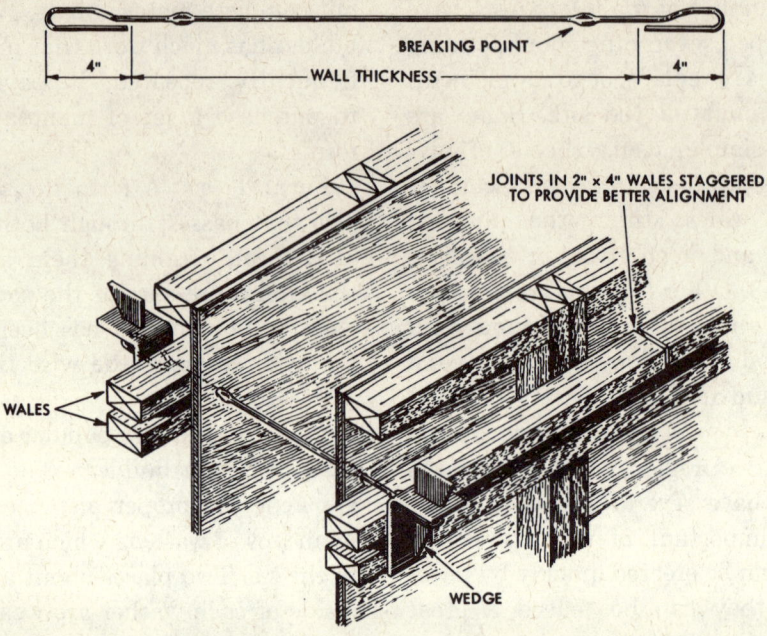

Fig. 5-11. Snap ties provide a means of spacing the walls at the proper distance apart, and also clamping the whole assembly together.

made of 2″ × 4″ members and 1″ × 6″ sheathing. They can be made quickly on the job site and may be taken apart and used for other building purposes. See Figs. 5-12 and 5-13.

Alternative Procedure for Building Forms for Low Walls Using "T" Footing. The procedure for building forms for low walls is essentially the same when "T" footings are used except that wedges are used under the sill to level the panels. It is assumed that the forms are made away from the excavation area and that the inner forms will be set first. See Fig. 5-14.

Openings in Concrete Walls

The frames for windows and doors that are located in the foundations are installed in some instances before the placing of concrete. In the case of some metal basement windows, the frames are put in place and wood forms are used to make the sill and sides of the window opening. For other windows a strip is nailed to the form which makes a recess in the concrete when it is placed. When

Concrete Formwork

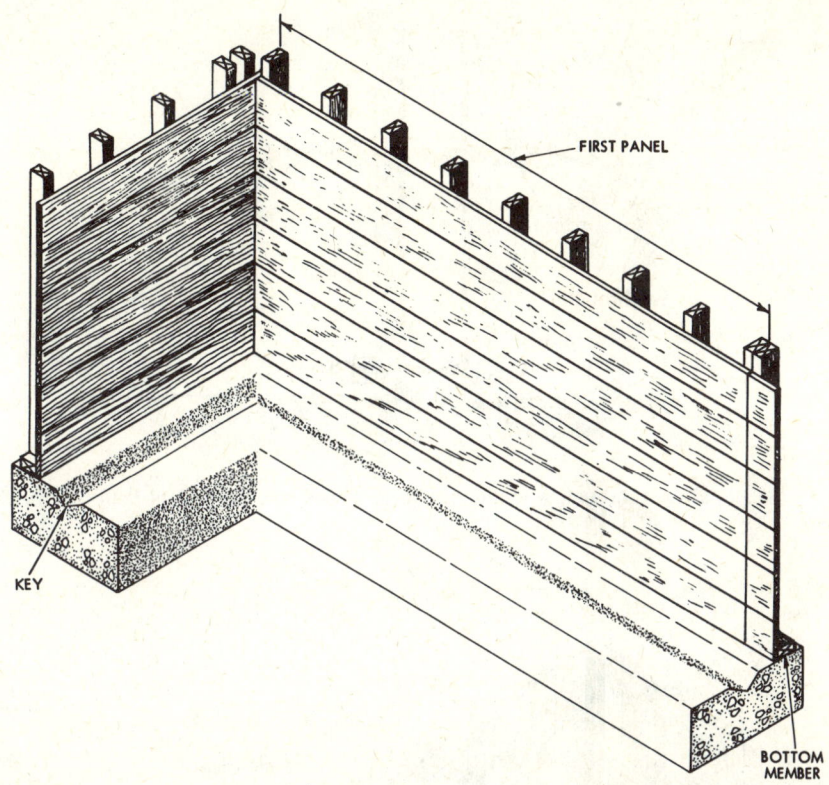

Fig. 5-12. Forms for low walls are made of 2" x 4" studs and sheathing. The outside form is usually erected first.

the form for the window is removed, a recess is left in the wall into which the metal sash is dropped. It is sealed with grout. See Fig. 5-15.

Some finished frames are put in place in the forms and are held by a key strip. The concrete stops against the frame. See Fig. 5-16.

Other openings are made by using a buck which is removed after the concrete is placed, leaving blocks or strips in the wall to which the frame is later fastened. One important thing to remember is that the buck must be made so that it can be removed without too much trouble. The corners of the window buck are mitered, and the bottom piece is cut through, so that it will slip out easily. See Fig. 5-17.

Forms for Steps

There are many different methods of forming for steps. The important

Concrete Block Construction

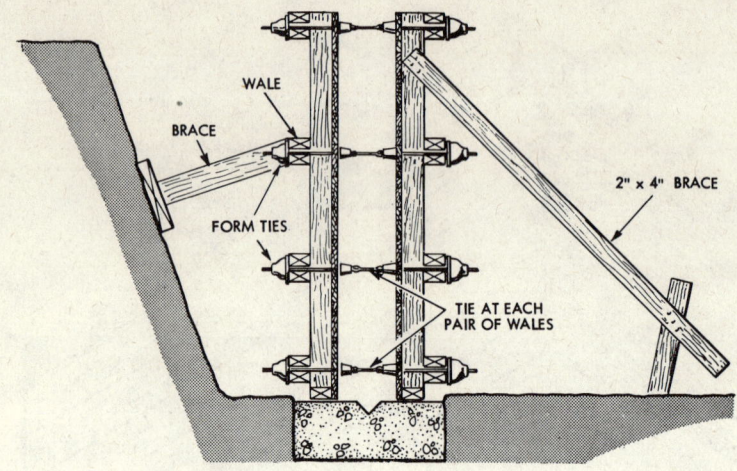

Fig. 5-13. Sectional view through a foundation form shows how the wall is held together and braced.

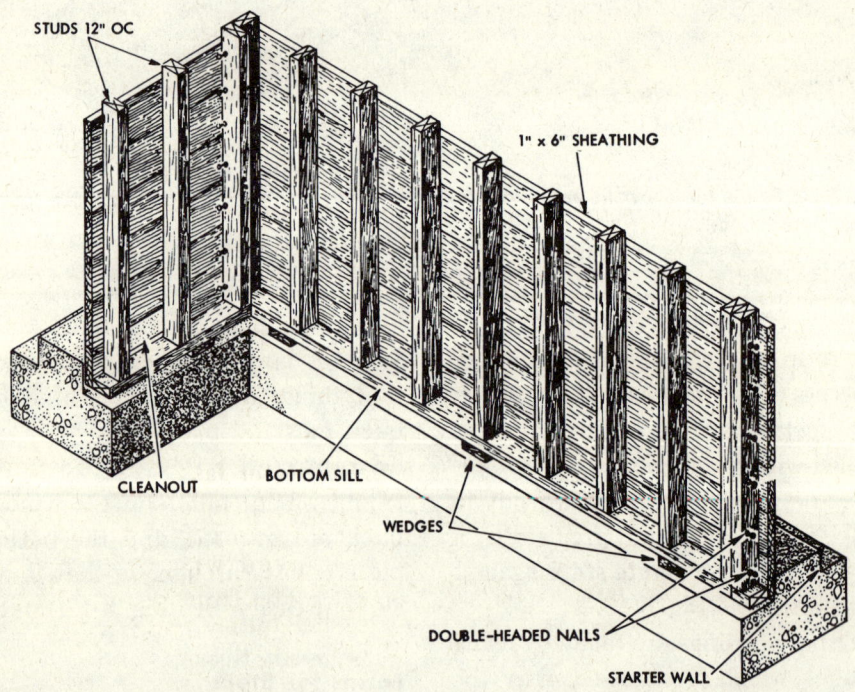

Fig. 5-14. Panel forms used with a "T" footing. Note the wedges used to level the forms. The inside panels are erected first.

Concrete Formwork

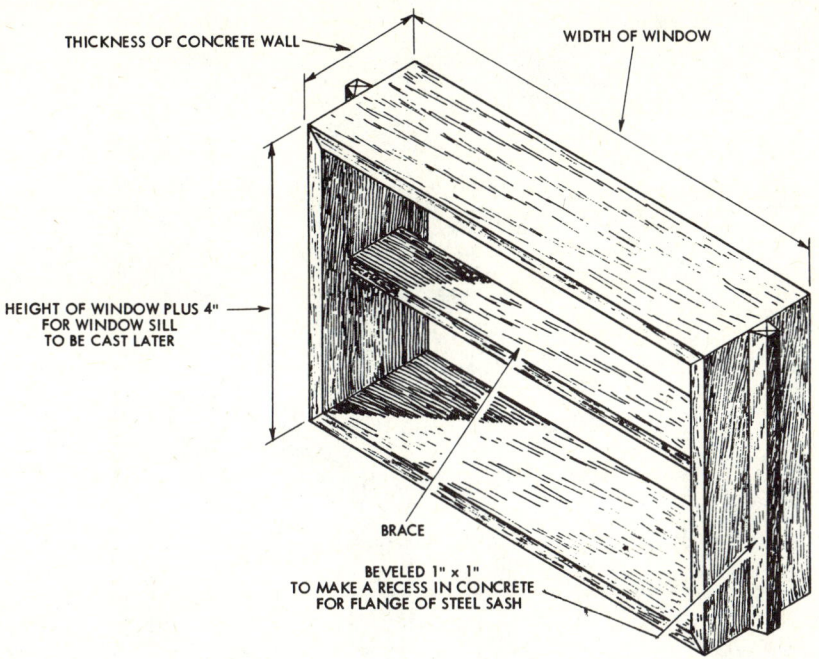

Fig. 5-15. The rough form for metal framed basement windows is removed after the concrete has set, leaving a recess for the window frame.

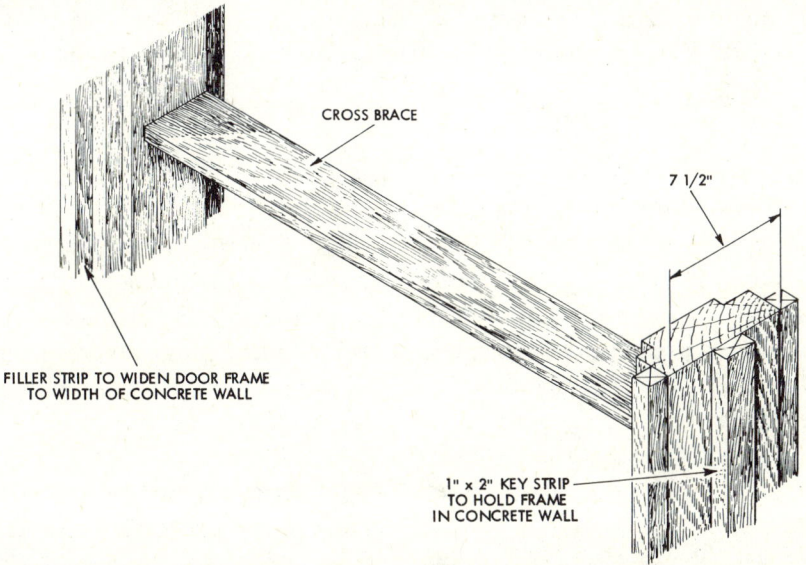

Fig. 5-16. A pre-installed door frame in a concrete wall. The key strip holds the frame in place.

Concrete Block Construction

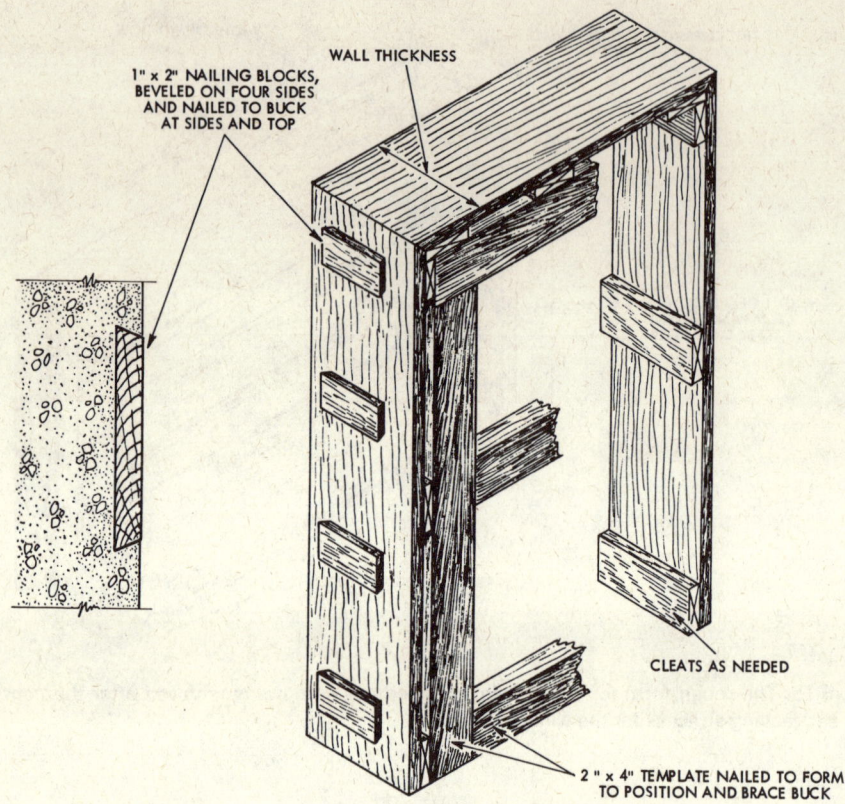

Fig. 5-17. A rough buck is made so that nailing blocks are left in the wall.

considerations are where the steps are located in relation to adjoining structures, and how they are to be supported. In most cases, however, the materials used are the same, and the bracing methods are similar. The riser forms are usually nominal 1 inch boards. The side forms or braces are made from 2″ × 6″ or 2″ × 8″ stock.

Fig. 5-18 shows a typical forming method for basement steps.

Fig. 5-19 shows two designs for sidewalk steps, one employing curbs. These may also be used as approach steps for building entrances.

Fig. 5-20 shows a simple method of forming for a small porch and steps resting on earth and a foundation.

The steps shown in Fig. 5-21 are self-supporting, reinforced with steel bars, and have a foundation which is not integral with the sidewalk. Such

Concrete Formwork

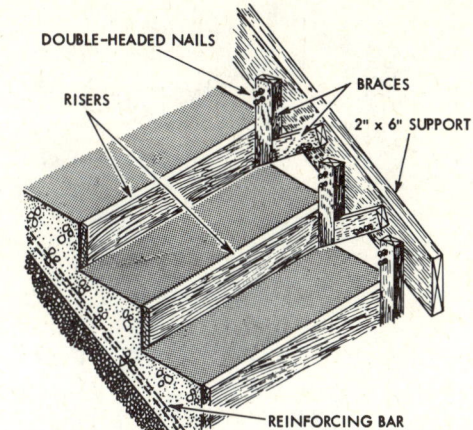

Fig. 5-18. Formwork for basement steps.

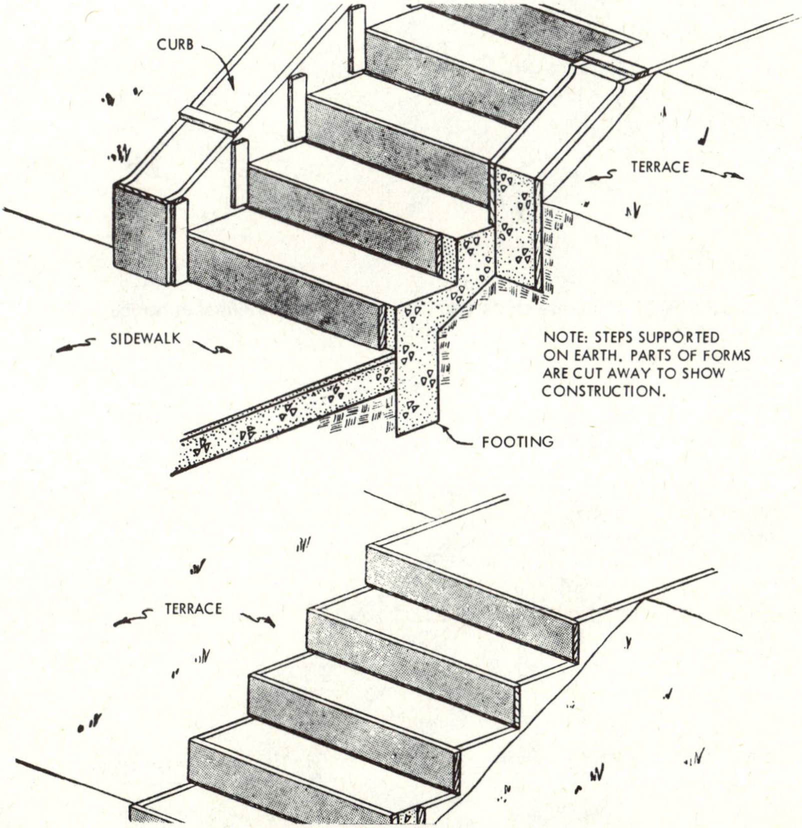

Fig. 5-19. Steps for changes in elevation of sidewalks.

Concrete Block Construction

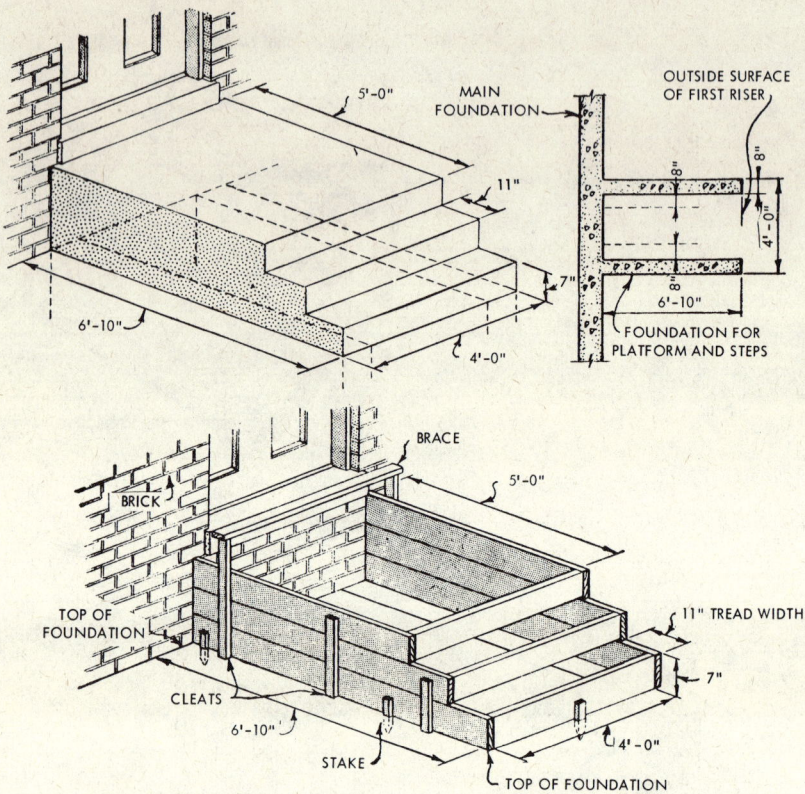

Fig. 5-20. Concrete steps and platform for a residential entrance.

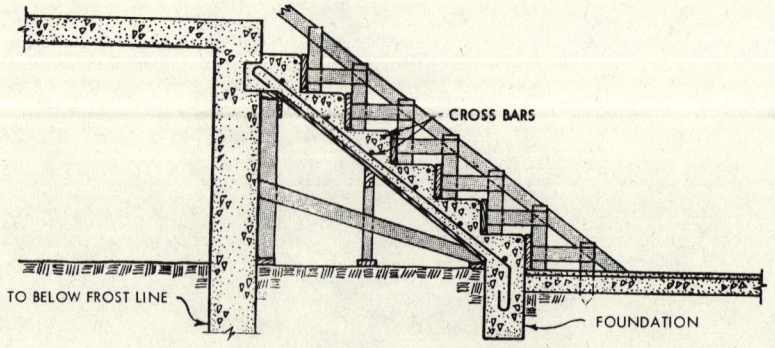

Fig. 5-21. Self supporting steps.

Concrete Formwork

steps are commonly used where a concrete front porch for a residence is several feet above grade. Note how the top of the steps is notched into the porch foundation wall.

Steel Reinforcement

Reinforcing is frequently used in footings, foundations, and steps to add strength and alleviate stresses. Reinforcing is usually designed by engineers and installed by professional steelworkers. The materials used are either deformed steel bars or welded wire fabric as shown in Fig. 5-22.

Concrete piers, pilasters and columns are also reinforced. Fig. 5-23 shows reinforcing steel in place for a column.

Fig. 5-23. Reinforcing steel for a concrete column.

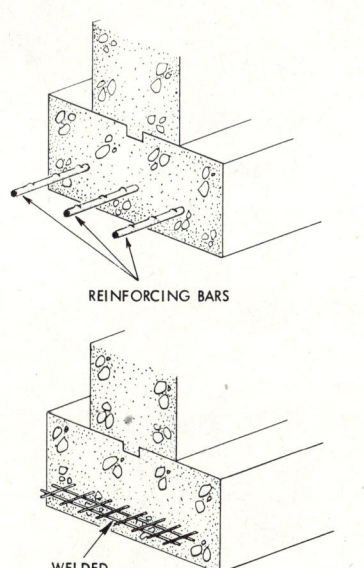

Fig. 5-22. Steel reinforcing in concrete footings.

Placing Concrete in Forms

Proper placing of concrete in forms is one of the most critical operations in building construction. Footings and foundations must carry the weight of the rest of the building. It is essential that the forms be completely filled with concrete and that the aggregate and cement proportions be consistent throughout. Remember that a good concrete mix will be stiff and difficult to work or compact. However, there are certain techniques which, if followed, will assure a sound, solid structure.

In all formed structures, whether they be footings, foundations, walls or others, the first placing should be at the end or ends of the form. Subsequent placing is done continuously

87

Concrete Block Construction

until the form is full. Horizontal movement of the concrete after it is placed in the form should be avoided. That is, the concrete should be placed as close as possible to its final position.

During or immediately after placing, the concrete must be compacted tightly against the forms to avoid air pockets or voids both internally and on the surface. This may be accomplished on smaller structures by *lightly* tapping the sides of the form with a hammer. Too heavy tapping, however, will cause the heavier aggregate to segregate and settle to the bottom. This will not only cause an uneven consistence in the mixture, but may also cause the forms to spread and separate at the bottom.

The most common method of compacting on all sizes and types of structures is by the means of mechanical vibrators. Vibrators, used correctly, assure complete consolidation of the concrete. There are no set rules as to the length of time concrete should be vibrated, but in most cases, 10 to 15 seconds for each placing is sufficient. This is another skill that the cement mason

Fig. 5-24. Compacting concrete in forms with a vibrator. (Adolphi Studio)

Concrete Formwork

Fig. 5-25. Float finishing the top surface of a foundation.

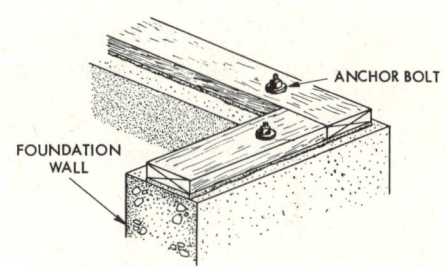

Fig. 5-26. Anchor bolts in a concrete foundation.

must learn by experience. Fig. 5-24 shows mechanical vibrators being used while concrete is being placed.

After the form is filled and compacted to the specified level, the top surface is finished with a hand float. See Fig. 5-25.

At this point, if the foundation is to be used as a base for frame construction, the anchor bolts for the sills should be placed. It is the cement mason's responsibility to check the building plans for the correct locations and to install the anchor bolts. See Fig. 5-26.

Concrete Walls. Concrete walls are placed and compacted in the same way as foundations. It may be impractical, however, to try to place all the concrete up to full height in one operation. In these cases, a few vertical feet are placed and compacted as for a foundation. Then succeeding layers, called *lifts,* are placed and compacted until the full height is reached. (From 12 to 15 inches per lift is recommended.) If vibrators are used, the vibrator head is allowed to penetrate through the new lift and at least 6 inches into the preceding lift. This makes for a unified structure with a uniform surface after the forms are removed.

Fig. 5-27 shows a completed foundation-basement wall system for a small residence. Note that the areaways, porch and garage foundations, and other structures and openings were formed in such a way that all the parts became one continuous piece of concrete. This prevents any part from settling away from the rest, insuring a firm and continuous support for the rest of the building.

Removal of Forms

Generally four days should elapse before the forms are removed if time will permit. The panels are usually removed in the reverse order from which they were placed. Form tie clamps are knocked off and the wales removed first. The forms are pried from the walls with care in order not to damage the concrete. The ties pull out of the forms and remain projecting from the wall. It is wise to wait a day or two longer before removing the tie ends. This is done by twisting or pulling on the tie end so that it breaks at the "break back" point within the wall. The hole in the wall is then filled with grout and finished flush with the surface.

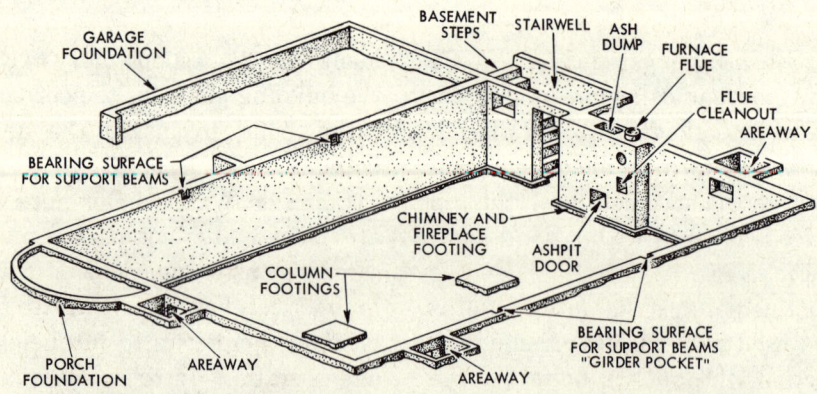

Fig. 5-27. Completed concrete foundation for a small basement type residence.

Concrete Formwork

Foundations for Homes with Slab-At-Grade

An increasing number of homes are being built in all parts of the country in which a concrete floor is laid directly on the ground. See Fig. 5-28. Certain precautions must be made in order that the floor be satisfactory. The Small Homes Council suggests the following: The earth around the house must be graded so that water will drain away properly. The entire area where the floor will be laid should be covered with 4 inches of washed gravel or crushed rock in order to reduce the capillary rise of moisture. A membrane should be provided over the gravel strong enough to resist puncturing when the concrete is placed. This membrane serves as a vapor barrier to keep moisture from entering the slab from the ground. Polyethylene film, asphaltum board ⅛ inch thick, or reinforced duplex paper with asphaltum center may be used. Overlap paper 4 inches. One additional problem to solve in cold climates is heat loss. The heat loss is primarily around the perimeter of the house,

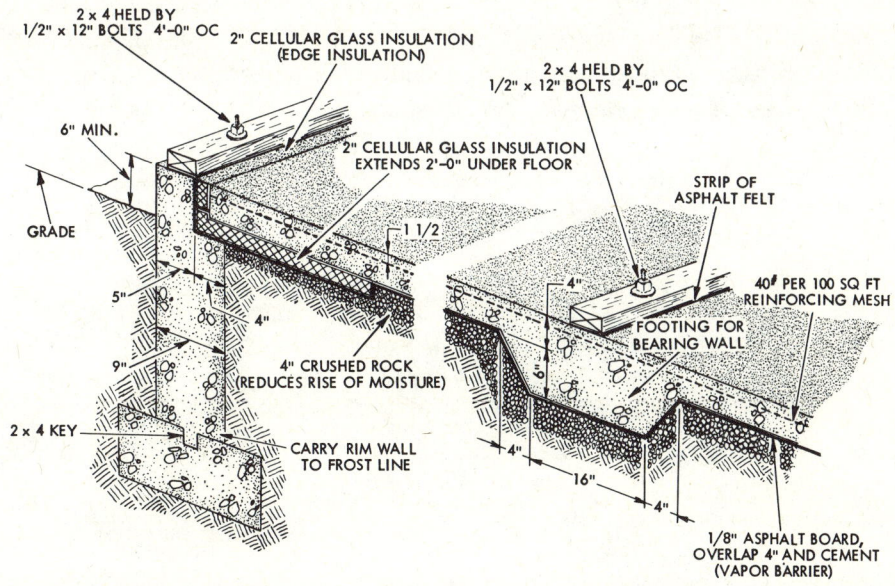

Fig. 5-28. A concrete floor laid on the ground requires a vapor barrier, and in cold climates, must have edge insulation.

Concrete Block Construction

and to counteract the loss and prevent condensation resulting from the cold floor, edge insulation is required. Two-inch thick rigid waterproof insulation extending 2 feet from the walls is suggested. Where panel heat is used in the floor, the insulation should cover the entire floor area.

In some areas the foundation wall is omitted entirely and a simple perimeter support is constructed instead by merely thickening the edge of the slab. See Fig. 5-29.

In some regions of the South, footings are laid both for the exterior wall and the bearing partition by making trenches in the firm earth. Reinforcing bars are used in the footings and concrete block is used for the foundation wall. A polyethylene film is spread over the earth where the slab is to be laid. The floor slab will be finished with terrazzo and in order to make it as rigid as possible, wire mesh is imbedded in the concrete. See Fig. 5-30.

In some areas where the soil is too unstable to permit the use of conventional footings and foundation walls, grade beams may be used. See Fig. 5-31. (Grade beams are continuous beams running around the house perimeter; they rest on piers.) Holes are dug at the perimeter of the building, a maximum of 8 feet apart, to a depth sufficient to bring them to solid soil well below the frost line. Concrete is placed into the holes, or into shells made for that purpose, to form piles. Forms are made to contain the grade beams which rest on the piles. A steel rod (a dowel) serves to position the grade beam. Horizontal reinforcing bars add strength to the grade beams. This construction may be used with slab-on-ground foundations and for houses with crawl spaces.

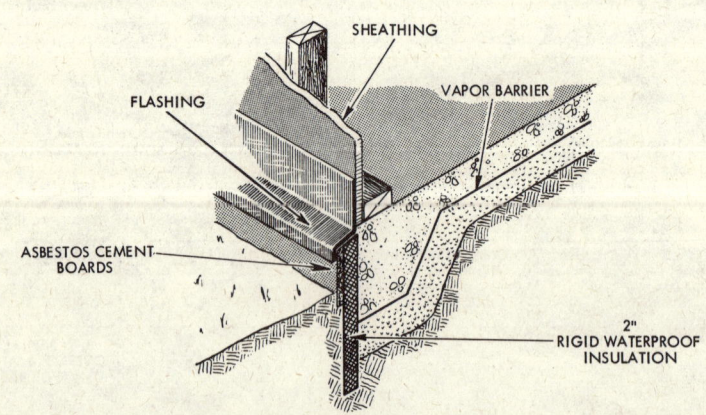

Fig. 5-29. A simple perimeter support for light construction in warm climates.

Concrete Formwork

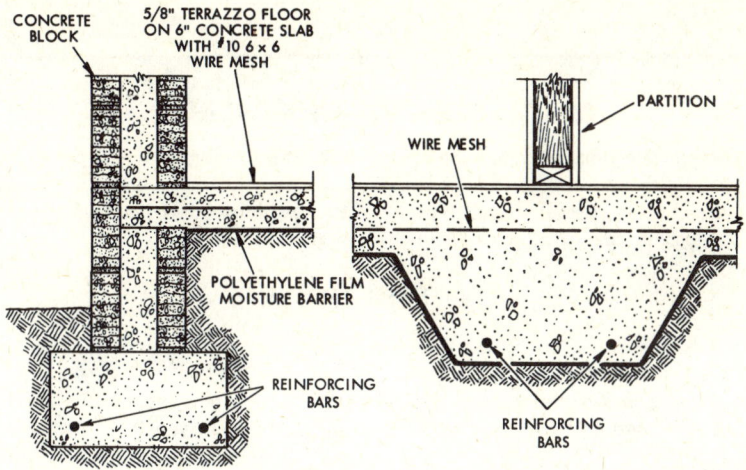

Fig. 5-30. Method used in warm climates for houses made with concrete block exterior walls and terrazzo floors.

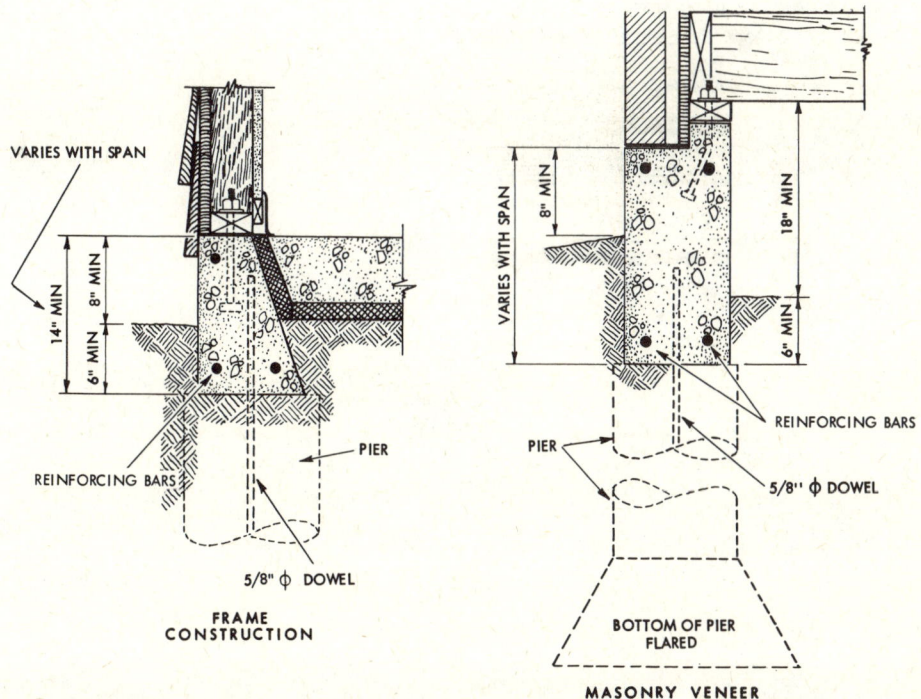

Fig. 5-31. Examples of grade beam and pier construction.

Concrete Block Construction

Checking On Your Knowledge

The following questions give you the opportunity to check up on yourself. If you have read the chapter carefully, you should be able to answer the questions. If you have any difficulty, read the chapter over once more so that you have the information well in mind before you go on with your reading.

DO YOU KNOW

1. Why footings must be straight and level and rest on undisturbed soil?
2. The purpose of keys in footings?
3. The advantages of using a *T type* footing?
4. The materials used in *built-in-place* forming?
5. What the most widely used material for the surface of concrete formwork is?
6. The advantages of using patented forms?
7. Two types of form ties?
8. The materials used in building forms for low walls?
9. How openings in concrete walls are provided for?
10. The important considerations in building forms for steps?
11. The purposes of steel reinforcing in concrete?
12. Where the first placing of concrete in forms should be?
13. Two methods of compacting concrete in forms?
14. Where grade beams and piers are used?

Footings: Design and Construction

Chapter 6

Footings comprise the first actual structural work to be done in the building of most structures. They are of great importance to the strength, appearance, usefulness, and safety of any building in which their use is required. Without good footings, a structure may easily develop unsightly cracks, off-level floors, and untrue doors and windows.

Inexperienced masons and designers seldom realize fully the real importance of footings or appreciate the caution which must be exercised in their design and building. Unless footings are carefully and exactly constructed, the block walls that are built on them will not be true and sound.

Theory of Footings

In order to present the theory of footings, a typical example will be explained using a common type of foundation. This foundation is shown in cross section in Fig. 6-1. Note that the foundation has no footing and that it is 12" thick and 8'-0" in height. The load on the foundation from the building can be assumed to be 2,250 pounds per lineal foot.

Soil Condition

While the foundation supports the weight of the structure above it, the foundation in turn must be supported by the soil on which it stands. Concrete weighs about 150

Concrete Block Construction

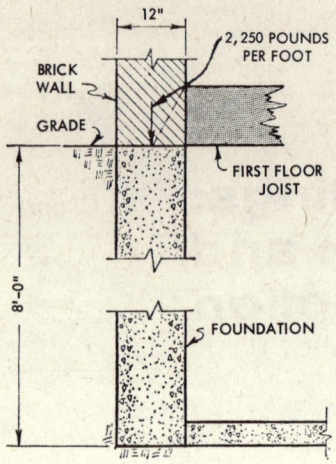

Fig. 6-1. Cross section of foundation without footing.

pounds per cubic foot, so a lineal foot of this particular foundation will weigh 150 × 8, or 1,200 pounds. This weight added to that which the foundation must support makes a total of 3,450 pounds per lineal foot which the soil must support. If the soil is not strong enough to support this load, the foundation will gradually settle, causing cracks and other annoyances in the structure above. It is possible for a foundation to sink far enough to cause the structure to collapse. For this reason, the strength or firmness of the soil must be considered when a building is being planned and provisions made so as not to overload it per square foot.

Soils vary greatly in their ability to support heavy loads. Table 6-1 gives the safe loadings for six common types. From this table it can be seen that soft clay, which is encountered most frequently, can safely support only one ton or 2,000 pounds per square foot.

The foundation shown in Fig. 6-1 transmits a load of 3,450 pounds to the soil per square foot. If the soil is assumed to be soft clay, it obviously cannot support the foundation. Unless some other provisions are made, the foundation will sink dangerously. However, if the bottom of the foundation is widened sufficiently, the load per square foot will be decreased to the extent that the soft clay will be able to support the load safely.

Distribution of Foundation Load

Fig. 6-2 shows one method of distributing the foundation load over a greater soil area. This structural part is known as a footing and is shown at *A B C D*. To find the area per lineal foot which is necessary to support the foundation load without sinking, divide the load (3,450) by the safe load per square foot of the soil (2,000). Thus, 3,450 ÷ 2,000 = 1.725 square feet. Since this is approximately two square feet, it can be assumed that the load of the foundation will be distributed over this area. Therefore, the load from the foundation, when distributed over two square feet of surface,

Footings: Design and Construction

TABLE 6-1. SAFE LOADS FOR VARIOUS SOILS

TYPE OF SOIL	SAFE LOAD IN TONS PER SQUARE FOOT*
SOFT CLAY	1
DRY, FINE SAND	2
COMPACT COARSE SAND	3
COARSE GRAVEL	4
HARD PAN OR HARD SHALE	10
SOLID ROCK	25

*NOTE: IF LOCAL BUILDING CODE SPECIFIES BEARING CAPACITY OF SOIL, USE THOSE FIGURES.

amounts to 1,725 pounds per square foot. This is less than the maximum strength or firmness of the soil and the foundation will not settle or sink.

As indicated in Table 6-1, some soils are safely able to support more than 3,450 pounds per square foot. In such cases footings are not actually required. However, most builders use them even under such circumstances as a safety factor against the slightest settling.

How far below grade footings are built depends on basement heights, if any, and on the frost level. All footings must be below the frost line in cold climates to avoid heaving and sinking as the soil freezes and thaws. Ordinarily, frost rarely goes deeper than 6'-0" in northern parts of the United States.

Footing Side and Bottom Shapes

One of the most important items concerning footings has to do with the shapes of their sides and bottoms. Unless these shapes are carefully considered in the design and building of footings, their usefulness and safety are greatly diminished.

Sloping Ground. Sometimes a residence or other structure must be built on sloping ground in such a way that the bottoms of the footings cannot all be at the same level. In such cases the footings should be

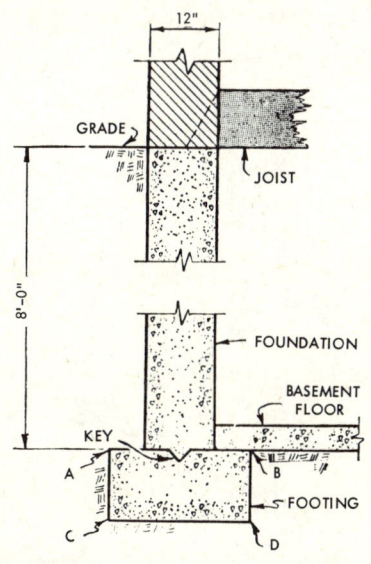

Fig. 6-2. Cross section of foundation with footing.

Concrete Block Construction

"stepped" as shown in Fig. 6-3. The difference in level is made up by a series of horizontal surfaces, each as long as the degree of slope will permit. Steps such as DC and BA must be perfectly horizontal. Risers such as CB must be perfectly vertical. This means that careful excavation work is important. If the steps sloped from B to A, for example, or if the risers leaned from the vertical, the footings might slip (move) or break under heavy loads. This would cause damage to the structure.

Fig. 6-4 illustrates another condition sometimes encountered where footings are built at right angles to the slope of the ground. In a case of this kind, the bottom of the excavation must be perfectly level or horizontal. The bottom of the footing, AB, will then be level and it will be easier to get the top of the footing, CD, level. The sides of the footing must be perfectly vertical.

Level Ground. Excavations for footings in level ground must be made as carefully as those where the ground sloped. The footings themselves require the same care in both situations.

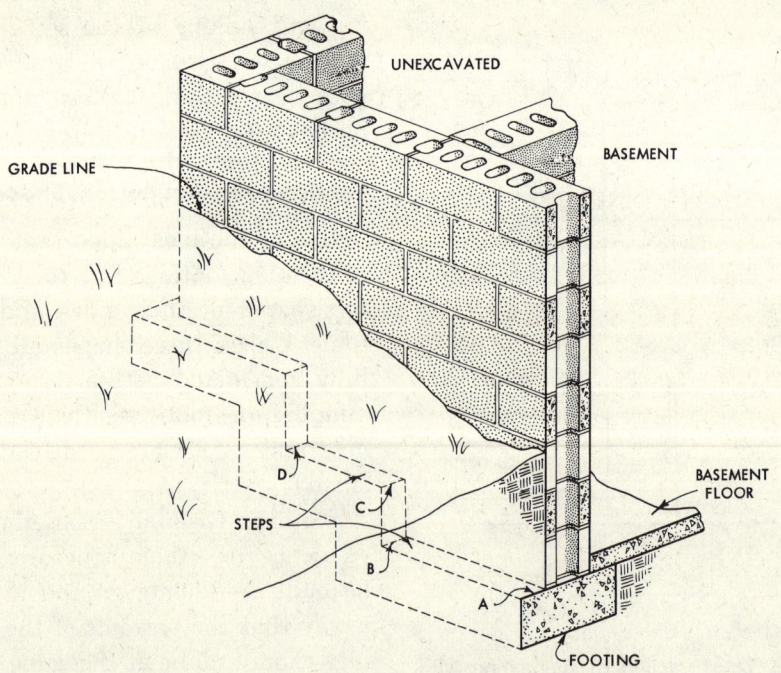

Fig. 6-3. Method of stepping wall footings in sloping ground.

Footings: Design and Construction

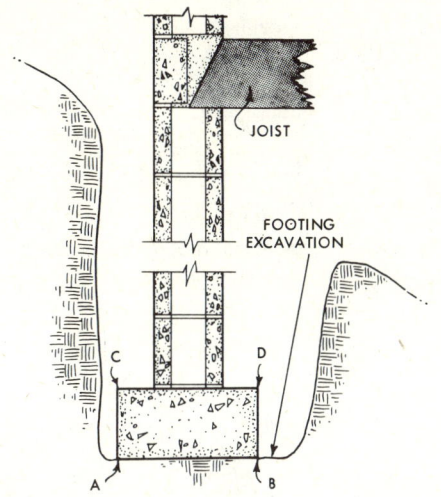

Fig. 6-4. Footing at right angle to sloping angle.

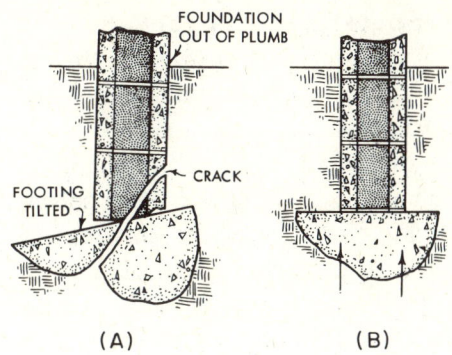

Fig. 6-5. Improperly shaped footings.

In (A) and (B) of Fig. 6-5 are illustrated two examples of careless excavation and lack of forms at the time the concrete was placed. These factors combined to produce footings which were not only of little value but which were actually dangerous. The footing at (A), because of its thin, irregular section, has tilted under the load from the foundation, causing both itself and the foundation to crack, throwing the foundation out of plumb. A condition of this nature might easily cause collapse of a structure. The footing at (B), because of its improper shape, could crack at both places indicated by the arrows. If such cracking occurs, the result would be the same as if no footings had been built.

When footings are required, and in most cases they are, they must be designed and built with all the care described and explained in succeeding pages.

Kinds of Footings

Common foundation footings are shown in Figs. 6-2 and 6-4. This is the type used most generally for residences, apartment buildings, small stores, or any structure where the loads are not great and where the soil is uniformly dense. If the soil has pockets where it is weaker and is not dependable, reinforced concrete footings may be required.

Concrete Block Construction

Concrete Foundation Footings

It sometimes happens that a building, as for example a store or apartment building, may be built up to the property line, thus making the use of the kind of footing shown in Fig. 6-2 impossible. In such instances, a footing as illustrated in Fig. 6-6 may be used. The required width of the footing is indicated as *AB*. The footing is slightly off center from the foundation. The step is permissible for concrete economy and does not lessen the effectiveness of the footing.

Fig. 6-7 shows another method of saving concrete when the footing has to be wide. This type requires double the amount of formwork, but in many cases the concrete saving is a distinct advantage.

As previously pointed out, there are instances where, because of the nature of the soil, footings are not absolutely necessary. If the soil is firm enough to permit the omission of forms, the bottom of the trench can be widened as shown in Fig. 6-8 to form a wider contact point with the soil. This forms a good footing and is an added protection against sinking and cracks.

Sometimes the footings under old foundations are not below the frost line. As a result, there is alternate heaving and sinking caused by the freezing and thawing of the ground. This condition can be corrected by excavating around and below the old footing and building a new one as illustrated in Fig. 6-9. This job requires additional foundation as can be seen from the illustration. Work of this kind requires a great deal of labor and material. Moreover, the structure must be supported during the time the new foundation and footing are being constructed. For these reasons, the job should not be undertaken unless the structure is important or unless general remodeling is being done.

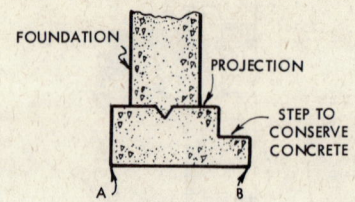

Fig. 6-6. Stepped-down footing for use when building is on property line.

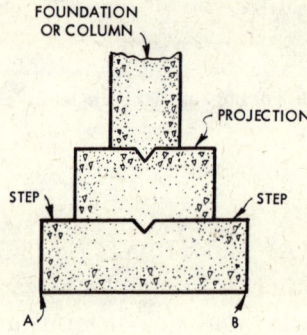

Fig. 6-7. Stepped-down footing.

Footings: Design and Construction

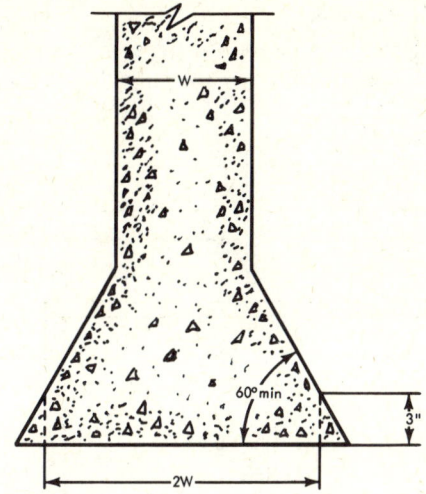

Fig. 6-8. Wide bottom of foundation serving as footing in firm ground.

In regions where frost is not a consideration, lightweight buildings are sometimes built on a concrete slab, the edges of which have been thickened to form footings. A footing of this kind is shown in Fig. 6-10. The footing thus formed supports the wall loads and prevents any possibility of the slab's cracking.

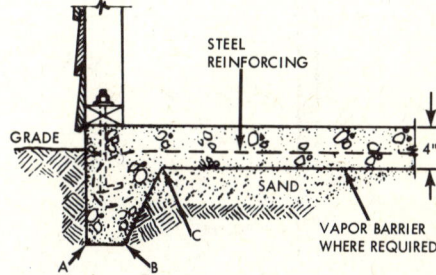

Fig. 6-10. A floating slab may be used when a foundation is above the frost line.

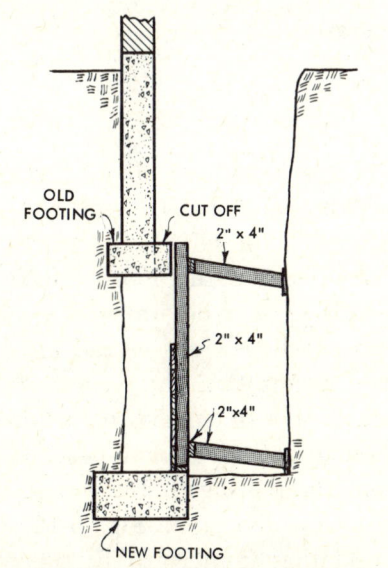

Fig. 6-9. Increasing depth of old foundation.

The plan view in Fig. 6-11 shows that one side of the building is up against the property line. This requires a footing similar to that of Fig. 6-6. At section C-C in Fig. 6-11, such a footing is shown together with the proper proportions. Suppose that the structure has foundations 10″ thick. Then, according to C-C in Fig. 6-11, W is equal to 10″ and ½ W is equal to 5 inches. If X is assumed to be 3″, then the footing is 20″ wide at the bottom, the projection is 5″, and the step is two inches.

101

Concrete Block Construction

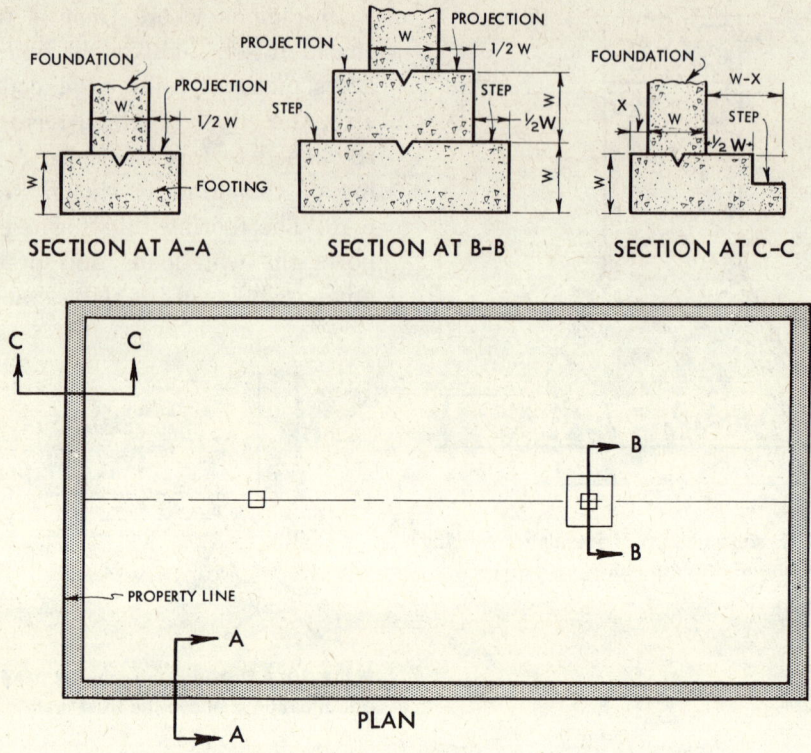

Fig. 6-11. Proportions for foundation and column footings.

The footing for *A-A* in the plan view of Fig. 6-11 is not on a property line and is similar to the footing illustrated in Figs. 6-2 and 6-4. The foundation above *A-A* in Fig. 6-11 is 10″ thick, so the footing is 20″ wide across the bottom, 10″ thick and has a 5″ projection on both sides.

For houses, store buildings, and other large structures, it is best to calculate the footing sizes according to the following example. The problem is to design the footing shown at *A* in Fig. 6-12. The soil may be assumed to be soft clay.

When calculating footing loads, it is necessary to determine the total load per lineal foot of the footing. This means that the weight of all structural work must be found, including both live and dead loads from the footing to the top of the structure. Thus, in Fig. 6-12, the foundation from *A* to *B*, the wall from *B* through *C* to *D*, the roof

Footings: Design and Construction

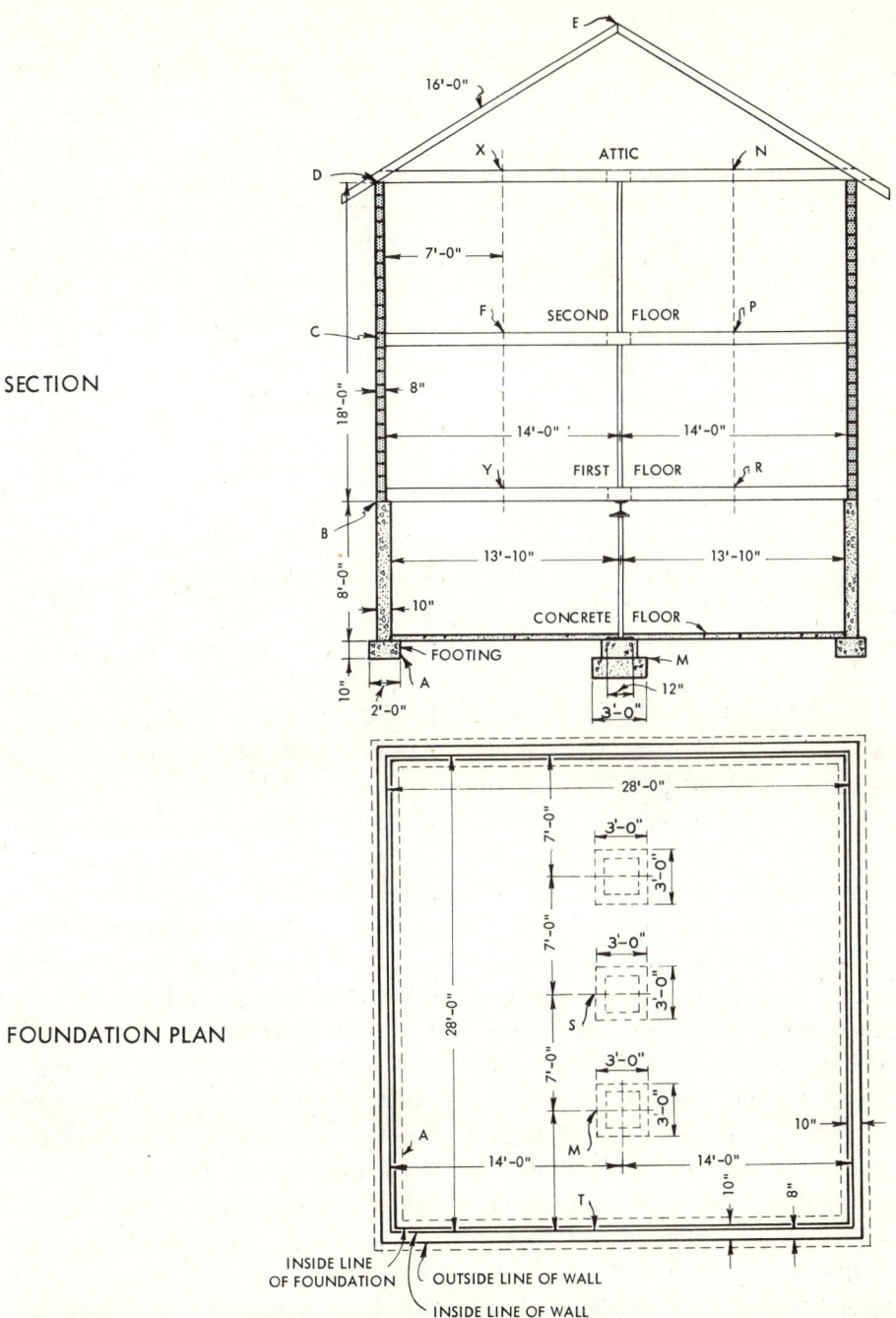

Fig. 6-12. Section and plan views of a two story masonry residence.

from D to E, the attic from D to X, the second floor from C to F, and the first floor from B to Y all must be considered.

The concrete for the foundation will weigh 150 pounds per cubic foot. Since the foundation is 10″ wide or almost one foot in width, it is easier when making calculations to think of it as being a full 12″ wide. A section of foundation 1′-0″ long and 8′-0″ in height, therefore, will weigh 8 × 150 or 1,200 pounds.

The masonry material for the wall BD weighs 60 pounds per cubic foot. Since 8″ = ⅔ of one foot, the volume of a section of wall 1′0″ long, 8″ wide, and 18′-0″ high would be 18 × ⅔, or 12 cubic feet. The weight of this section would then be 12 × 60, or 720 pounds.

If the roof has a combined live and dead load of 35 pounds per square foot and a rafter length of 16′-0″, then the total roof weight for a 1′-0″ length of wall is 16 × 35, or 560 pounds.

If the attic floor has a combined live and dead load of 56 pounds per square foot and if the span supported by the wall is 7′-0″, then the total floor weight for a 1′-0″ length of wall is 7 × 56, or 392 pounds.

If the second floor has a combined live and dead load of 60 pounds per square foot and a span of 7′-0″, then the total weight for a 1′-0″ length of wall is 7 × 60, or 420 pounds.

If the first floor load is assumed as being equal to the load from the second floor, then the complete loading in pounds is as follows:

Foundation load	1,280
Wall load	720
Roof load	560
Attic floor load	392
Second floor load	420
First floor load	420
Total load	3,792

Soft clay soil will not safely support over 2,000 pounds per square foot. The required area of the footing is therefore 3,792 ÷ 2,000, or approximately two square feet. Since the weight of the foundation used in the calculations is greater than it actually would be, the two foot area will be adequate. It should be remembered that this area is for one lineal foot of footing.

This footing can be constructed so that it is similar to that shown at A-A in Fig. 6-11. Following the proportions set down in the discussion of Fig. 6-11, the value of W or depth of the footing is 10 inches. Ordinarily, a 5″ projection on either side of the footing would be sufficient. This would give the footing a width across its bottom of 20 inches. However, the 20″ is 4″ short of the 2′-0″ necessary. Increasing the width of the projections to 7″ will not seriously change the proportions. But if a greater bottom width had been necessary, the thickness would have to be increased in order

Footings: Design and Construction

to keep the ratio of width to thickness about 2 to 1.

Where the soil is strong enough so that little or no footing is required and where the foundation is not as deep as in the case of structures not having a basement, a wide-bottom foundation such as explained in connection with Fig. 6-8 is provided for by gradually increasing the width of the foundation at the bottom. Thus, if the foundation is 10″ thick, the widening should start at a point 20″ from the bottom and gradually widen so that it is 20″ across the bottom.

For thickened edges of concrete slabs as explained for Fig. 6-10, the bottom of the thickened area AB is twice the thickness of the slab. The sloping inner side BC is usually about 60° although the degree of slope is unimportant so long as it is present. If a footing of this kind is built on soft or weak soil, the weight of the wall above plus a portion of the roof weight must be calculated just as was described for the building in Fig. 6-12. The distance AB should be made sufficiently wide to distribute the load satisfactorily over the soil.

Concrete Column Footings

The most commonly used footing for columns of various materials is the plain square kind shown in Fig. 6-13. This variety serves the purpose for all types of columns where

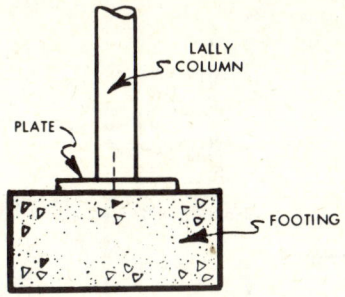

Fig. 6-13. Common column footing.

moderate loads are involved and can be built with a minimum amount of labor, material, and formwork. The footing shown in Fig. 6-7 frequently is employed for columns, especially where the width, AB, must be more than that shown in Fig. 6-13.

In larger buildings one finds either wood or steel columns, depending upon the structural plan and the loads to be supported. Where wood columns are employed, a combination anchor and footing works out to good advantage. Such a footing is shown in Fig. 6-14.

Another method of support for wood columns is to provide a concrete base, or *plinth* which rests on the footing. See Fig. 6-15. The plinth is leveled by setting it in a full bed of mortar. If the column is in a basementless building, the top of the plinth should be at least 8 inches above the finish grade. If the column is in a basement, the plinth should

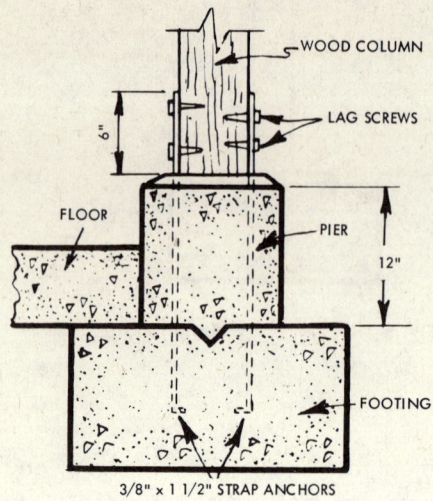

Fig. 6-14. Method of anchoring wood posts to footing.

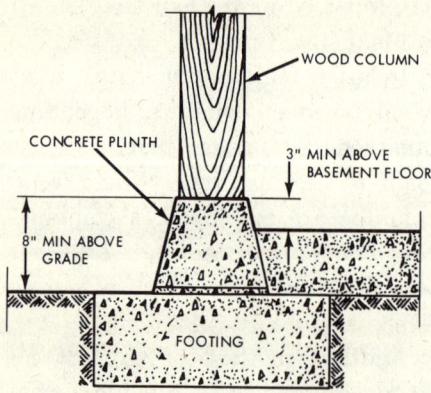

Fig. 6-15. Concrete plinth used as base for wood column.

extend at least 3 inches above the top of the finished floor slab.

Since columns represent concentrated loads, footings for them should be designed with the greatest of care. A point to be remembered when considering column footings is that the loads from them will vary much more than will loads from foundations and walls.

Column footings may be simple squares or rectangles, as in Figs. 6-13 and 6-14 or they may be stepped as shown in Figs. 6-6, 6-7, and 6-11 if the width across the bottom is great enough to warrant it. The footing shown at B-B in Fig. 6-11 is more often used for columns than it is for foundations. The proportions are similar to those previously explained for the footing in A-A. Thus, for masonry columns 12" square, the value of W is 12", the projection is 6", the step is 6", the total height is 24", and the bottom width 24 inches. When steel columns such as the Lally columns shown in Fig. 6-13 are used, the width of the bottom plate governs the value of W. When wood columns are used, the thickness of the timber governs the value of W except where a pier is used as in Fig. 6-14. In such instances the pier thickness governs the value of W.

The following examples are typical of problems which arise when footings are being designed for columns. As a first exercise, suppose it is necessary to calculate the required size for the column footing at M in Fig. 6-12. The same soil condition exists as before and a steel Lally column is to be used.

To the footing at M is transmitted the load from one end of the basement beam running from the column at M to T and one end of the beam running from the column at M to the column at S. Thus, the total floor and partition loads for attic, second, and first floors must be calculated between line XY and NR in the section view, and between T and S in the plan view. The floor spans from X to N, F to P, and Y to R are all 14' exactly. The distance between S and T in the plan view is 14 feet. The area of each floor to be considered, then, is 14' × 14' or 196 square feet. The attic floor load was given as 56 pounds per square foot in the problem involving foundation footings. The total attic floor load which must be supported, then, is 196 × 56 or 10,976 pounds. The second and first floors each have an area of 196 square feet and a floor load of 60 pounds per square foot. The load on each floor is therefore 196 × 60 or 11,760 pounds.

Since the partitions are right over the beam, an approximate weight of 110 pounds per lineal foot will be assumed for them. The partitions on the second and first floors are each 14'-0" long. The two partitions add up to 28'-0" in length which at 110 pounds per lineal foot amounts to 3,080 pounds.

The total weight in pounds supported by the beams between MT and MS is as follows:

Attic floor load	10,976
Second floor load	11,760
First floor load	11,760
Partition load	3,080
Total load	37,576

Each beam supports half of this load, or 18,788 pounds. The end of each beam transmits half of its load to the column under it. Thus, each beam transmits 9,394 pounds to the column. Therefore, the column at M, in supporting one end of the beam between TM and one end of the beam between MS, has a total load of 18,788 pounds to support.

If the soil can safely support 2,000 pounds per square foot, then the bottom area of the footing must be 18,788 ÷ 2,000, or approximately 9.39 square feet. For ease in calculation, this area can be called an even 9 square feet. This means that the bottom of the footing must be at least 3'-0" square.

Following the proportions for the footing B–B in Fig. 6-11 the value of W is governed by the plate on which the steel column rests. Assume that this plate is 12" square. Then with W equal to 12", the projection will be 6", the step 6", the total depth 24", and the bottom width 36 inches. These proportions work out perfectly.

Some designers cut down some-

Concrete Block Construction

what on the floor loads assuming that not all portions of the floor area will have all their maximum live load at the same time. For example, the attic floor load per square foot was taken at 56 pounds. Of this, 20 pounds may be considered as dead load and 36 as live. In such calculations, it is always the live load that is cut and the maximum allowable is one-half. The second and first floor loads were calculated on the basis of 60 pounds per square foot. Of this load, 25 pounds is dead load and 35 live load.

The examples in this book use larger than ordinary loads per square foot in order to be on the safe side. The building codes in the various cities specify exact live and dead loads and they can always be used when making calculations.

As a second exercise, suppose it is desired to design the footing for the 12″ by 12″ concrete column at G in Fig. 6-16. Assume that the beam EG supports 32,000 pounds and that the building site has damp clay and fine, sandy soil. If the beam supports 32,000 pounds, then column G supports one-half of 32,000 pounds, or 16,000 pounds. The concrete column is large so its weight should be added to the other load. Solid concrete weighs about 145 pounds per cubic foot. If the

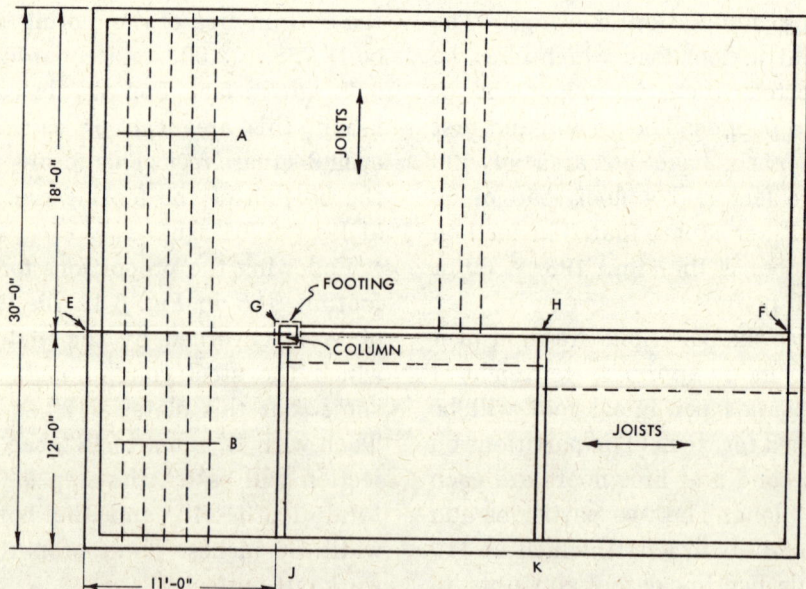

Fig. 6-16. Plan for basement showing necessity for column footing.

Footings: Design and Construction

the column is 7'-0" high and 12" x 12" on the sides, it contains seven cubic feet of masonry materials and weighs 7 × 145, or 1015 pounds. The total weight is, therefore, 17,015 pounds.

If the soil can safely support 4,000 pounds per square foot, the required footing area is 17,015 ÷ 4,000, or approximately 4.25 square feet. This can be called an even four square feet. The footing must be a minimum, then, of two feet square. A simple footing such as shown at A-A in Fig. 6-11 and having a depth of 12" would be best for this particular problem.

Suppose it is desired to construct the footing for one of the 6" x 6" wood columns shown in Fig. 6-17. The soil can be assumed to be capable of supporting 4,000 pounds per square foot. Each column supports two beam ends. If each beam end transmits 6,500 pounds to the column on which it rests, each column, therefore, must support 13,000 pounds. The area necessary to support this weight is 13,000 ÷ 4,000, or 3.25 square feet. To determine the dimensions of the sides of this footing, the square root of 3.25 is found. This is 1.8 feet which is about 1'-9" as the dimension of the side. A simple footing like that at A-A in Fig. 6-11 can be used. The depth should be about 12 inches.

For precast concrete post footings such as those shown in Fig. 6-15 the required bottom width, *AB*, can be determined in exactly the same manner as explained for more complicated structures. Depth *AC* can be equal to or somewhat greater than *AB*. Depth *DA* should be from 3'-0" to 4'-0" at most, depending upon the frost level. The heavier the poured concrete block, the more stability the supported structure has against windstorms and the like. The precast post can be made 6" x 6" or 8" x 8" depending on the beams to be supported. Either size will work out satisfactorily for light

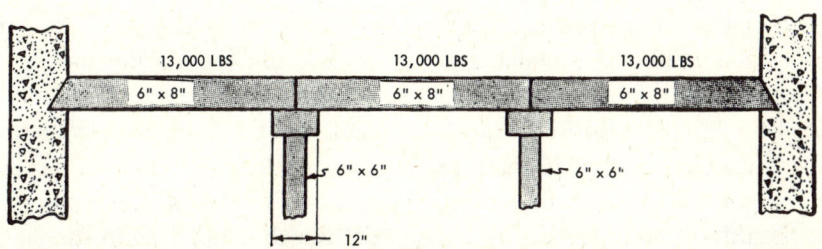

Fig. 6-17. Typical wood beams and columns.

Concrete Block Construction

structures. Precast posts are generally made about 4'-0" long. A 6" x 6" post of that length weighs 145 pounds, whereas the 8" x 8" post weighs about 260 pounds. It is well to consider the weight of the post when designing the bottom dimension *AB*.

Concrete Chimney Footings

Chimneys, especially those built for fireplaces, weigh a great deal. As a matter of fact, a chimney and fireplace for an ordinary two story residence weighs approximately 30,000 pounds. This concentrated load must be adequately supported not only to safeguard the chimney against cracks and leaning, but to protect the adjoining walls as well. The footing shown in Fig. 6-18 is the kind generally used where a fireplace and chimney are located in an outside masonry wall. The chimney and wall footings are placed as one. Chimney footings should allow an ample factor of safety and should be used to some extent even on very firm soil.

Chimney footings are designed like column footings except that simple footings are always used. The weight of a chimney is calculated by figuring the number of cubic feet of brick in the structure and multiplying that figure by 120 pounds. The weight of the tile flue lining also should be considered. An ordinary two-flue chimney having a

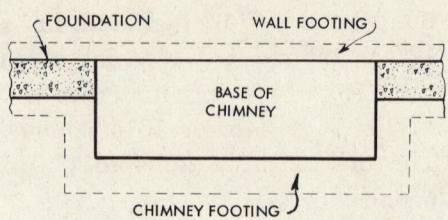

Fig. 6-18. Footing for chimney located in outside wall.

small vent for a gas heater and one fireplace in a two story house should weigh between 35,000 and 45,000 pounds.

In order to understand the design of chimney footings, assume that it is necessary to construct the footing for the chimney shown in Fig. 6-18. If the weight of the chimney is given at 35,000 pounds and the soil's degree of firmness allows it to support up to 2,000 pounds per square foot, the required footing area will be 35,000 ÷ 2,000, or 17.5 square feet. If the chimney measures 6'-0" × 2'-0", or 12 square feet, little or no footing will be needed. However, in order to make a firm base upon which to build the chimney and to guard against any possible settlement and resultant cracks, the foundation footing (see Fig. 6-18) should be enlarged so that it extends beyond the chimney base at least 6" and preferably 8 inches. For the sake of convenience, the depth can be made the same as the foundation footing.

Footings: Design and Construction

Concrete Pilaster Footings

Pilasters sometimes support heavy loads such as those, for example, from beam ends. Therefore, they must have adequate footings. The shape of the footings for any kind of pilaster, whether it be constructed of brick, concrete, or concrete blocks, should be as shown in Fig. 6-19. Such footings are designed exactly as were chimney footings and should also be a part of the foundation footings.

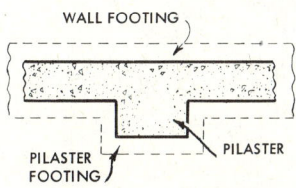

Fig. 6-19. Concrete footing for pilaster.

Concrete Porch and Stair Footings

In many cases the first floor level of a residence is higher than the adjacent street level. This may be due to sloping ground or the need to have the basement floor above the seepage point in the surrounding soil, or because the street sewer is at a shallow depth. In any event, if concrete porches and steps such as shown in Fig. 6-20 are required, footings A and B should be at least 6″ concrete walls extending to a depth below the frost line. The footings under the porch should be as shown in the plan view of the porch footing. All three walls should extend to a depth below the frost line. If insufficient footings are built above the frost line, cracks are likely to occur at the locations indicated by X in the plan and section views.

The footing under the ends of the steps is important because, unless this footing is sufficient and is carried below the frost line, cracks are apt to occur at the locations denoted by Y in the plan and section views.

Porches and steps of the general kind such as shown in Fig. 6-20 are costly to build in terms of labor and material. Unless they are properly built and with secure footings, they are almost certain to crack and sag. Even in climates where frost is not a consideration, footings to a lesser depth are necessary to prevent settlement or sagging.

When the porch floor is supported by the earth underneath it, no reinforcing is necessary. A recommended construction is shown in Fig. 6-20. If there is no earth fill or if the fill cannot be depended upon, then the floor should be reinforced as shown in Fig. 6-21. The size and spacing of the reinforcing bars necessary for porch slabs of varying spans and thicknesses are given in Table 6-2.

The slab for concrete cast-in-place steps should be 5″ to 6″ thick

111

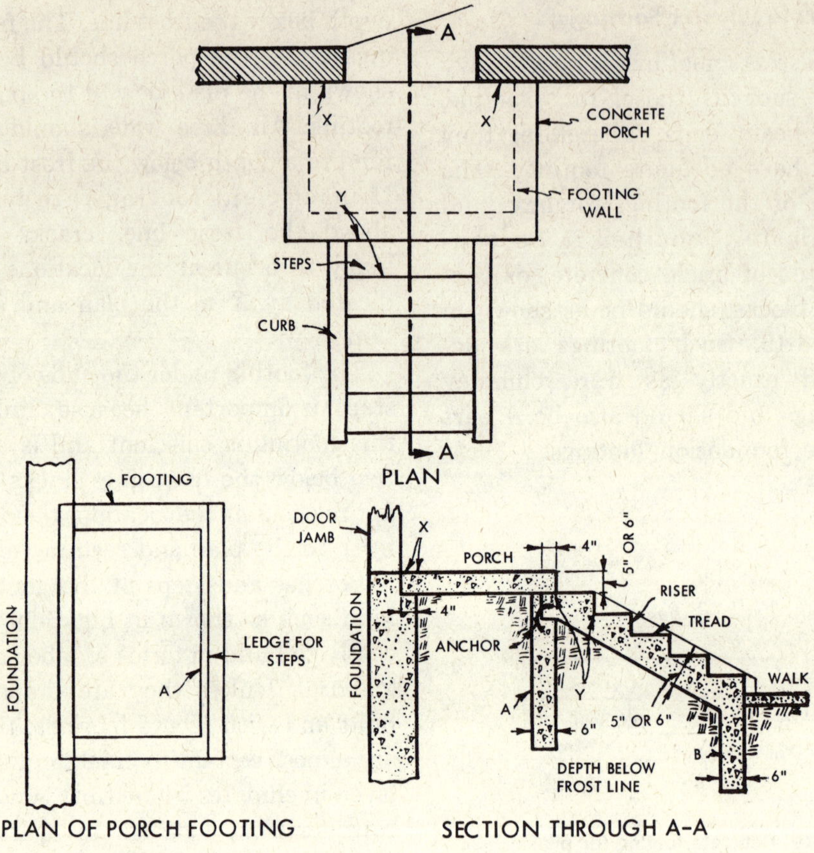

Concrete Block Construction

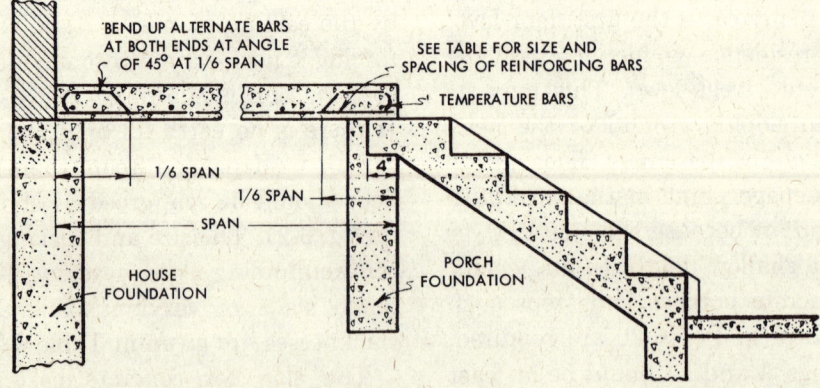

Fig. 6-20. Footings for porch and steps.

Fig. 6-21. Cross section of reinforced concrete porch floor.

112

Footings: Design and Construction

TABLE 6-2. REINFORCING BARS REQUIRED FOR PORCH SLABS

SPAN	THICKNESS	SIZE OF BARS	SPACING OF BARS
4'0"	4-1/2"	1/4"	8"
5'0"	4-1/2"	1/4"	6"
6'0"	4-1/2"	3/8"	9"
8'0"	5"	3/8"	6"
10'0"	5"	3/8"	4"

as shown in Fig. 6-20. The top of the slab should have bearing on wall A to prevent the possibility of any movement taking place. Walls A and B should have a depth to below the frost line or, where frost does not have to be considered, at least 2'-0" below ground surface. These walls should be at least 6" thick. Wall B should be placed at the same time as the stair slab. The risers in such stairs should have a certain relation to the width of the treads and at the same time should not be more than 6" to 7½" in height. For exterior steps, low risers and broad treads are generally preferable. The rise should be about 10" for a comfortable flight of steps. Curbs should be from 6" to 10" wide.

Reinforced Concrete Footings

Ordinarily, reinforced concrete footings are not required for small buildings because the loads are not great enough to make them necessary. However, for large buildings where the foundation and column

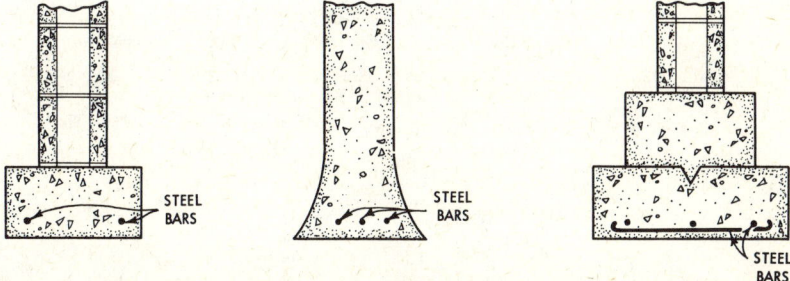

Fig. 6-22. Concrete footings reinforced with steel bars.

Concrete Block Construction

loads are exceedingly large, the use of reinforced concrete provides a stronger footing as well as a saving in material cost since a reinforced footing need not be as large as a plain footing because of the relatively greater tensile strength of reinforced concrete. See Fig. 6-22. The design of this type of footing requires use of intricate mathematics and is not explained here for that reason. Whenever reinforced footings are thought necessary, a structural engineer should be consulted.

Checking On Your Knowledge

The following questions give you the opportunity to check up on yourself. If you have read the chapter carefully, you should be able to answer the questions. If you have any difficulty, read the chapter over once more so that you have the information well in mind before you go on with your reading.

DO YOU KNOW

1. Why the condition of the soil on which the foundations or footings will rest is important?
2. How to calculate the distribution of foundation loads?
3. How footings are designed to compensate for sloping ground?
4. What the weight of concrete per cubic inch is?
5. How to design footings for buildings built up to the property line?
6. How to provide footings in firm soil where regular footings are not necessary?
7. What kind of footings may be used for lightweight buildings in frost-free areas?
8. The safe carrying capacity of soft clay soil?
9. What type of footing is most commonly used for columns?
10. The average weight of a chimney and fireplace for a two story residence?
11. What type of footing is always used for chimneys?
12. When porch floors should be reinforced?
13. When reinforced concrete footings are required?

Foundations: Design and Construction

Chapter 7

Of equal importance as the footings previously described is the design and construction of foundations. Most concrete block walls used in residential and commercial construction will be supported by solid concrete or concrete block foundations. Correct design and careful construction of foundations is absolutely essential to the total soundness and durability of a building. The concrete mason will many times be involved with the construction of foundations prior to the erection of walls so it is necessary that he have a thorough knowledge of the purposes of foundations and the best practices involved in constructing them. This chapter, along with chapters 5 and 6, provides the necessary guidelines for the proper methods of constructing foundations to assure an ultimately safe and sound building.

Theory of Foundations

The theory of foundations can be explained most easily through a careful consideration of the important purposes they serve. A study of the following functions performed by foundations will demonstrate that the cost of properly designed and carefully built foundations is an excellent investment. Any attempt at cutting the cost of construction of such foundations will prove to be false economy.

Foundations Provide Support. In all structural work the question of proper support must be considered constantly because every part of any building depends upon some other part or parts of the same building for its own support. For example, the roof of a two story residence is usually supported by two or more outside walls. Portions of the attic, second, and first floors are also supported by the outside walls. These walls are in turn supported by the foundations. The important part played by the foundation in supporting this weight can be much better understood by studying Figs. 7-1 and 7-2. The section drawing in Fig. 7-1 shows the roof, outside walls, floors, partitions, and foundations for a residence. The pictorial view indicates those same items plus a cutaway which shows part of the basement and first floor in section. From both views it can be seen that the roof is supported by the outside walls. For example, one-half of the roof, or AE, is supported by the outside wall AC. The other half of the roof is supported by the opposite outside wall. Partition GK supports the attic floor between points F and H. Therefore, the AF portion of this floor is supported by outside wall AC. In like manner, partition KN and column NQ support the second and first floors between points JL and MO. Thus, portions BJ and CM of the second and first floors are also supported by outside wall AC. The portions of floor supported by the opposite outside wall are determined in the same manner.

Suppose that the residence shown in the pictorial view in Fig. 7-1 could be cut or sawed into two parts, making the cut along line X–X vertically so that it passed through points F, J, M, and P. Suppose that the larger portion of the residence is moved away so that the remaining part is as shown in Fig. 7-2. Outside wall AC in Fig. 7-2 is the same as outside wall AC in Fig. 7-1. Portions of floor AF, BJ, and CM in Fig. 7-2 are the same portions of floor indicated by the same letters in Fig. 7-1. Thus, Fig. 7-2 shows those portions of the roof and floors which are supported by one of the outside walls. The opposite outside wall supports like portions of the roof and floors. It can easily be seen that only two outside walls are necessary in most cases to support the roof and floors of a building. The other portions of the floors in Fig. 7-1 are supported by interior partitions GK and KN and by column NQ.

From the foregoing descriptions it can readily be seen that foundation CD in Figs. 7-1 and 7-2 must support all of the weight, not only from the roof and portions of the floor, but from outside wall AC as well. This combined or total weight is considerable as will be shown in the following analysis.

That part of the roof supported by the outside wall AC in Fig. 7-2 is shown by the letters $AESR$. This is just half of the roof and the dimensions are 17'-6" × 35'-0". The area of this portion of the roof is 17.5 × 35 or approximately 613

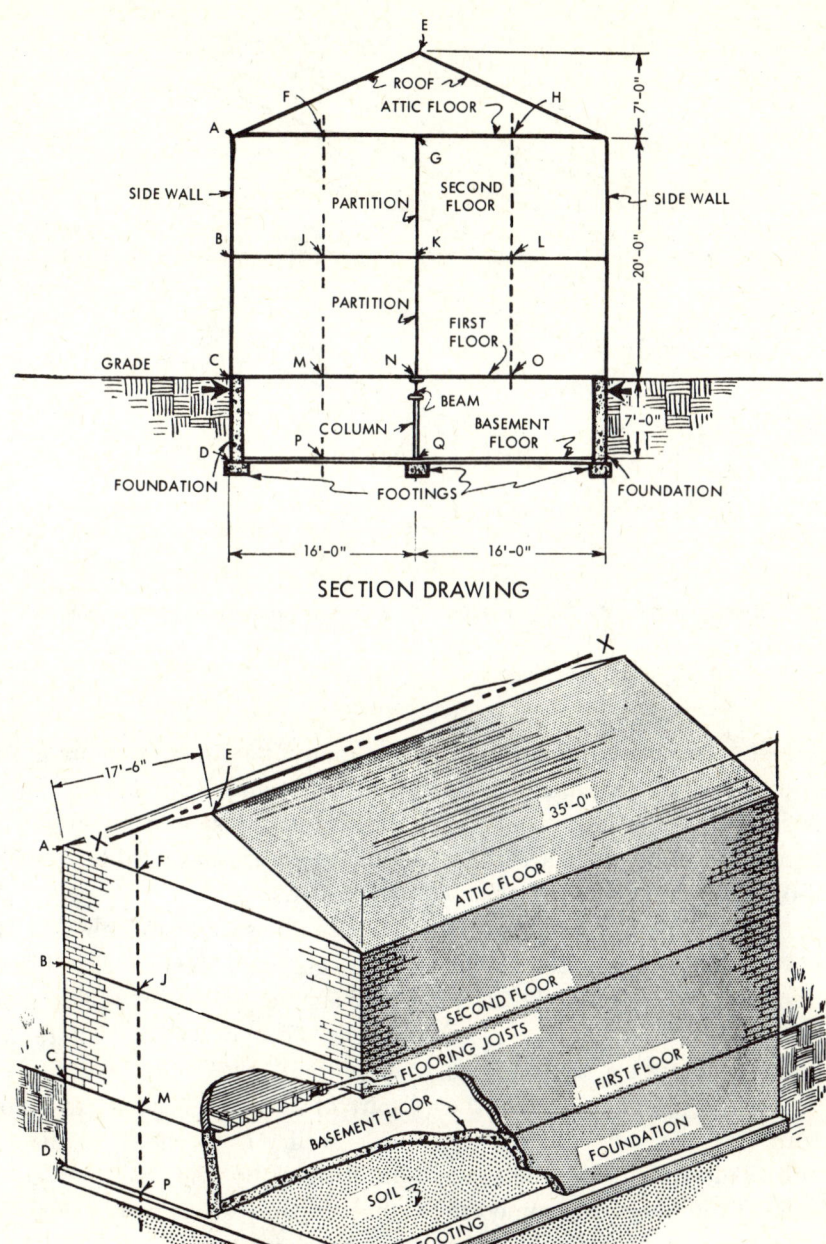

Fig. 7-1. A residence and the foundation supporting it.

Concrete Block Construction

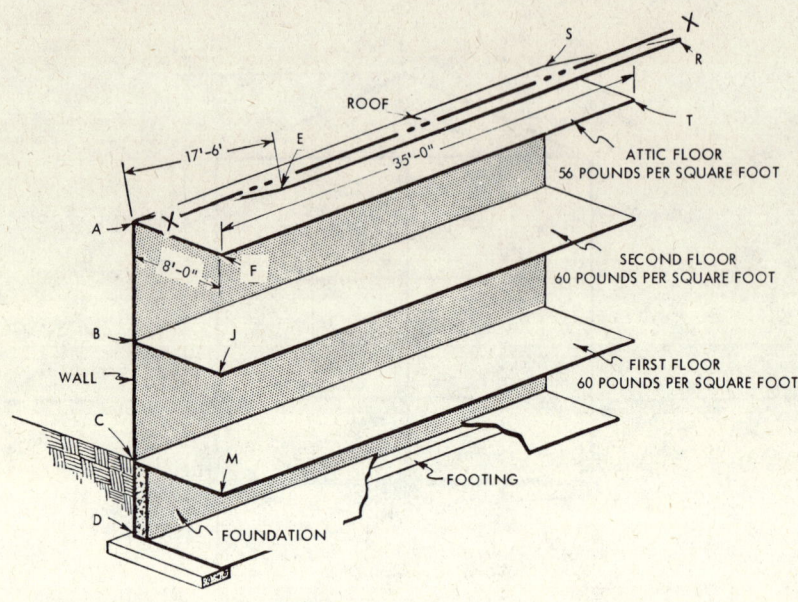

Fig. 7-2. Parts of the roof, floors and outside walls are supported by the foundation.

square feet. The portion of the attic floor supported by this same outside wall is shown by the letters *AFST*, the dimensions for which are 8'-0" × 35'-0". This gives an area of 280 square feet. The portions of the second and first floors supported by the outside walls have exactly the same areas.

Roofs and floors are assumed to have a certain weight due to the structural materials of which they are built. This weight is called the *dead load*. They are also assumed to have a certain weight due to people, furnishings, and other movable objects. This is known as the *live load*. Both loads are spoken of in terms of

so many pounds per square foot. Both live and dead loads must be taken into consideration when planning any structure. Table 7-1 shows such loads.

It can be seen from Table 7-1 that the combined load for a pitched roof such as shown in Figs. 7-1 and 7-2 is 35 pounds per square foot. Therefore, the total load for that part of the roof supported by outside wall *AC* is equal to the area multiplied by the load per square foot. In this case it would be 613 × 35, or 21,455 pounds. Table 7-1 also shows that the combined live and dead load for an attic floor is 56 pounds per square foot. The total

Foundations: Design and Construction

load from that part of the attic floor supported by outside wall *AC* is therefore 280 × 56, or 15,680 pounds. In like manner, the total load from the second floor is 280 × 60, or 16,800 pounds. The total first floor load is also 16,800 pounds. If it is assumed that the outside walls are built of brick and are 8″ in thickness, then each square foot of wall area, according to Table 7-2, weighs 10.4 × 8, or approximately 83 pounds. The wall dimensions are 20′-0″ × 35′-0″, which makes an area of 700 square feet. At a weight of 83 pounds per square foot, the wall will constitute a load on the foundation of 700 × 83, or 58,100 pounds.

The total load in pounds, including the roof, floors, and walls, is:

Roof	21,455
Attic Floor	15,680
Second Floor	16,800
First Floor	16,800
Wall	58,100
Total load	128,835

The foundation along a length of 35′-0″ supports a load, therefore, of

TABLE 7-1. LOADS FOR AVERAGE RESIDENCES

STRUCTURAL ITEM	COMBINED LIVE AND DEAD LOADS (POUNDS PER SQUARE FOOT)	LIVE LOADS ONLY (POUNDS PER SQUARE FOOT)
ROOFS--PITCHED	35	25
ROOFS--FLAT	40	30
ATTIC FLOOR	56	40
SECOND FLOOR	60	40
FIRST FLOOR	60	40
2x4 PARTITIONS	12	....

NOTE: THESE LOADS VARY GREATLY IN BUILDING CODES OF VARIOUS CITIES. THE LOADS GIVEN HERE ARE TYPICAL.

TABLE 7-2. WEIGHTS OF MATERIALS

MATERIAL	WEIGHT IN POUNDS PER CUBIC FOOT	WEIGHT IN POUNDS PER INCH THICKNESS
BRICK MASONRY	125	10.4
CONCRETE	150	12.5
CINDER BLOCKS	...	6
CONCRETE BLOCKS	...	8
RUBBLE STONE	...	12.5

128,835 pounds. For each lineal foot of the foundation the load is 128,835 ÷ 35, or 3,681 pounds. The foundation must be strong and firm to support such a load without allowing settlement, uneven floors, plaster cracks, and many other annoying and even dangerous possibilities.

Foundations Guard against Frost Action. It is a well-known fact that when water freezes its volume increases. The same situation exists when moist soil freezes. In the case of soil, the increase in volume causes an upward movement which is called heaving. This heaving causes any structure to move upward with the expanding soil unless the foundations for such structures extend below the lowest freezing point in the soil. When the soil thaws, it settles to its original volume. A building would settle with the soil if the foundations did not extend below the point at which the settlement takes place. Therefore, foundations are used to prevent any possible upward or downward movement. Such movement causes plaster cracks and other annoyances and might even endanger a building.

Foundations Provide Basements. The only way in which basements can be provided below grade is through the use of foundations which cannot be harmed by moist earth. The foundations also prevent the sides of the basement from caving in. In the section view of Fig. 7-1, two arrows are shown which indicate the direction of the soil pressure on the sides of the foundation walls. The foundations resist this pressure and also serve as a means of keeping basements dry.

Foundations Protect against Termites. In many parts of the United States, ant-like insects called termites attack and eat any wood which comes in contact with the soil in which they are found. Foundations and termite shields raise and isolate all wood parts of a structure above the soil, thus guarding it from attack by the tiny insects.

Kinds of Foundations

There are as many kinds of foundations as there are kinds of buildings. Some of them are good while others are poor. Some of them serve the purpose for which they were intended while others fail. Perhaps the most common reason for failure of foundations is the desire in builders to save on structural costs. Such economy is false and a bad investment. Good foundations are expensive but their cost is one of the best

Foundations: Design and Construction

investments in any structure. In the following general explanations, only those types of foundations which are recommended by engineers and building codes are considered.

Concrete Foundations

Fig. 7-3 shows a typical concrete foundation for an average residence. This foundation has the advantage of being integral or all in one piece. All parts of it were placed at the same time with the result that when it hardened, it became one solid piece of concrete. This prevents any part of the foundation from settling away from the rest. Thus, it insures a firm and continuous support for the residence.

In Fig. 7-3 the portion of the illustration at *A–A* shows the foundation which extends from the ground level down to the footings which are below the basement floor level. The foundation at *C–C* is for the garage. The circular foundation at *E–E* is for a front entrance porch. At *B–B* is shown an areaway which is necessary for basement windows which are below ground level. Areaways are shown also at *Z* and *R*. The foundation at *F* is a retaining wall around exterior stairs. At the middle of the rear portion of the foundation is the fireplace and chimney foundation. Note the cleanout doors. Note the recesses or pockets in the foundation at points marked *1*, *2*, *3*, and *4*. These recesses serve as bearing surfaces for the two beams which will be used to support the interior sections of the house in the same manner as the beam shown in the section view of Fig. 7-1. The various foundation refinements mentioned in connection with Fig. 7-3 will be more fully explained and illustrated in succeeding pages.

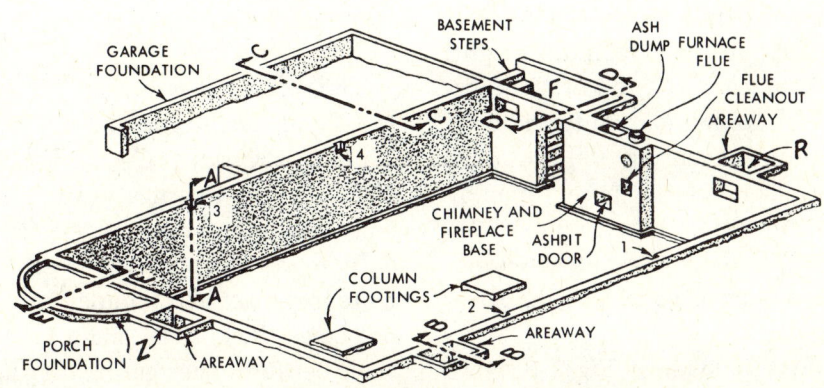

Fig. 7-3. Concrete foundation for small residence.

121

Concrete Block Construction

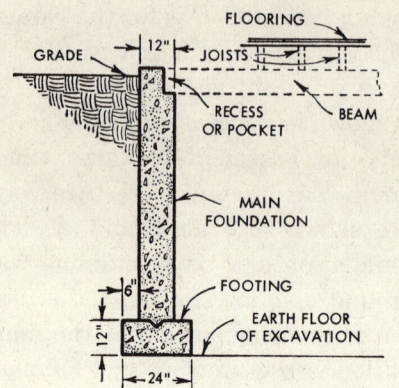

Fig. 7-4. Section at A-A of main foundation in Fig. 7-3.

one in Fig. 7-4 except that the first floor level in Fig. 7-5 is considerably above grade. This necessitates a much shorter foundation. Note that in a case of this kind, the wall of the structure rather than the foundation is depended upon to support the beam ends. In all cases where first floor levels are above the grade line and where full-height basements are required, the concrete foundation is built only up to the grade line.

The illustration in Fig. 7-4 shows the main foundation and footing in section as they appear at *A–A*. Note that the recess or pocket for the beam bearing surface is visible. If this figure is visualized in connection with Fig. 7-3, the main foundation will then be easier to understand.

This type of concrete foundation is the one most generally used. Its thickness and the thickness of the footing depends upon the load it must support and upon its height. The channel in the top of the footing locks the foundation to the footing, thus preventing the sideward displacement of the foundation by earth pressure. The channel also serves to help prevent moisture from seeping through into the basement.

The section view in Fig. 7-5 shows a concrete foundation similar to the

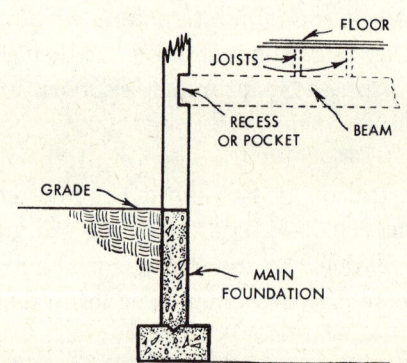

Fig. 7-5. Section of foundation wall where grade is below first floor.

The section view in Fig. 7-6 gives the details of the garage foundation which was shown at *C–C* in Fig. 7-3. Note that no footings are required and that the foundation extends only to a depth below frost line. Note, too, that this foundation need not be as thick as the main foundation because the garage is light when contrasted with the residence.

122

Foundations: Design and Construction

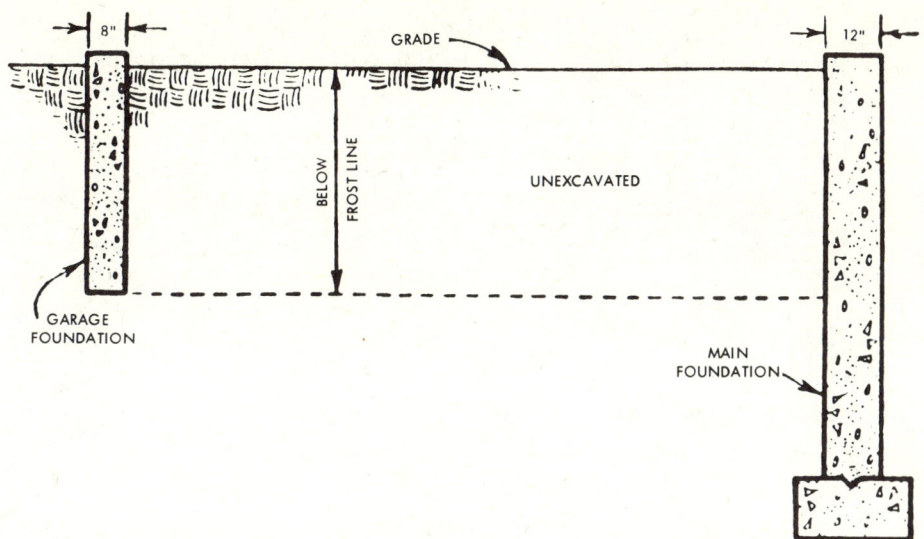

Fig. 7-6. Section at C-C of garage foundation in Fig. 7-3.

The section view in Fig. 7-7 shows the details of the porch foundation which was designed as E–E in Fig. 7-3. This foundation, like the one for the garage, is only 8″ thick. It requires no footing and extends down only to a point below the frost line.

Details of the areaway walls are shown in Fig. 7-8. Note that only 6″ walls are required and that the frost depth need not be considered. The areaway walls do not support any part of the structure and since they are an integral part of the foundation, could not easily be pushed upward due to the heaving of the ground. Note, too, that the better areaways will have a concrete floor slightly below the sill of the window as well as a drain and sloping floor for rain water and melting snow.

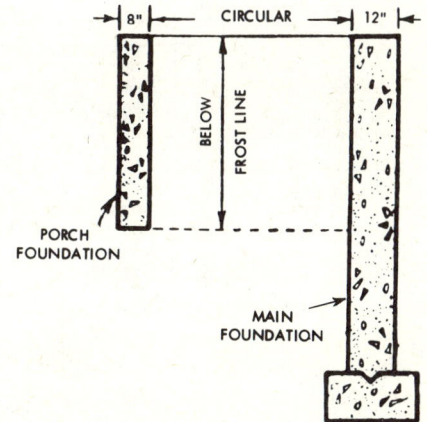

Fig. 7-7. Section at E-E of porch and main foundation in Fig. 7-3.

123

Concrete Block Construction

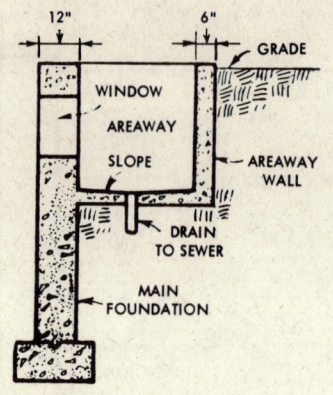

Fig. 7-8. Section at B-B of areaway wall in Fig. 7-3.

Fig. 7-9 shows both plan and section views of the exterior stairway of Fig. 7-3. The section view of Fig. 7-9 is taken along the line $F-F$ in the plan view. Note that the stair retaining wall is only 8" thick but that because of its height and weight, a footing is advisable. The stair wall and the steps are placed at the same time so that they are all of one piece. This prevents any possible displacement of the steps due to frost action.

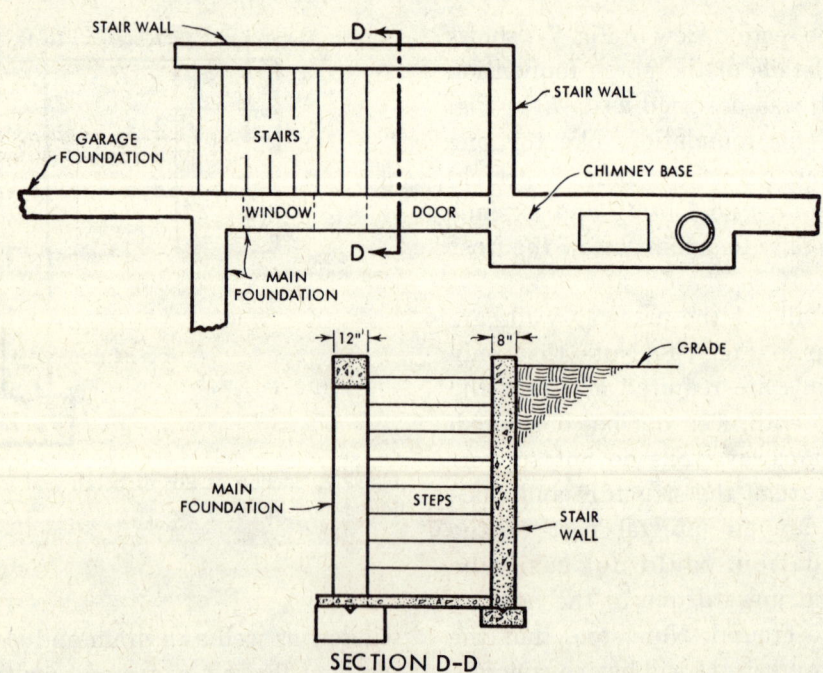

Fig. 7-9. Plan and section views of stair wall at F in foundation in Fig. 7-3.

Foundations: Design and Construction

Concrete Pilasters. Pilasters, shown in Fig. 7-10, are used to stiffen long foundations and also to serve as increased bearing surface for the ends of beams. Stiffening of concrete foundations is seldom necessary except in cases where they are very high and over 20'-0" long in any direction. For the ordinary residence, store building, or other small structure, there is seldom any need for pilasters. Exceptionally high foundations are subject to considerable soil pressures and pilasters act as braces in helping to resist this pressure.

Generally speaking, concrete foundations are of sufficient thickness and strength to provide safe bearing surfaces for beams as was shown at points *1*, *2*, *3*, and *4* in Fig. 7-3 and in Figs. 7-4 and 7-5. However, it sometimes happens that a beam supporting an exceptionally heavy load imposes too great a burden on the foundation. In such cases a pilaster is necessary.

Concrete Block Foundations

The use of concrete blocks for foundations under small residences and other such buildings is usually preferred when cast-in-place concrete is not used. As the second most common material used for building such foundations, concrete blocks are rapidly laid and, if the mason is careful, make good foundations.

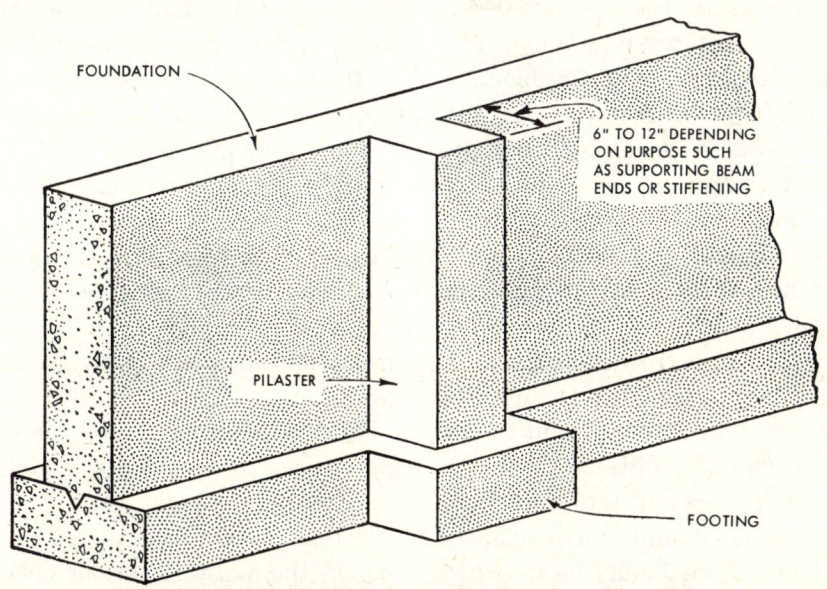

Fig. 7-10. Concrete foundation with integral pilaster.

Concrete Block Construction

When the concrete footing for concrete block foundations is sufficiently hard, the outline of the foundation can be marked using a chalk line or chalk. This line serves as a guide in placing the first row or course of blocks. It is a good suggestion to lay the first row of blocks without mortar all the way around the foundation in order to determine the joint spacing and whether or not any blocks have to be cut in order to piece out the required foundation on each side of the building.

The vertical space for mortar joints between the blocks is usually specified to be ⅜". However, small variations are permitted to allow the corner blocks to be exactly on the chalk outline.

After the spacing and placement of the blocks has been decided upon, the blocks are removed and a full mortar bed as wide as the block is spread along the footing using the chalk outline as a guide. This mortar bed should be very thick; at least one inch or more to insure solid bedding. The blocks should have their vertical edges buttered, as shown in Fig. 7-11, before being placed in position. Each block should be pressed firmly into its mortar bed so that the joint is not more than ½" between the block and the footing and not more than ⅜" between it and the previously laid block. Care should be taken to see that the blocks all follow the outline made along the footing and that the top edges of the blocks are all exactly the same height.

When the first row has been laid, the corners of the foundation should be built up at least several rows high if not to complete height. Care should be taken to break joints as shown in Figs. 7-11 and 7-12.

Staggering the joints in the manner shown binds the wall firmly together. Use the level often to keep the foundation plumb and the top surfaces of the blocks even and level. As shown in Figs. 7-11 and 7-12, double rows of mortar are laid along the blocks. Note that the end of each block is carefully buttered before it is lifted in place and pressed into position.

When the corners of the foundation have been built up, the intermediate rows of blocks on each side of the building are laid up to a line which is stretched from corner to corner. The line is moved up one course for each course laid. The outside top edge of each block must just touch this line as it is placed in position. In this manner the wall is made straight and the top of each row of blocks is at exactly the same level.

The paragraphs above describe practices that are basic to good masonry. Chapter 8 will describe in detail how these practices are put to use in the many situations encountered on a construction job.

Footings: Design and Construction

Fig. 7-11. Vertical edges of blocks are "buttered" with mortar before laying.

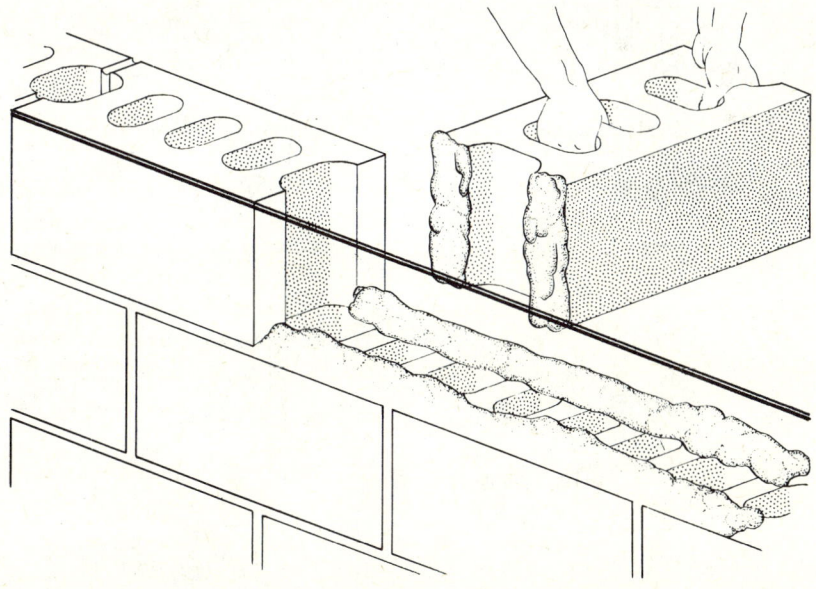

Fig. 7-12. Method of holding block for placing against the block previously laid.

Concrete Block Construction

A typical concrete block foundation is shown in (A) of Fig. 7-13. Dimensions for all blocks should be exactly the same and no blocks with broken edges or corners should be used.

At points where such foundations support the ends of beams which are to be heavily loaded, the blocks underneath and on either side of the beam from the footing to the beam bearing surface should have their cores filled with concrete. This practice gives the foundation a strength about equal to that of a cast-in-place foundation.

When concrete block walls are to be built above the foundation as in (A) of Fig. 7-13, half units can be used at beam bearing points to provide ample bearing surface, as shown by letters *EF*. When brick walls are specified, the bricks are simply laid around the beam end as shown in (B). If frame (wood) walls are to be used, the plate on which the beam rests should be anchored to the foundation as shown in (C). Anchor bolts should extend down at least 15″ in the block foundation and should be spaced at no more than 8′ intervals.

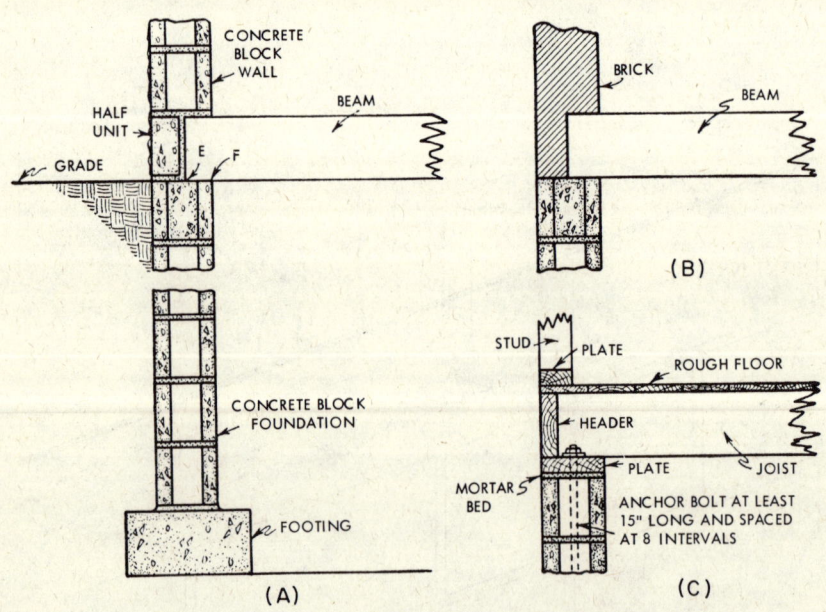

Fig. 7-13. Section of concrete block foundation.

Foundations: Design and Construction

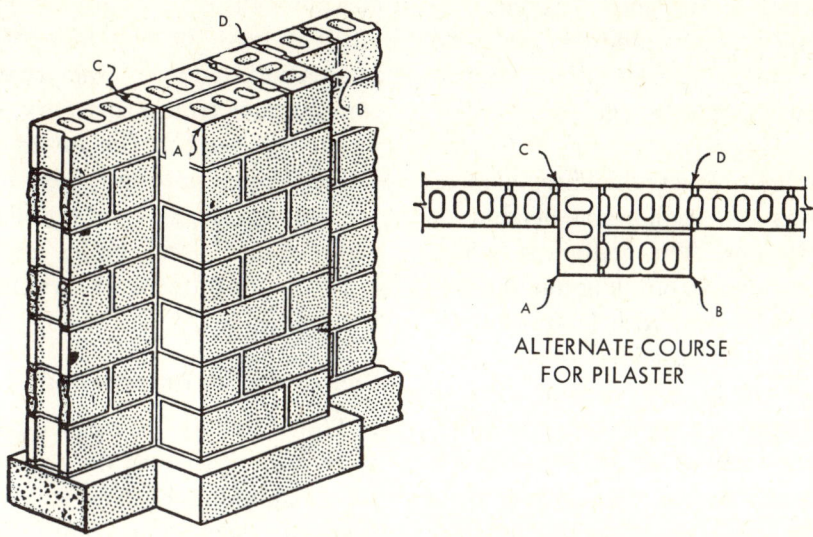

Sec. 7-14. Section of concrete block foundation and pilaster.

Concrete block foundations such as shown in Fig. 7-13 are especially applicable to all smaller structures for which outside walls of masonry materials are planned.

Concrete Block Pilasters. In concrete block foundations, pilasters are employed for the same purposes explained for concrete foundations.

However, in concrete block walls, pilasters are necessary as stiffening agents even in foundations of ordinary height if the foundations exceed 30 feet in length. Also, where heavily loaded beams have their bearing in such foundations, rather large pilasters (see Fig. 7-14) usually are required.

Design of Foundations

Most cities throughout the United States publish building codes setting forth definite and rigid specifications regarding, among other things, the design of foundations for various types of buildings. Since these codes are the law, architects and masons must follow them to the letter. This means that in localities where such codes exist, foundations

129

need not be designed. Instead, the architect merely indicates them on the plans as being built in accordance with existing regulations.

Generally speaking, building codes give exact thickness dimensions as well as allowable heights for foundations. The materials which may be used in building foundations are listed along with limitations on outside wall thicknesses and the number of floors. For example, the building code published by Highland Park, Illinois, states that for two story brick residences the foundation must be 12" thick if built of regular, plain concrete.

With this in mind, it is always a good policy for a mason to ascertain if there is a building code in any city or town in which he anticipates building foundations. Should such a code exist, he must carefully follow all specifications as to thicknesses and heights for his foundations.

In small towns and rural areas, building codes are not common. As a result, foundations must be designed for each building. If plans prepared by architects are not available, the mason must do the required designing.

Concrete Foundations

Concrete foundations for residences, apartment buildings, and other small structures can be designed satisfactorily, specifications being based on the thicknesses of outside walls above the foundation, on the depth below grade of the foundation, and on the type of construction (frame, masonry, etc.) which will rest on the foundation. Table 7-3 illustrates a typical building code for thickness of foundation walls. Again, local building codes must be consulted and strictly adhered to.

Concrete Block Foundations

There are no rules commonly agreed upon, such as were set forth for concrete foundations, in connection with foundations built of concrete blocks. However, the strengths of such foundations can be easily calculated and the load limitations established for most purposes. See Table 7-3 for thickness requirements.

The compressive strength of good concrete blocks can be safely assumed to be 80 pounds per square inch gross area if the blocks are laid in portland cement mortar. In other words, if an 8" × 12" concrete block has a gross area of 96 square inches (8 × 12 = 96, including holes), it can safely support a load of 96 × 80, or 7,680 pounds. If a foundation is built of 8" × 12" concrete blocks, it can support 7,680 pounds per lineal foot, provided portland cement mortar is used.

In the section in this chapter on the theory of foundations, the weight on each lineal foot of foun-

Foundations: Design and Construction

TABLE 7-3. THICKNESS OF FOUNDATION WALLS

FOUNDATION WALL CONSTRUCTION		MAXIMUM DEPTH BELOW GRADE (feet) (SEE NOTES 1 AND 2)		
TYPE	THICKNESS (INCHES)	FRAME	MASONRY VENEER	MASONRY
HOLLOW MASONRY	8	4 (6)	4.5 (6)	5 (7)
	10	5 (7)	5.5 (7)	6 (7)
	12	7	7	7
SOLID MASONRY	8	5 (7)	5.5 (7)	6 (7)
	10	6 (7)	6 (7)	6.5 (7)
	12	7	7	7
MASS CONCRETE	8	7	7	7

NOTE 1. DEPTH BELOW GRADE MAY BE INCREASED UP TO THOSE SHOWN IN PARENTHESES WHERE SUCH INCREASE IS WARRANTED BY SOIL CONDITIONS AND LOCAL EXPERIENCE AND IS REQUIRED BY THE BUILDING OFFICIAL.

NOTE 2. WHERE HEIGHT OF UNBALANCED FILL (HEIGHT OF FINISH GRADE ABOVE BASEMENT FLOOR OR INSIDE GRADE) EXCEEDS SEVEN (7) FEET, FOUNDATION WALL THICKNESS SHALL BE DETERMINED BY STRUCTURAL ANALYSIS.

dation for a typical residence was calculated as 3,681 pounds. Thus, an 8" concrete block foundation is over twice as strong as is necessary.

The weight per lineal foot of foundation can be calculated for any small building by following the same procedures described for the residence in the first section of this chapter. Then the strength of any size concrete block foundation can be determined to see if it will be strong enough to do the job.

Concrete Block Pilasters. The strength of concrete block pilasters is calculated in exactly the same manner as explained for concrete block foundations. Determine the gross area in square inches of the pilaster, including the foundation (or area *ABCD* in Fig. 7-14), and multiply the result by 80 if portland cement mortar is used. By comparing the strength of the pilaster with the beam-end load it is to carry, the proper size of the pilaster can be checked. Pilasters can be made larger or smaller to suit load demands. The strength of such pilasters can be appreciably increased by filling the holes with concrete.

Concrete block pilasters are also used in concrete block foundations as stiffeners at 30' intervals where the foundation is exceptionally long. The pilaster shown in Fig. 7-14 is considered of adequate size to act as a stiffening agent.

Checking On Your Knowledge

The following questions give you the opportunity to check up on yourself. If you have read the chapter carefully, you should be able to answer the questions. If you have any difficulty, read the chapter over once more so that you have the information well in mind before you go on with your reading.

DO YOU KNOW

1. The four main functions of foundations?

2. What the most common reason for failure of foundations is?

3. How far foundations should extend into the ground?

4. What means are used to strengthen foundations against side pressure from soil?

5. What the second most common material used for foundations is?

6. The physical requirements for concrete blocks to be used for foundations?

7. When pilasters are necessary in concrete block foundations?

8. The compressive strength of good concrete block?

9. How the strength of concrete block pilasters may be increased?

Concrete Block Masonry: Units and Building

Chapter **8**

The term *concrete masonry* is applied to various sizes and kinds of hollow or solid block, to brick, and to many sizes and kinds of concrete building units, all of which are molded from concrete and laid by masons. The concrete is made by mixing portland cement with water and such materials as sand, gravel, slate, crushed stone, cinders, slag, expanded shale or clay, or other types of aggregate.

Concrete masonry is of great interest to all who are concerned with the planning and erection of masonry projects. This type of masonry is economical and allows easy planning and quick erection. It has excellent sound reduction and insulating properties, great durability to weathering and other destructive agents, and high fire resistance. Concrete masonry is available in a great variety of shapes, textures, and colors, which makes it readily adaptable to all commonly used styles of architecture.

The purpose of this chapter is to describe some of the more commonly used kinds of concrete units; to explain in greater detail the types of construction they can be used for; to set forth helpful and useful facts relative to textures, colors, wall patterns, mortar, and joints; to show and explain typical details of construction; to show how typical erection is carried on; and to present other miscellaneous items of a helpful nature.

Concrete Block Construction

Materials and Manufacture

The materials used in making concrete building units (block) are portland cement, various kinds of aggregate, and enough water to bind the mixture. The proportions will vary considerably according to the size, density, appearance requirements, etc. The kind of aggregate used in the mixture is the main factor in determining the properties of the finished product. The two kinds of aggregate are normal weight and lightweight.

Normal Weight Aggregate

These are the naturally occurring materials normally used in making all kinds of concrete. They are sand, gravel or crushed stone (usually some form of limestone). The proportion of sand to coarse aggregate will vary according to the strength and texture desired, as will the size of the coarse aggregate. Because of the relatively thin shells of most concrete block units, the size of the coarse aggregate will seldom exceed $3/8''$. Normal weight aggregate produces a heavier, more dense unit with slightly higher compressive strength than those made with lightweight aggregate. A hollow load-bearing unit of $8'' \times 8'' \times 16''$ nominal size will weigh about 40 to 50 pounds.

Lightweight Aggregate

These aggregates are commercially manufactured products which are sold under several names. They are produced from clays, shales, slag or cinders which are expanded in very high temperature rotary kilns. This produces a porous, rock-like substance which is then ground into the desired sizes. Although the compressive strength of the units made with this type of aggregate is slightly less than normal weight units, they may be, in several instances, interchangeable. Units made with lightweight aggregates usually have better heat and sound insulating qualities. Lightweight units, because their aggregate is a commercially manufactured product, are necessarily more expensive. An $8'' \times 8'' \times 16''$ hollow, load-bearing lightweight unit will weigh from 25 to 35 pounds.

Concrete Block Manufacture

One of the most important aspects of concrete block masonry is its economy. The units cost considerably less than other types because they are made from inexpensive and readily available materials and may be manufactured in huge quantities in a short time. Although manufacturing plants vary in size or capacity, they all employ the same basic steps in manufacture: receiving and storing materials, batching and mixing, molding, curing, packaging and delivery. Modern plants are automated to a greater or less extent. Usually, after the materials are delivered and batched, they are fed into mixers in proportions controlled by electronic meters. After mixing, the materials are fed into molding machines which employ both vibrating and tamping actions. The molding machines are automatically regulated to control the density and texture of the units. There is only enough water in the mixture to make it fluid enough to feed into the machines and so that the units will hold their shape when taken from the molds.

Curing

The method first used for curing concrete blocks was to store the freshly molded units (called *green units*) so that they were exposed to normal atmospheric conditions until thoroughly cured. This usually took about 28 days. The development of modern technological methods, using heated air and steam, revolutionized concrete block manufacture by greatly reducing the time of curing from several days down to a matter of hours.

Unlike clay brick units, concrete blocks must be cured in the presence of moisture. If the green units are subjected to hot dry air, they will lose moisture too rapidly, causing excessive shrinkage and cracking. These units will be weak and brittle and generally unfit for almost any kind of construction. The principal methods are low pressure steam curing and high pressure steam curing.

Low Pressure Steam Curing. This takes place in tunnel kilns similar to those used in curing clay bricks except that warm moist air is used instead of dry heat. Normal atmospheric pressure is maintained throughout the cycle. After the green units are stacked in the kiln, they are left to sit for 1 to 3 hours at normal temperatures (70 to 100 degrees) to attain initial hardening. This is called the "holding" period. Then steam is injected into the kiln and the temperature gradually raised to a maximum of 150 to 165 degrees for normal weight units and 170 to 180 degrees for lightweight units. When the maximum temperature is reached, the steam is turned off, allowing the units to "soak in" the residual moisture in the kiln. The low pressure curing cycle takes about 24 hours in the kiln; the units attain most of their ultimate strength in 2 to 4 days.

High Pressure Steam Curing. This takes place in air-tight steel cylinders called *autoclaves*. Auto-

Concrete Block Construction

Fig. 8-1. Green units entering an autoclave for curing. (Illinois Brick Co.)

claves are from 6 to 10 feet in diameter and 50 to 100 feet long. See Fig. 8-1. After a holding period of from 2 to 5 hours, steam under pressure is gradually injected into the autoclave until the air pressure is 150 psi and the steam temperature is 366 degrees. This process requires at least 3 hours. The units are then steamed from 5 to 10 hours, depending on the thickness of the units. After steaming, the pressure is quickly released, usually in less than ½ hour. This sudden release of pressure, called "blow-down," creates a vacuum-like atmosphere, causing a rapid loss of moisture from the units without allowing time for shrinkage. The units are ready for use immediately after removal from the autoclave. The entire cycle, from removal from the mold to cubing and delivery, usually takes less than 24 hours. High pressure steam cured units are uniformly strong, stable, and highly resistant to shrinkage.

Fig. 8-2 illustrates the manufacture of concrete building units.

Concrete Block Masonry: Units and Building

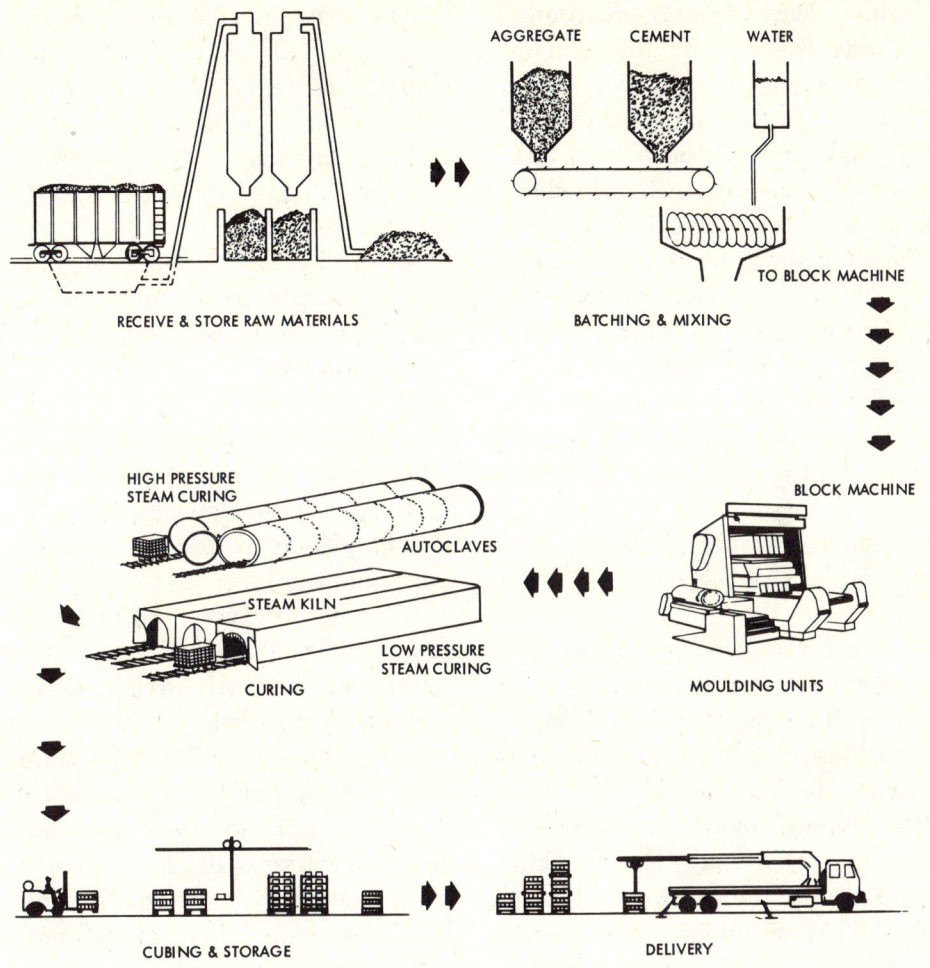

Fig. 8-2. Manufacturing flow chart.

Concrete Block Units

The American Society for Testing and Materials (ASTM) classifies concrete masonry units into two *grades* according to degree of resistance to frost action in different geographical areas, and into two *types* according to the amount of moisture in each individual unit (again in re-

Concrete Block Construction

lation to local climatic conditions).

Grade N units are intended for use in areas where they will be subjected to frost action (freezing and thawing), and will be in direct exposure to moisture, such as in above and below grade exterior walls. These units may be used either with or without a protective coating. The minimum allowable compressive strength per unit is 800 psi.

Grade S units are limited to use in above grade exterior walls with weather protective coatings and in walls not exposed to weather. The minimum allowable compressive strength of Grade S units is 600 psi per unit.

All concrete masonry units retain a small amount of moisture after curing. If the structure in which they are laid is subjected to hot, dry conditions, they may shrink slightly as the retained moisture evaporates. This may eventually cause cracking in the mortar joints. For this reason, the ASTM has designated as *Type I* units with specified low maximum moisture content for geographical areas with low relative humidity. The desert regions of the American southwest is an example of where Type I units would be specified.

Type II units have no specified moisture content limitations and are generally used throughout the country where the average relative humidity is moderate to high.

Note: All block manufactured by the autoclave process, as previously described, will be well within the moisture content limitations.

In building specifications, grades and types are usually listed together as Grades N-I, N-II, S-I, and S-II.

Unit Classification

The ASTM also classifies concrete masonry units as building brick, solid load-bearing block, hollow non-load bearing block, and hollow load-bearing block.

Concrete building brick are solid units manufactured in dimensions much the same as clay masonry units (bricks). They are used in much the same manner.

Solid load-bearing block have little or no coring and are used mostly where very great compressive strength is required.

Hollow non-load-bearing block are thin shelled, lightweight units intended primarily for use in non-load-bearing partitions, but in some cases may be used in above grade, non-load-bearing exterior walls if protected from the weather.

Hollow load-bearing block have by far the greatest range of uses of all the types of units. They combine the qualities of compressive strength with light weight and flexibility of design, size, and shape. Throughout this chapter, wherever the term "block" is used alone, it will refer to hollow load-bearing units. Most of the concrete block manufactured is of this type.

Concrete Block Masonry: Units and Building

Shapes and Sizes of Concrete Masonry Units

Typical shapes and sizes of concrete masonry units are illustrated and named in Fig. 8-3. It should be understood that both heavy and lightweight units can be obtained in these shapes and sizes, and that the typical units illustrated in Fig. 8-3 constitute only those most commonly used. Many other shapes and sizes are available or can be made to order. Most masons refer to concrete masonry units as *concrete blocks* or simply as *block*. All of the three core block illustrated in Fig. 8-3 are obtainable as two core block, the difference in structural properties between the two types being only slight. The dimensions shown are true whether the two or three core variation is used. The following paragraphs describe briefly the qualities and uses of the various concrete masonry units shown in (A) through (BB) of Fig. 8-3.

Stretcher Block. The block shown at (A) is perhaps the most used of all concrete block in the construction of farm buildings, garages, etc., and for all types of buildings where stucco, or other surfacing materials such as brick veneer, is to be used as exterior surfacing.

Corner Block. (B) is used for corners and for simple window and door openings, numerous illustrations of which are shown in this chapter.

Double Corner or Pier Block. (C) is designed for use in laying piers or pilasters, or for any other purpose where both ends of the block would be visible.

Bullnose Block. (D) serves the same purpose as corner block, but it is used where rounded (bullnose) corners are desired.

Wood Sash Jamb Block. (E) is used with stretcher and corner block around the more elaborate window openings. The recess in the block allows room for the various casing members as, for example, in a double-hung window.

Header Block. (F) and (G) are the same as stretcher block, except that a shelf has been provided to facilitate bonding them with brick masonry. (Fig. 8-41, page 160 illustrates the use of a header block.)

Solid Top Block. (H) is the same as stretcher block except that the upper four inches of the block are solid. It is used as the bearing surface on which floor and ceiling joists rest. It may also provide the bearing surface for light girders, such as residential center beams, although gir-

Concrete Block Construction

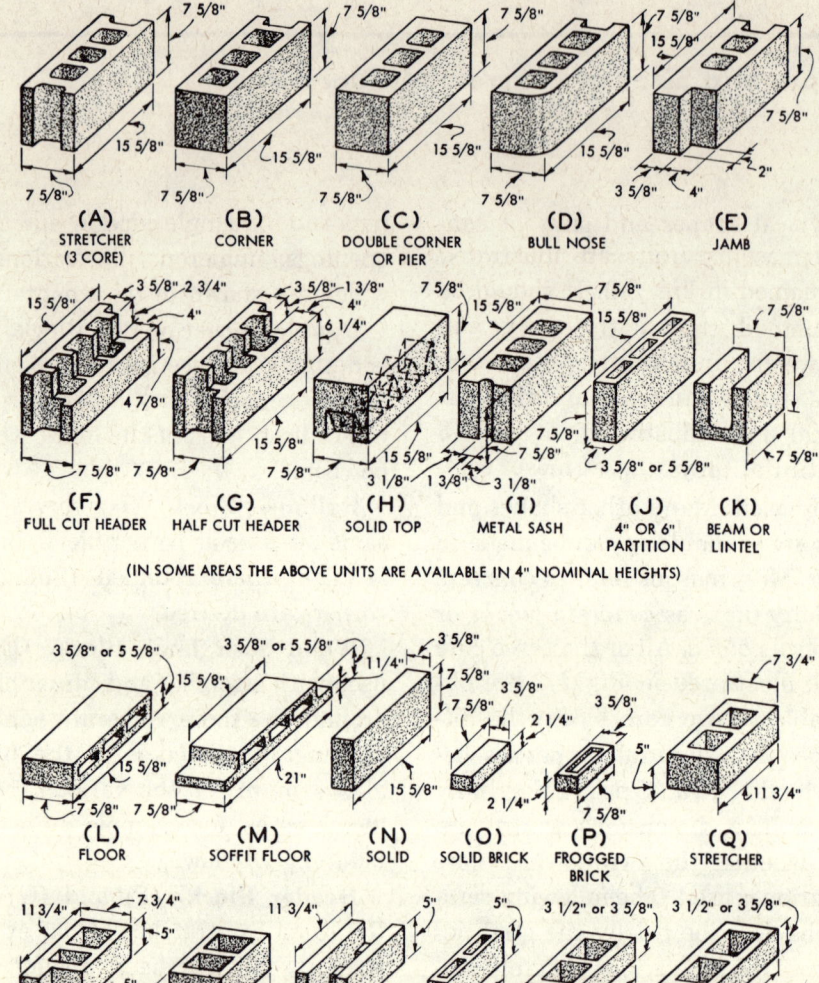

Fig. 8-3. Concrete blocks come in various shapes and sizes to serve many purposes.

Concrete Block Masonry: Units and Building

ders which are intended to carry heavy loads are usually supported by pilasters.

Metal Sash Block. (I) is used for window openings in which metal sash is to be employed. The slot in the block allows room to anchor the jamb members of such sash.

4 in. or 6 in. Partition Block. (J) is used in constructing non-bearing partition walls. It comes in $3\frac{5}{8}''$ and $5\frac{5}{8}''$ widths, allowing construction of either a 4″ or 6″ wall.

Beam or Lintel Block. (K) is used for the construction of reinforced block beams or lintels. The block is laid end-to-end forming a channel. Reinforcing bars are placed in the channel, after which it is filled with concrete. The beams or lintels may be cast in place on shoring or precast and installed later. See Fig. 8-46.

Special Concrete Blocks. The blocks shown in (L) through (BB) of Fig. 8-3, as well as blocks of other shapes and sizes, are used for a large variety of purposes. The filler block used in the construction of concrete filler block floors are shown at (L) and (M). The solid block, shown at (N), is used primarily as a facer unit in framing floor joists in a concrete masonry wall. The concrete bricks shown at (O) and (P) are used in laying concrete brick walls. The remaining units are variations of the blocks previously discussed, and provide some of the range of sizes necessary to meet various construction problems. The variation in sizes also allows the erection of patterned walls, of which more is said in the section dealing with wall patterns.

Actual and Nominal Block Sizes. The sizes shown in Fig. 8-3 for the various blocks are the *actual* sizes. For example, the block shown at (A) has actual dimensions of $7\frac{5}{8}''$ x $7\frac{5}{8}''$ x $15\frac{5}{8}''$. However, it is common practice to speak of or designate such block in terms of *nominal* dimensions. Using this system, these units are then called 8″ x 8″ x 16″ block. This practice is followed in the succeeding pages.

Actual dimensions are made fractional so that, combined with a $\frac{3}{8}''$ mortar joint, all dimensions come out to even inch sizes. Thus, a $15\frac{5}{8}''$ stretcher block with its $\frac{3}{8}''$ mortar joint, equals 16 inches. The same explanation holds true for heights and widths. The $\frac{3}{8}''$ mortar joint has been adopted as the standard-sized joint for concrete masonry construction. This does not mean that mortar joints cannot vary in size. In general, the thinner the mortar joint, the stronger the wall. It is not recommended that mortar joints exceed $\frac{1}{2}''$ in thickness. Since the *actual* dimensions of concrete masonry units make allowance for a $\frac{3}{8}''$ mortar joint, it is easier in calculating wall sizes to adhere to the standard mortar joint thickness.

Although the majority of manufacturers observe the standard sizes

Concrete Block Construction

for concrete masonry units shown in Fig. 8-3 there remain a few whose block may vary slightly in size. It is always wise to ascertain the exact sizes of block available before planning wall dimensions.

Special Concrete Blocks

Besides the standard building units described above, there are other types of units available for special decorative purposes. They may be the regular building units with special surfaces, or specially molded shapes. Some of the more common types are described in the following paragraphs.

Scored Block. Regular stretcher and corner units may be ordered with scoring on the outside face. This creates an artificial joint which gives the appearance of different sized units in the wall. See Fig. 8-4.

Textured Block. Regular sized building units may be specially molded with a raised pattern on the face surface. This allows for a great variety of geometric designs and creates interesting light and shadow patterns. See Fig. 8-5.

Face or Glazed Block. These blocks are also available in most regular building sizes. They have one or more surfaces with a glaze or facing of hard, smooth material such as ceramic or stone. Because of the smooth surface, they may be washed easily and are often used in walls where sanitation is important, such

Fig. 8-4. Scored block.

as in hospitals, kitchens, toilet facilities, etc. See Fig. 8-6. They are also available in a variety of patterns.

Slump Block. A mixture of special consistency is used in the manufacture of this block so that when the units are released from their molds before complete setting they will sag or *slump*. This method of manufacture produces irregularities in the blocks which provide an interesting medium artistically. This type of block may be laid in coursed or ashlar patterns in random lengths of 12″ to 24″. The blocks vary from $1\frac{5}{8}″$ to $3\frac{5}{8}″$ in height. Many of the slump block are integrally colored.

Slump block may be laid in coursed or ashlar patterns, as shown in Fig. 8-7. Walls patterned with slump block are especially popular for interiors and exteriors of homes and commercial buildings, as well as for fireplaces, planter boxes, chimneys, and other decorative details.

Split Block. Rough hewn textures are quite often desirable in home

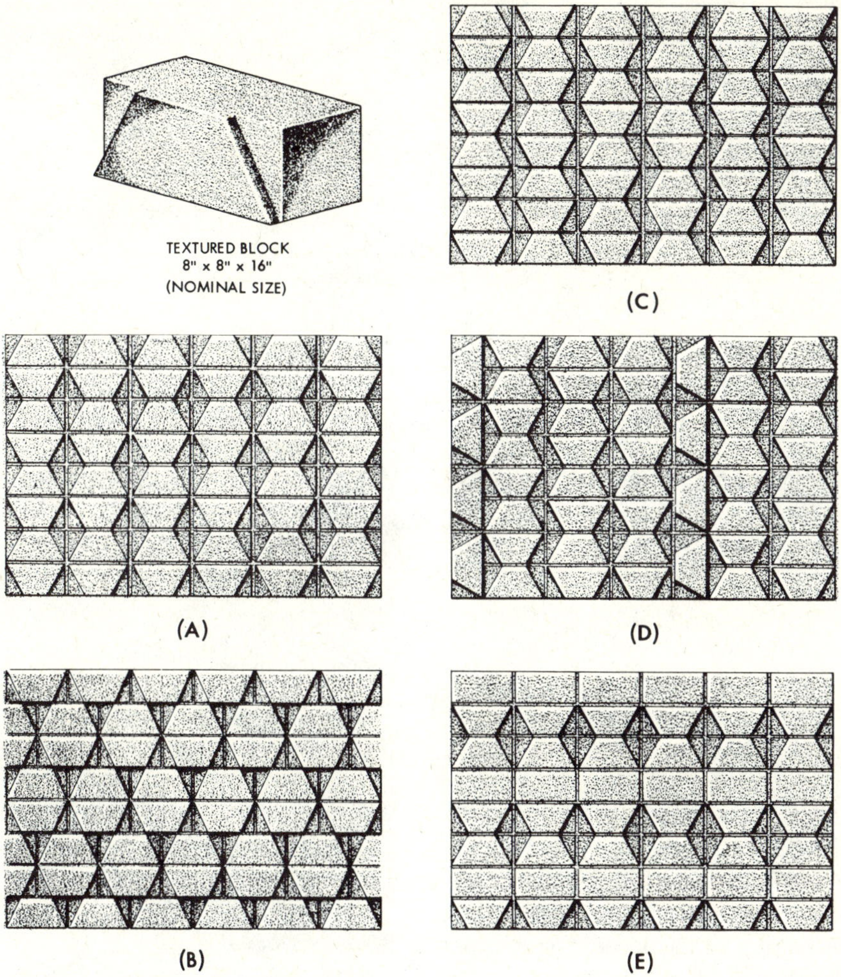

Concrete Block Masonry: Units and Building

Fig. 8-5. Textured or shadow masonry block add beauty and variety to interior and exterior walls.

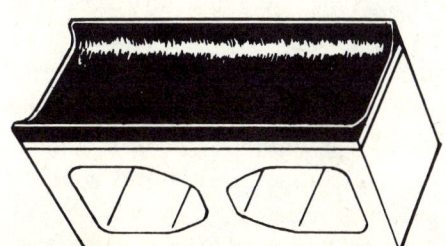

Fig. 8-6. Faced or glazed block.

Concrete Block Construction

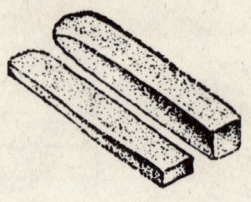

Fig. 8-7. Slump block.

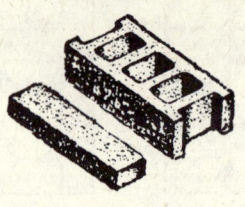

Fig. 8-8. Split block.

construction, or in churches and other public buildings. Split block is produced by splitting or fracturing concrete masonry units lengthwise. The colors of exposed aggregates and the natural color of the cement binder produce a wide range of color choices. A great number of these units have a coloring pigment intermixed. The use of such units presents rough-hewn walls for both exterior and interior walls. See Fig. 8-8.

Color. Many manufacturers make blocks in a variety of colors. The colors are achieved by the use of nonfading mineral pigments or by the use of special cement paints. Colored blocks produce pleasing walls, especially for residences. Almost any color may be reproduced.

Wall Patterns

The following pages illustrate a few typical wall patterns built with concrete masonry units. Many of the units which appear here are relatively new, but they are receiving wider recognition continually and are generally available. The variations achieved in these walls are the result of a number of factors. Changing the course heights and bonding patterns are the most obvious. Variation in the treatment of mortar

Concrete Block Masonry: Units and Building

joints can also produce interesting effects, and some examples of this are shown. Finally, changing of block styles affords still another method of altering the appearance of a wall.

Fig. 8-9 shows four examples of wall pattern variations which may be made using the standard 8" x 8" x 16" block. Both examples in the top row of Fig. 8-9 have tooled horizontal joints, but the one to the right has flush rubbed vertical joints, while the one to the left has tooled vertical joints. In this manner, a wall laid in the typical running bond (left) may be given a horizontal accent (right). The lower left example in Fig. 8-9 shows a basket weave pattern, and the lower right the vertically stacked pattern.

A variation on the basket weave pattern shown in Fig. 8-9 is made in Fig. 8-10 using 4" x 4" x 16" units.

Split block adapts itself widely in wall patterning. The illustration to the left in Fig. 8-11 shows split block in quarter-bond pattern, while the illustration to the right shows split block in several lengths and heights laid in random ashlar pattern. A third variation in wall patterning using split block is shown in Fig. 8-12. Here, the horizontal joints were raked, certain units were separated, and the mortar recessed to produce the diamond pattern shown.

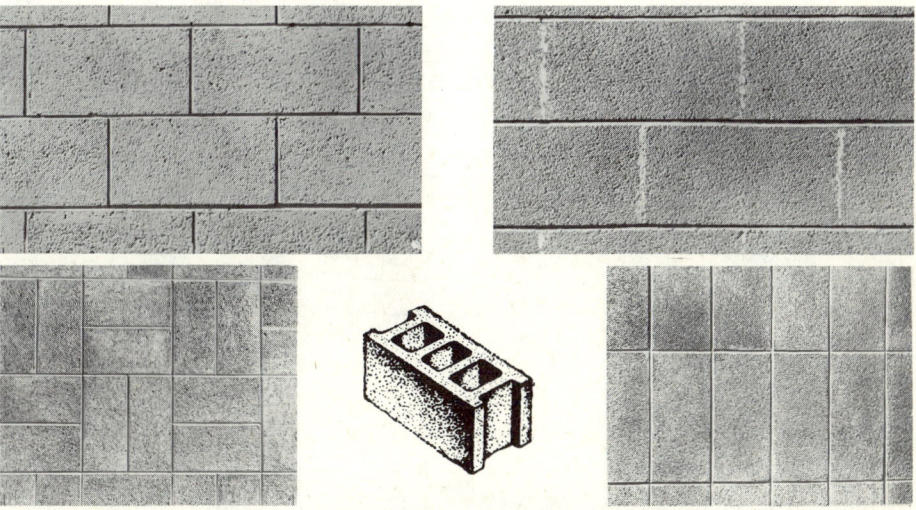

Fig. 8-9. Standard block.

Concrete Block Construction

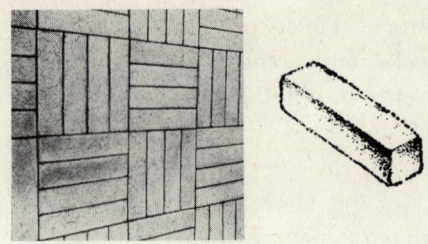

Fig. 8-10. 4″ x 4″ x 16″ units.

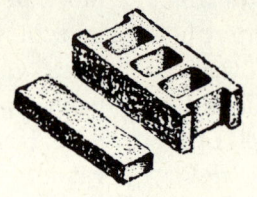

Fig. 8-11. Split block.

Fig. 8-12. Patterns may be achieved by light and shadow effects.

The striking light and shadow effect in Fig. 8-13 is created with units 4″ high. The mortar joints have been raked deeply to create the desired contrast. A coat of paint may be added, as has been done here, to emphasize the highlights. The clapboard effect in Fig. 8-14 is achieved

Concrete Block Masonry: Units and Building

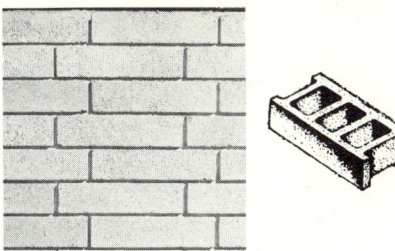

Fig. 8-13. 4" high units.

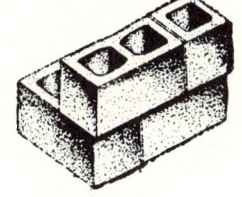

Fig. 8-14. Shadow block.

through the use of shadow block. The lower edge of each shadow block unit projects ⅝" from the face of the block below. This type of wall patterning harmonizes well with low ranch and Colonial style homes.

The wall patterns in Fig. 8-15 are made with similar units, but the treatment in each is totally different. To the right, polished units with a face size of 2" x 16" are employed. To the left, units with a face size of 2" x 16" (called concrete roman brick) are again used, but no special treatment was given the units themselves, and the bonding pattern is entirely different.

The effect in Fig. 8-16 results from a treatment known as "extruded mortar". It is produced by allowing the excess mortar to set as it extrudes without being trimmed off. The open lattice pattern in Fig. 8-17 is produced with overlapping 8" x 8" x 16" units. In making the interesting wall section in Fig. 8-18 the block sizes used were: 8" x 8" x 16", 8" x 8" x 8", and 12" x 8" x 8".

Fig. 8-15. Concrete Roman brick.

147

Concrete Block Construction

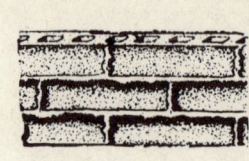

Fig. 8-16. Extruded mortar.

Fig. 8-17. 8" x 8" x 16" block.

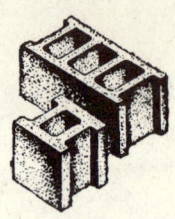

Fig. 8-18. Patterned wall.

Still another interesting way to vary wall patterns is to use different types of units in conjunction. An example of this is shown in Fig. 8-19, where ordinary stretcher units are combined with core blocks to produce an attractive interior partition.

The preceding illustrations show only a few of the many possibilities for wall patterns in concrete masonry. After the size and strength requirements are determined, the only limitation is the imagination of the builder.

Fig. 8-19. Patterned partition wall using core blocks.

Concrete Block Masonry: Units and Building

Concrete Block Construction

Units

As noted earlier, the most common concrete building unit is the *hollow load-bearing block*, measuring nominally 8″ x 8″ x 16″. The nominal dimensions include the actual manufactured size of the block *plus* the thickness of the mortar joint, ⅜″. (Note: The ⅜″ mortar joint is standard throughout the building industry and is always used unless another thickness is definitely specified.) Thus, the actual size of the block is 7⅝″ x 7⅝″ x 15⅝″. Fig. 8-20 shows a typical block of this type and the nomenclature of the parts that will be used in the remainder of this chapter.

Note in Fig. 8-20 that the cores taper in toward the top of the block affording a wider face shell. The units are always laid with the wide face shell up to provide a greater area for bed joint mortar. The unit shown in Fig. 8-20 is made with either three cores or two cores. Two-cored units (Fig. 8-20, right) have slightly different physical properties from the three-cored units. Two-cored units have larger holes and thus have less concrete mass and more core space; they weigh less and cost less. Also, as air does not readily conduct heat, two-cored blocks have slightly better insulating quality.

Note in Fig. 8-20, right, that the inside of the side face shells in the two-core units taper in toward the center web. This provides greater lateral strength than the three-cored units.

In most concrete structures, the main stress is from the top (compression). As three-cored blocks have greater concrete mass and

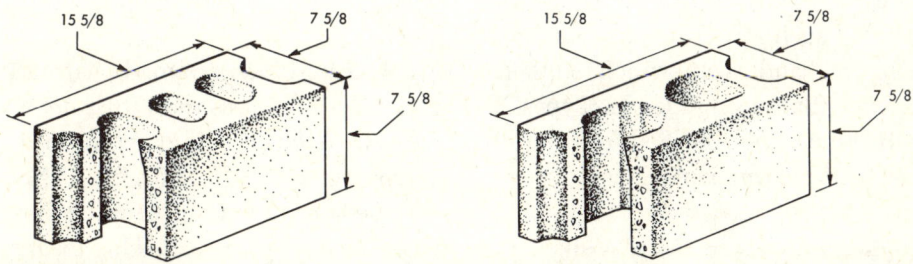

Fig. 8-20. Standard nominal 8″ x 8″ x 16″ hollow load bearing block. Left: Three cored unit. Right: Two cored unit.

larger bearing surface area, they have greater compressive strength and are specified for most jobs.

Preparation of Materials

As previously noted, the presence of excess moisture in concrete blocks will cause shrinkage upon drying. For this reason, blocks should never be wetted before laying. On the job, they should be stockpiled on raised platforms in order to prevent absorption of ground moisture. At the end of the work day, the stockpiled blocks should be covered with a watertight tarpaulin to protect them from rain. If the blocks are accidentally wetted, the work must be postponed until dry units are available. If practical, they should be stored indoors.

Mortar for concrete block masonry should be mixed according to the specifications for unit masonry as outlined in Chapter 3. For example, Type S mortar would be used for most load-bearing walls, particularly those exposed to severe weathering, and below grade structures exposed to earth. Type M mortar would be used in such structures as pilasters, columns, and piers which support heavier than normal loads. Types N and O might be specified for interior non load-bearing partitions.

Laying a Concrete Block Wall

Having learned what the common types of concrete masonry units are, and how to mix mortar properly, the next step is to learn how to correctly handle these materials in actual construction. The remainder of this section will describe the practical application of basic concrete masonry skills by showing how a simple concrete block wall is planned and erected.

Block Planning. The most economical concrete masonry walls are constructed using two standard block, namely stretcher and corner blocks, shown at (A) and (B) of Fig. 8-3. Good construction demands either that joints be staggered or that adequate reinforcement be used. Good appearance demands that the block be used uniformly in all courses. To comply with these demands, the designer of concrete masonry walls must carefully consider the lengths of the blocks plus mortar joints in deciding on the lengths of walls and the location and size of window and door openings. Heights of walls and heights of window and door openings also must be considered in connection with the height, plus mortar joint, of the block.

Concrete block are made with all dimensions $3/8''$ less than their nominal size. A block whose actual measurements are $7 5/8'' \times 7 5/8'' \times 15 5/8''$ may be considered for planning purposes as $8'' \times 8'' \times 16''$. This means that in planning concrete masonry walls, the mortar joints *and* the ma-

Concrete Block Masonry: Units and Building

sonry units themselves may be figured as a single dimensional size.

In planning a building, architects and designers select some basic grid dimension as a basic planning size. This grid may be of any size and value, but it is generally some multiple of 4 inches. By using such a system, called modular coordination, the architect can design his building to afford a minimum of waste material through a minimum amount of cutting. Planning in this way contributes considerably to the reduction of construction costs.

Concrete block structures should generally be laid out on an 8″ grid or some multiple of 8 inches. In planning this way, wall lengths, window and door openings, and wall heights will automatically conform to the standard sizes of concrete masonry units.

It is always wise for the mason to check dimensions given for a building before construction has actually begun. Suppose, for example, that in planning a small building whose walls are to be constructed of 8″ x 8″ x 16″ concrete block, it is desirable from the architectural standpoint to have one of the walls exactly 12′0″ long. Before this length can be definitely decided upon, the lengths of the block plus mortar joints must be considered.

Each ordinary stretcher block is *actually* 15⅝″ long. Adding a ⅜″ mortar joint to a stretcher makes it exactly 16″ long. Corner block are 7⅝″ wide.

One course of the wall in question is shown in Fig. 8-21, top. It can be seen that two corner blocks and eight stretchers fit nicely into the 12′-0″ wall length. This was determined in advance as follows:

The 12′-0″ dimension equals 144 inches. There must be a corner block at each corner. The two corner blocks, with their mortar joints, are 8″ wide and make a total of 16″ which subtracted from 144″ leaves a remainder of 128 inches. Dividing 128″ by 16″ gives a quotient of exactly 8. In other words, 8 stretcher blocks, allowing ⅜″ joints, fit between the two corner blocks, as shown in Fig. 8-21, top. However, these calculations count the mortar joint joint at A twice, which means that the wall will actually be ⅜″ short of the 12′-0″ dimension. This is not serious, for each of the other joints can be made a trifle larger to take up the slack.

To check the block layout shown in Fig. 8-21, top, note the smaller dimensions shown. Adding these will equal 11′-11⅝″ or 143⅝ inches. There are eight stretchers which, with their ⅜″ mortar joints, equal 16″ each. Eight times 16″ is 128 inches. The corner block at C with its joint equals 8″ which, added to the 7⅝″ corner block at B, gives 15⅝ inches. Adding 15⅝″ and 128″ gives a total of 143⅝″, which is just

151

Concrete Block Construction

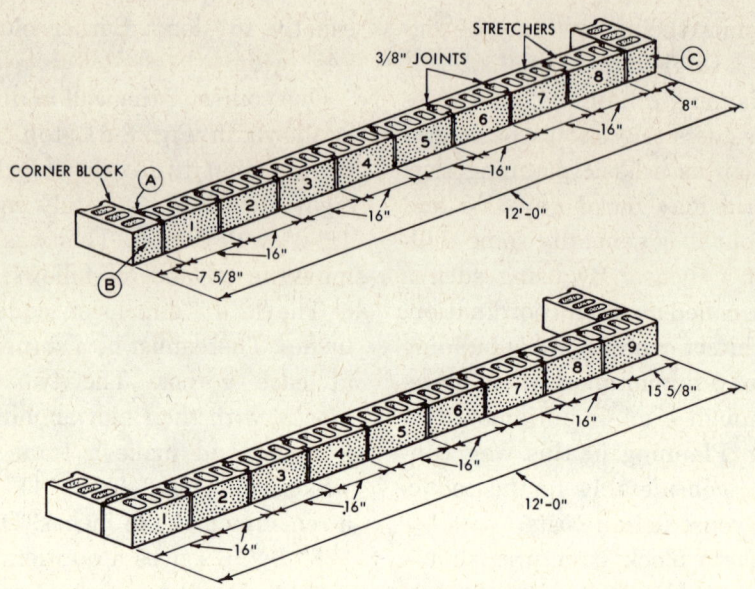

Fig. 8-21. First and alternate courses in a well planned block wall.

⅜″ less than the 12′-0″ dimension of the wall. The missing ⅜″ is absorbed by the other nine joints, as was pointed out in the last paragraph.

The next regular course above the course shown in Fig. 8-21, top, would have the corner blocks laid in the opposite direction, as indicated in Fig. 8-21, bottom. In this course, there are 9 stretchers (including the corner blocks, since they are in line with the regular stretchers) and 8 joints. There is one less joint than in the under top course. Therefore, one stretcher (No. 9) takes up only 15⅝″ in the wall. The length can be checked by multiplying 16″ by 8 and adding 15⅝″, which gives a total of 143⅝ inches. In this course again, each of the 8 joints must have a little added to it to fill out the required length of 12′0″.

Note: Instead of dividing reductions or increases among all joints, masons generally reduce or increase one or two joints. This is much easier and quicker, and where only small reductions or increases are involved, is hardly noticeable.

Following this procedure, the length dimensions for the walls of each job should be carefully considered, no matter what shapes and sizes of block are to be used. The heights of block walls should be checked with equal exactness. If

152

wall dimensions do not conform to the modular sizes of the block, an attempt should be made to change the wall dimensions.

In some cases it is impossible to change wall dimensions to conform with modular planning of the block. In this case, cut block must be used. Modern masonry saws ease the operation of cutting concrete masonry units, reducing the time necessary to cut block while increasing accuracy. One method of amending walls made unsightly by cut blocks would be to tool the joints flush and then paint.

Layout. Before any concrete block is actually laid in a wall, it is always wise to check the designer's dimensions and to determine an accurate block layout. To achieve this purpose, one course of blocks should be set around the footing without the use of mortar (Fig. 8-22). This allows you to determine if any cutting of blocks will be necessary. It also allows you to find if adequate allowance has been made for mortar joints. A chalked snap-line is sometimes used to mark the position of blocks in the first course. This helps in aligning blocks correctly as they are laid.

Once the block layout has been checked, the first course of the wall is laid. As shown in Fig. 8-23, a full mortar bed is spread and furrowed with a trowel to insure complete bedding of the face shells *and* webs of blocks in the first course. The corner block is laid first, and great care should be taken in positioning it correctly, as this block will act as a guide for the entire corner (Fig. 8-24).

All block should be laid with the thicker end of the face shell up, as this provides a larger mortar bedding area. Only the ends of the face shells are buttered for vertical joints, as shown in Fig. 8-25. To speed laying of the block, you can apply mortar to the vertical face shells of three

Fig. 8-22. Checking the layout.

Fig. 8-23. A full mortar bed.

Concrete Block Construction

Fig. 8-24. One block—guide to entire corner.

Fig. 8-26. Aligning block in the first course.

Fig. 8-25. Buttering face shell for vertical joint.

Fig. 8-27. Bringing block to grade.

or four blocks in one operation. Each block is then lowered into its final position and pushed downward into the mortar bed, producing well-filled vertical joints.

After the first few block have been laid, the mason's level is used as a straightedge to assure correct alignment of the block, as shown in Fig. 8-26. The block are brought to proper grade by use of the level, as shown in Fig. 8-27. Position block by light taps with the trowel. Some masons use the edge of the trowel for tapping so as to reduce the amount of mortar scattered around, while others prefer to use the trowel handle. Blocks are plumbed as shown in Fig. 8-28. Take great care in aligning, leveling, and plumbing the first course as it is essential in building a straight, true, wall in a minimum time.

Succeeding courses in the wall are usually laid with what is called "face-shell bedding". This means

Concrete Block Masonry: Units and Building

Fig. 8-28. Plumbing block.

five or six courses higher than the center of the wall to act as guides in laying the rest of the block. As each course is laid at the corner, it is carefully checked with a level to make sure it is level, plumb, and in alignment. Each corner block is likewise checked with a straightedge to make certain that the faces of the block are in the same plane, as shown in Fig. 8-30. This will further insure a straight, true wall.

that mortar is applied only to the horizontal face shells of the block, as shown in Fig. 8-29. Mortar for vertical joints can be placed on the vertical face shells of either the block to be placed, or the block previously laid. Some masons butter the vertical face shells of both the previously laid block and the block to be laid. Well-filled vertical and end joints are essential as moisture has a tendency to seep through. After the first course is laid the corners are built up

Fig. 8-30. Aligning block face.

Fig. 8-29. Face shell bedding.

A story- or course-pole, which is a board (usually 1" x 2") with markings 8" apart, is used to find the top of the masonry for each course, Fig. 8-31. In building corners, each course is stepped back half a block. This is sometimes called *racking the*

Concrete Block Construction

Fig. 8-31. Use of the story pole.

lead. Horizontal spacing of the block may be checked by placing a level diagonally across the corners of the block, as shown in Fig. 8-32.

Fig. 8-32. Checking horizontal spacing.

This is called "straightedging the rack". Each block must touch, and be completely flush with the level if the wall is to be plumb and true and in line with the corners. This step must be repeated often to prevent bulges or depressions in the wall and to keep the courses in line with the corners.

In laying block for the wall between corners, a mason's line is stretched from corner to corner for each course. The outside top of each block is then laid to this line. The manner in which you handle the block is important. Only practice can determine the most practical way for each individual to handle block. If you tip the block you are laying slightly toward yourself, you can see the upper edge of the course below. This will allow you to place the lower edge of the block you are handling directly over the course below, as shown in Fig. 8-33.

All final adjustments to a block must be made while the mortar is soft and plastic. Once the mortar has stiffened, shifting the block will break the mortar bond and cause cracks between the block and the mortar. If the block is disturbed after the mortar has begun to set, the block must be removed, stripped of all the old mortar, and relaid in fresh mortar.

As shown in Fig. 8-34, each block is leveled and aligned by tapping lightly with the trowel handle. In laying block between corners, the

Concrete Block Masonry: Units and Building

Fig. 8-33. Handling the block.

Fig. 8-34. Aligning the block by tapping.

level is used only to check the face of each block to keep it lined up with the face of the wall.

Mortar should not be spread too far ahead of the actual laying, as it will stiffen and lose its plasticity. This will decrease its bonding power and weaken the structure of the entire wall. Excess mortar squeezed from between the block as it is laid is cut off with a trowel (Fig. 8-35). This excess mortar is usually thrown back on the mortar board to be reworked into fresh mortar. Some masons apply the excess mortar to the vertical face shells of the block just laid. Any mortar which begins to stiffen after it has been spread should be removed and reworked on the mortar board. Mortar applied to the vertical joints of the block just laid and to the block being set insures well-filled joints (Fig. 8-36). Dead mortar picked up from the scaffold or floor should never be used. Full mortar bedding may be required in some localities, and should always be used where the greatest possible structural strength is necessary, as in pilasters, piers, and columns. This requires mortar on the cross webs of the block as well as on the face shells.

The installation of the closure block requires great care. The closure block should be laid in the opening without mortar to determine if there is adequate allowance for the mortar joints. If the block must be cut, care should be taken that the cut is accurate, since oversized joints are just as objectionable as joints which are too thin. All four vertical edges of the closure block and all edges of the opening should be buttered with mortar. The closure block should be lowered carefully into place (Fig. 8-37). If any of the mor-

Concrete Block Construction

Fig. 8-35. Cutting off excess mortar.

Fig. 8-37. Installing the closure block.

Fig. 8-36. Well filled mortar joints.

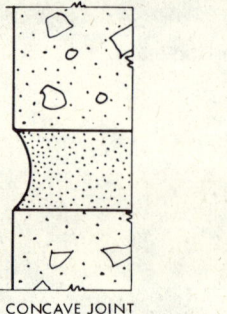

Fig. 8-38. Concave and V-shaped mortar joints.

tar falls out, leaving an open joint, the closure block should be removed, fresh mortar applied, and the operation repeated.

Well tooled joints will produce weathertight walls of neat appearance. Joints should be tooled after the mortar has stiffened, but before it has hardened. The length of time which it takes to set will be less in warm weather than in cold. Learn to check the mortar with your finger tips to determine when it is ready to strike. Tooling of the joints compacts the mortar and forces it tightly against the masonry on each side of the joint. Unless otherwise specified, all joints in concrete masonry walls should be tooled either concave or V-shaped. See Fig. 8-38.

The jointer, sometimes called a sled-runner, for tooling horizontal joints should be at least 22" long, preferably longer, and upturned at one end to prevent gouging of the mortar. A handle should be located

Concrete Block Masonry: Units and Building

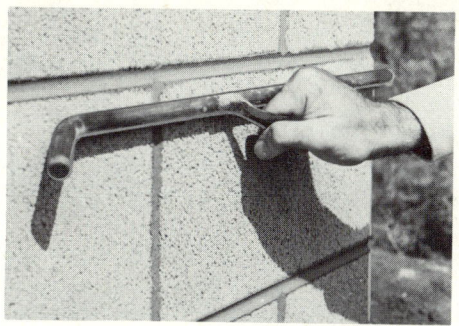

Fig. 8-39. Tool used for horizontal joints.

Fig. 8-40. Tool used for vertical joints.

approximately in the center of the tool for ease in handling. A tool made from a ⅝" round bar is satisfactory for concave joints (Fig. 8-39). Tooling of the horizontal joints should be done first, followed by striking the vertical joints with a small S-shaped jointer (Fig. 8-40). Any mortar burrs on the wall should be trimmed off after the joints have been tooled. This may be done with a trowel or by rubbing with a burlap bag.

Construction Details

After learning and practicing the basic skills necessary for laying a concrete block wall that is plumb and level with tight solid mortar joints, the next step is to learn the more complex construction details the mason will commonly encounter. The following section of this chapter will show in detail such structures as combination walls, various supporting structures, door and window openings, etc. A thorough understanding of these details is essential to good masonry.

Wall Details

The basic wall construction previously described will many times have modifications or additions in order to accommodate heavier loads or additional structures. The following paragraphs show details of these constructions.

Composite Walls. Fig. 8-41, left, shows the use of concrete blocks as backing for a brick wall. Note that at intervals, a header course of brick is employed to tie the tiers of brick and block together. The block used

Concrete Block Construction

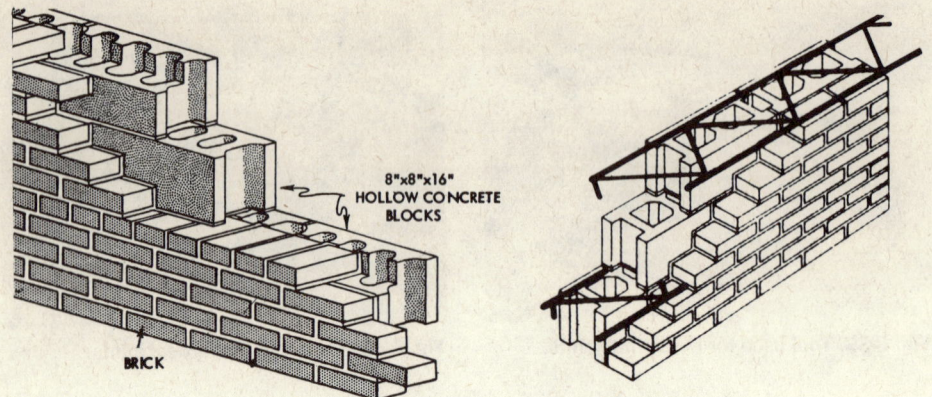

Fig. 8-41. Composite masonry walls.

in these courses are specially molded units with a notch provided to receive the brick headers. These units are called "full cut header block".

Fig. 8-41, right, shows another method of bonding a brick and block composite wall. The two tiers are tied together with manufactured metal ties.

Cavity Walls. A cavity wall is a form of masonry wall consisting of two parallel wythes of masonry separated by a continuous air space, usually about 2″ wide. One of the advantages of cavity wall construction is that the air space acts to prevent rain or moisture that has seeped through the outer wythe from penetrating the inner wythe. If moisture tends to collect in the cavity between the walls, flashing and weep holes are usually located at the base of the outer wall. The cavity also interrupts the continuity of the masonry and provides the additional insulation effect of an air space. An improvement of over 25 percent in insulating value was found for unventilated cavity walls compared with solid walls of the same material.

Cavity walls when properly built will withstand reasonable impact and the usual floor and roof loading of a two-story building. The fire resistance of cavity walls is not much different from walls with the same quantity of solid materials except for the ability to withstand loads. Cavity walls which are loaded toward the inner wythe have the greatest stability during exposure to fire. The advantages which cavity walls display may be lost through improper design, particularly with respect to flashing, openings, ties, and wall intersections.

The two wythes of a cavity wall should be securely tied together with non-corroding ties. For each 3 sq. ft. of wall surface, a rectangular tie of

Concrete Block Masonry: Units and Building

No. 6 gage wire should be used. The ties are embedded in the horizontal joints of both walls. Additional ties are required at all openings, with ties spaced about 3' apart around the perimeter and within 12" of the opening.

Generally, 10" cavity walls should not exceed 25' in height. Neither the inner nor the outer walls should be less than 4" thick, and the space between them should not be less than 2" nor more than 3" wide, if the most efficient insulating effect is desired. Usually the outer wall is 4" thick and the remaining wall thickness is made up by the air space and the inner wall.

If concrete masonry cavity walls are properly designed and built, with well tooled mortar joints and a covering of paint or stucco, the walls should be weathertight. This means that in general there should be no need to include special flashing and weep holes. However, in limited areas subjected to driving rains, or where experience has shown that water collects in the walls, extra flashing and weep holes will be necessary.

Under severe moisture conditions, the heads of windows, doors, and other wall openings, and the bottom course of masonry, are flashed so that moisture entering the wall cavity will be directed toward the outside wall. Only rust-resisting metal or other tested and approved materials should be used for flashing.

Weep holes should be placed 2 or 3 units apart in the vertical joints of the bottom course. Weep holes should never be placed below grade.

Weep holes can be made by placing well-oiled rods in the mortar joint, removing them after the mortar has hardened; or short pieces of hemp rope, sash cord or fiberglass insulation may be placed in the end joints near the bottom of the outside wall. This material allows moisture to seep out and insects cannot get in. Care should be taken that the inside openings of weep holes are not clogged by mortar droppings. Place a 1" x 2" board across a level of wall ties to catch the droppings. As the masonry reaches the next level for placing ties, the board is raised, cleaned, and laid on the ties placed at this level.

Fig. 8-42, left, shows the basic arrangement of a ten inch cavity wall. Both wythes are constructed of partition block which are nominally 4" thick. To increase the size of a cavity wall, the inner wythe is generally thickened. Thus, for a 12" cavity wall, the outer wythe would still be 4" block and the inner wythe would be 6" block. One type of wall tie is illustrated and the spacing recommended is indicated. Fig. 8-42, right, illustrates a brick and block cavity wall using continuous metal ties.

Horizontal Reinforcement. Reinforcement added to the horizontal mortar joints of concrete masonry

Concrete Block Construction

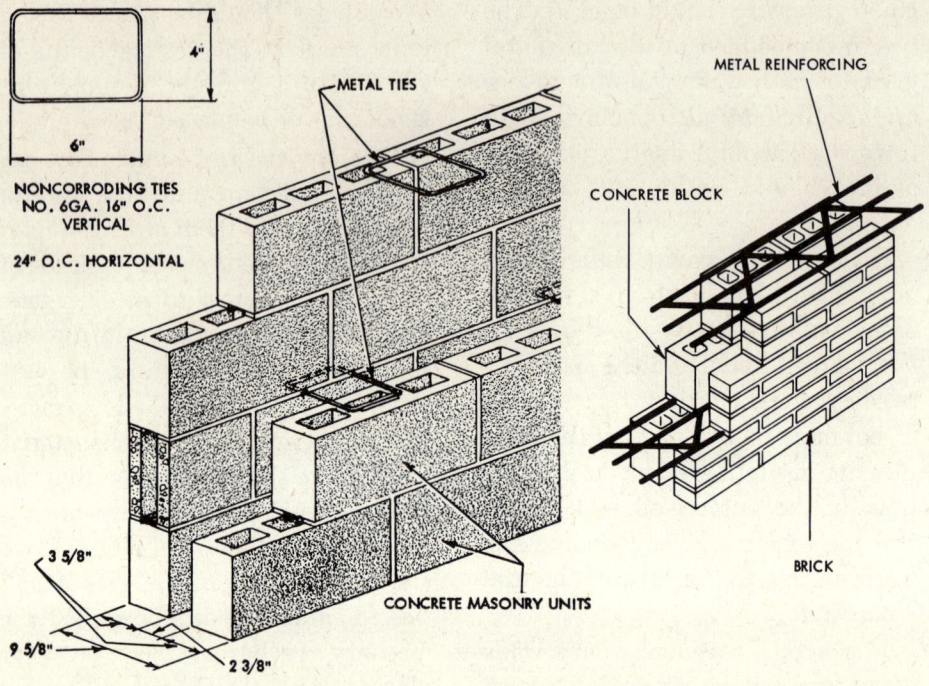

Fig. 8-42. Typical masonry cavity walls.

walls develops appreciably higher bond stress in the wall and aids in reducing cracks in the masonry units due to shrinkage. Concrete masonry units tend to expand when dampened and to contract when dried. While this does not affect independent units which are not part of a wall but are laid into a wall, such shrinkage or expansion tends to create cracks in the units. This shrinkage may be reduced either by the use of control joints or horizontal reinforcement. One method of horizontal reinforcement is to use two ¼" round steel reinforcing bars,

one placed in each face shell joint. These bars should be placed in alternate courses above and below window openings. Bars should also be carried over door openings and should be bent around corners. Bars should be lapped a minimum of 10 inches. See Fig. 8-43.

Horizontal reinforcement may also be achieved by the use of prefabricated welded cross wires. Such reinforcement can be used in either single wythe walls or to tie brick faced or cavity walls together. The cross wires in this type of reinforcement act to replace the more usual

Concrete Block Masonry: Units and Building

Fig. 8-43. Steel bars used as horizontal reinforcement.

wall ties necessary for brick faced or cavity walls. Prefabricated reinforcement may be purchased with cross wires which are crimped into a drip. This drip provides a barrier to any moisture which collects on the cross wire, preventing it from entering the inner wythe of a cavity wall. Horizontal reinforcement increases the ability of a concrete masonry wall to withstand side pressure caused by water, soil, or wind pressure considerably.

The degree to which horizontal reinforcement is used is determined by the qualities desired of a concrete masonry wall. Used in every third course and above all window and door openings, horizontal reinforcement aids materially in developing lateral strength in a wall, while largely reducing cracking due to shrinkage. Horizontal reinforcement used in every course of a concrete masonry wall reduces shrinkage cracking to a minimum while developing walls with great lateral strength. Fig. 8-44 shows one type of modern, prefabricated horizontal tie.

Concrete Block Construction

Fig. 8-44. Horizontal joint reinforcement provides added lateral strength for a concrete block wall. (Dur-O-Wal Products, Inc.)

Steel Bar Reinforcing. In areas where concrete block walls are subjected to greater than normal lateral stresses such as earthquakes or high winds, the walls may be reinforced with deformed steel bars. The bars are placed in the footing or foundation at regular intervals so as to run vertically through the head joints and block coring in each course. The cores or joints are filled with mortar or grout as each course is laid up. This is called "rodding the core". This type of reinforcing is also employed at corners and at door and window openings. See Figs. 8-45 and 8-47.

Steel bars are used in the same manner and for the same reason in such horizontal structures as bond

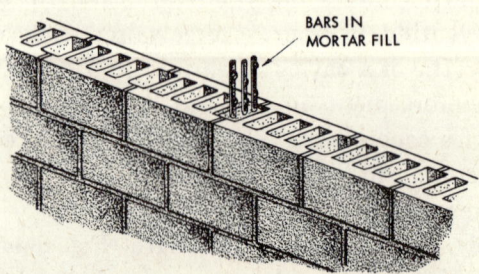

Fig. 8-45. Steel bars used for vertical reinforcing.

164

Concrete Block Masonry: Units and Building

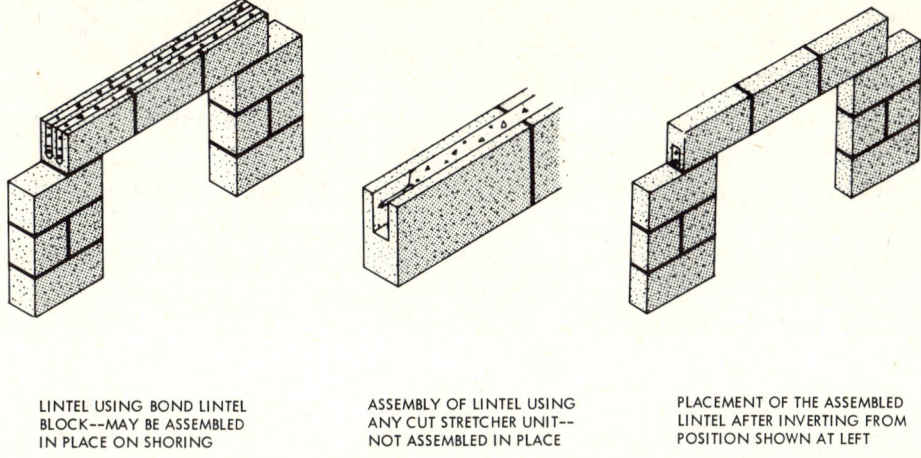

LINTEL USING BOND LINTEL BLOCK--MAY BE ASSEMBLED IN PLACE ON SHORING

ASSEMBLY OF LINTEL USING ANY CUT STRETCHER UNIT-- NOT ASSEMBLED IN PLACE

PLACEMENT OF THE ASSEMBLED LINTEL AFTER INVERTING FROM POSITION SHOWN AT LEFT

Fig. 8-46. Lintels made with concrete block, mortar, and reinforcing steel bars. (Illinois Brick Co.)

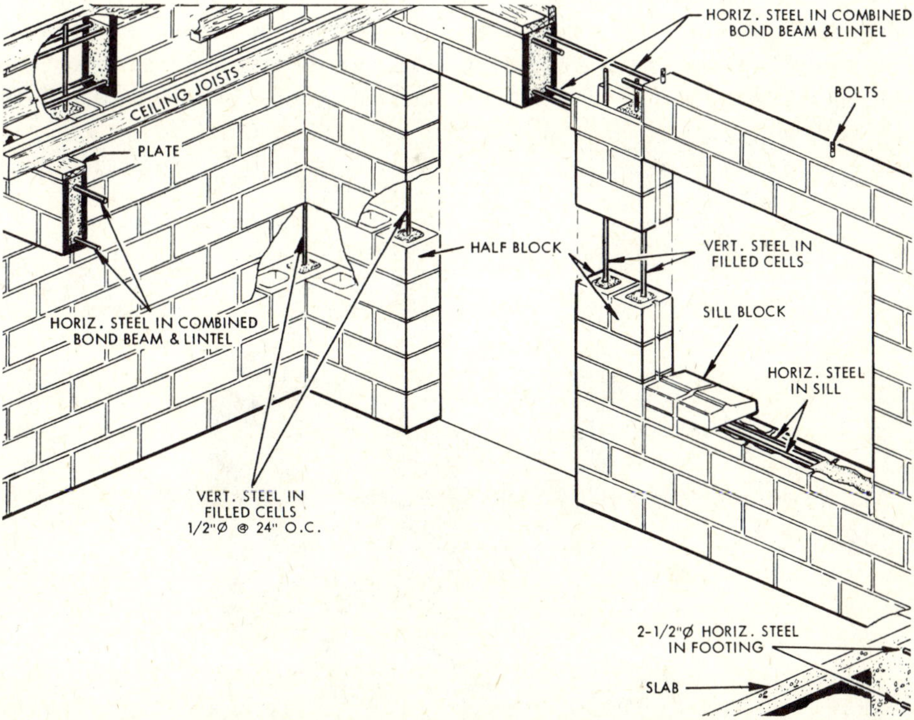

Fig. 8-47. Steel reinforcing may be used in several ways.

Concrete Block Construction

beams and lintels. See Figs. 8-46 and 8-47. Note: A bond beam is uually the top course of each story height.

Fig. 8-47 illustrates many ways in which steel bars are used as reinforcement in concrete block construction.

Note: In Fig. 8-47 that the diameter of the steel reinforcing bars is given as the actual diameter in inches and fractions. This is only to give examples of typical sizes of bars used for specific purposes. On regular working drawings, specifications, and shipping tags, the size is given as a number corresponding to the diameter of the bar in eighths of an inch. For example, a one-half inch bar would be listed as #4, a one-inch bar as #8, etc.

Fig. 8-48 shows the use of a precast solid concrete lintel in combination with a steel angle in a brick-faced wall with concrete block backing.

Joist Support. Joists usually support a rather heavy floor load, and careful provisions must be made to support their ends in the concrete block walls. There are several ways in which such support may be secured. Fig. 8-49 shows several typical methods, all of which are acceptable.

Fig. 8-49(A) illustrates one of the simplest methods. Here the ends of regular stretcher blocks are cut to allow room for the joist ends. All joists must be beveled as shown at (E). In the event of a fire or accident which results in a collapse of the

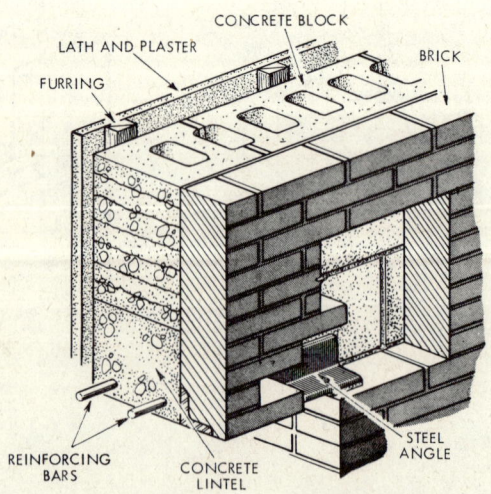

Fig. 8-48. Solid reinforced lintel in a brick and block wall.

Concrete Block Masonry: Units and Building

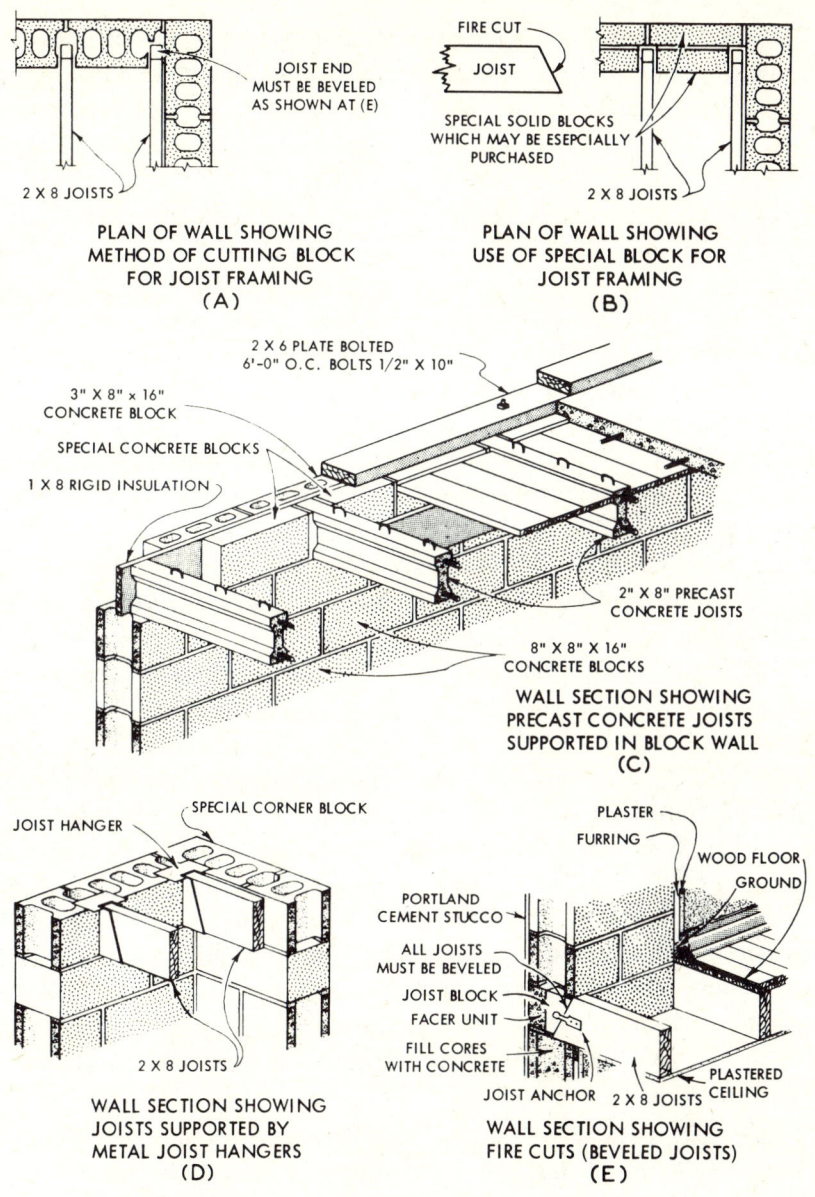

Fig. 8-49. Details of joist bearings in concrete block walls.

floor, beveled joists will fall free from their positions in the wall. Joists with square ends will act as levers, prying their way free and destroying the wall. The course of blocks directly under the joists

167

should be solid or have all cores filled with concrete. The bearing of the joists should be a minimum of 3 inches.

In Fig. 8-49(B), the use of special blocks for joist framing is shown. All other conditions explained for (A) apply here.

At Fig. 8-49(C), the method of supporting precast concrete joists in a block wall is illustrated. Note that special size blocks are required.

In Fig. 8-49(D), the use of metal joist hangers is illustrated. Here the joists need not be beveled. The hangers, of which several kinds are available, are set into the block at their vertical joints.

Fig. 8-49(E) is a more complicated method of support. This method is of particular use for residential construction.

It will be noted that all joists shown in Fig. 8-49 are 2" x 8" in size. This was done in order to simplify the presentation of construction details in floor framing. 2" x 10" joists are normally necessary, and when framing around such joists, special blocks, as shown at Fig. 8-49(B), are required.

Pilasters and Columns. Sometimes the loads on beams are so great that a large bearing surface and pilaster or pier are required. In such cases, pilasters or piers as shown in Fig. 8-50 are necessary. Pilasters can be made of standard stretchers and corner blocks as part of regular walls, or specially sized units may be used. Piers are constructed with double corner or pier blocks. All cores in the pilaster or pier blocks should be filled with concrete for maximum strength under heavy loads.

Columns built of concrete block can be made using two or three blocks in each course, as shown in the pier and pilaster construction in Fig. 8-50. In some parts of the country, circular blocks having a 12" diameter can be purchased to use in column building.

Fig. 8-51 shows details of a corner pilaster and a typical mid-wall pilaster.

Columns are free-standing units constructed in the same manner as pilasters and piers. They are used mainly as center supports for joists, beams, etc.

Beam Supports. In most residences and other larger buildings, there are one or more beams which have to be supported at one end by the walls or foundations. Such beams generally carry heavy loads and therefore must be carefully supported.

In Fig. 8-52, left, a typical case where a block wall supports one end of a beam is shown. The beam should have at least 3" of bearing. This is important where heavy loads are involved in order to avoid the shearing off of the edges of blocks. All blocks under the beam (see blocks

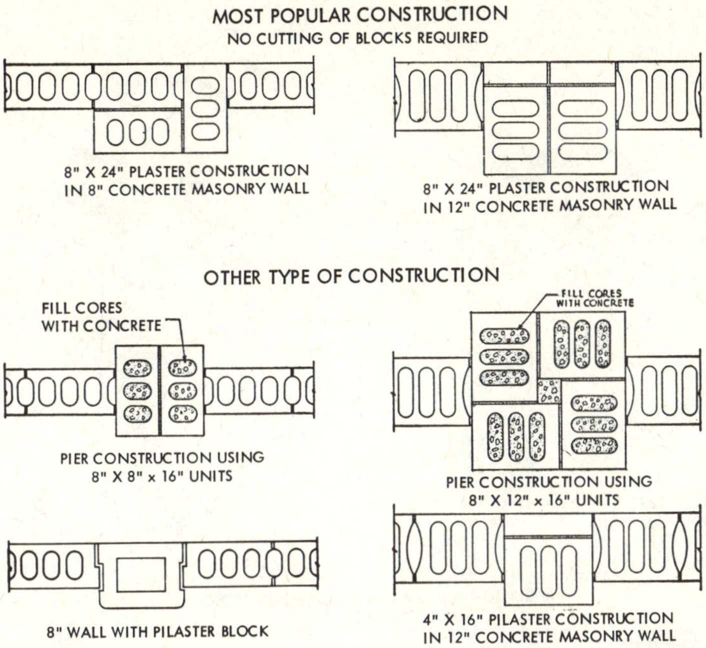

Concrete Block Masonry: Units and Building

MOST POPULAR CONSTRUCTION
NO CUTTING OF BLOCKS REQUIRED

8" X 24" PLASTER CONSTRUCTION IN 8" CONCRETE MASONRY WALL

8" X 24" PLASTER CONSTRUCTION IN 12" CONCRETE MASONRY WALL

OTHER TYPE OF CONSTRUCTION

FILL CORES WITH CONCRETE

PIER CONSTRUCTION USING 8" X 8" X 16" UNITS

FILL CORES WITH CONCRETE

PIER CONSTRUCTION USING 8" X 12" X 16" UNITS

8" WALL WITH PILASTER BLOCK

4" X 16" PILASTER CONSTRUCTION IN 12" CONCRETE MASONRY WALL

Fig. 8-50. Pilasters and piers used for added strength. (National Concrete Masonry Association)

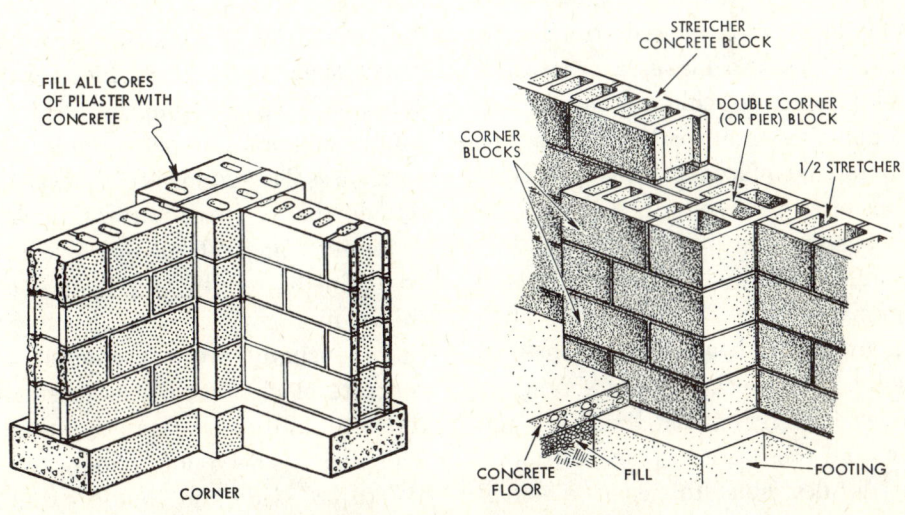

Fig. 8-51. Corner and mid-wall pilasters.

169

Concrete Block Construction

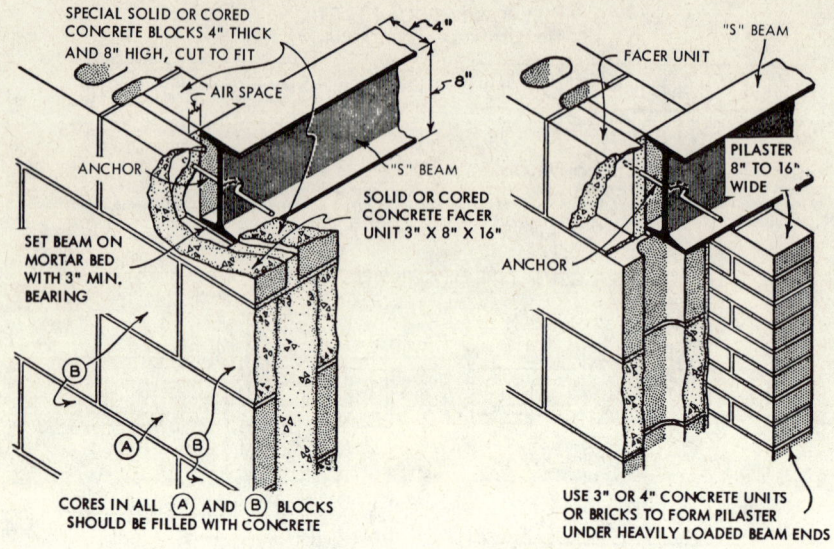

Fig. 8-52. Typical method of supporting beams in concrete block walls.

A and B in the elevation view) should have their cores filled with concrete. This practice strengthens each block and makes a practically solid concrete column capable of supporting great loads. Anchor pins should be placed at least 4″ from face of wall.

The top view of the section at Fig. 8-52, left, shows how facer units and special solid or cored blocks are filled in around the beam to make the wall solid. The special blocks should be placed snugly against the beam web to hold the beam in place, although it is desirable to leave a small amount of play to allow for expansion of the beam due to temperature changes.

Sometimes beams carry such heavy loads that the 8″ block wall is not sufficiently strong by itself to safely support the beam ends. In such cases, larger blocks can be used. Should this be inadequate, the wall or foundation can be given considerable added strength by pilasters, as shown in Fig. 8-52, right. Such pilasters usually are constructed of concrete blocks, but bricks or small concrete units also may be used. The pilasters need not be more than 12″ to 24″ wide and should extend from the beam down to the footing.

Concrete Block Masonry: Units and Building

Concrete Floor Support. In buildings where fireproof construction is mandatory, reinforced concrete floors are necessary. Fig. 8-53 shows two typical methods of supporting such floors in block walls.

In Fig. 8-53(A), where the floor thickness is not equal to 8″, facer units and concrete bricks can be used together with the thickened edge of the concrete floor to build up and provide support for the wall. In Fig. 8-53(B), a more complicated method is required because the thickness of the precast concrete joists plus a concrete floor amounts to more than 8 inches.

Note in both (A) and (B) that an air space is provided to allow for expansion or contraction of the joists due to changes in temperature. This space can be filled with insulation to help make the wall more resistant to the passage of heat at the points where there are no cores.

The most important features to keep in mind with regard to joist and floor supports are that at least 3″ of bearing are required, and that the walls must be built up, as shown in Figs. 8-49, 8-51, 8-52, and 8-53 so as not to impair their strength or stability.

Concrete Block Joist Floors. Along with the greatly increased production of concrete block for use in walls and partitions, there has arisen a strong interest in the use of hollow concrete units as fillers in the construction of one-way ribbed slab floors. Concrete filler blocks are made of lightweight aggregate and have hollow spaces which total 40 to 60 percent of the gross volume of

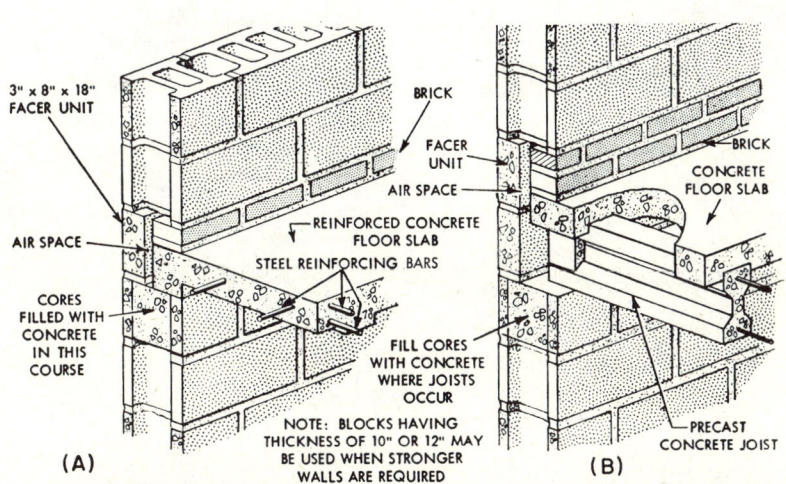

Fig. 8-53. Details of support for concrete floor in a masonry wall.

Concrete Block Construction

the unit itself. This effects a marked reduction in the dead load of floors constructed of concrete filler block, as compared with a solid slab of equal load carrying capacity.

This type of construction can be used in both floor and roof finishing, and combines precast concrete block with the cast-in-place concrete slab and joists. The concrete blocks provide both the forms for the joists of the floors and a flat ceiling which can be painted or plastered direct. In the example shown in Fig. 8-54, where filler block units 15⅝" long are used, the design for this type of floor system requires a uniform spacing of joists 21" on centers. The joists, then, are actually 5⅜" wide. The joist depth is the sum of the thicknesses of the block filler and the concrete slab. While the dead load of such a floor is less than a slab floor of equal load carrying capacity, the total depth of the floor is increased.

This method of floor construction is simple to build and requires no

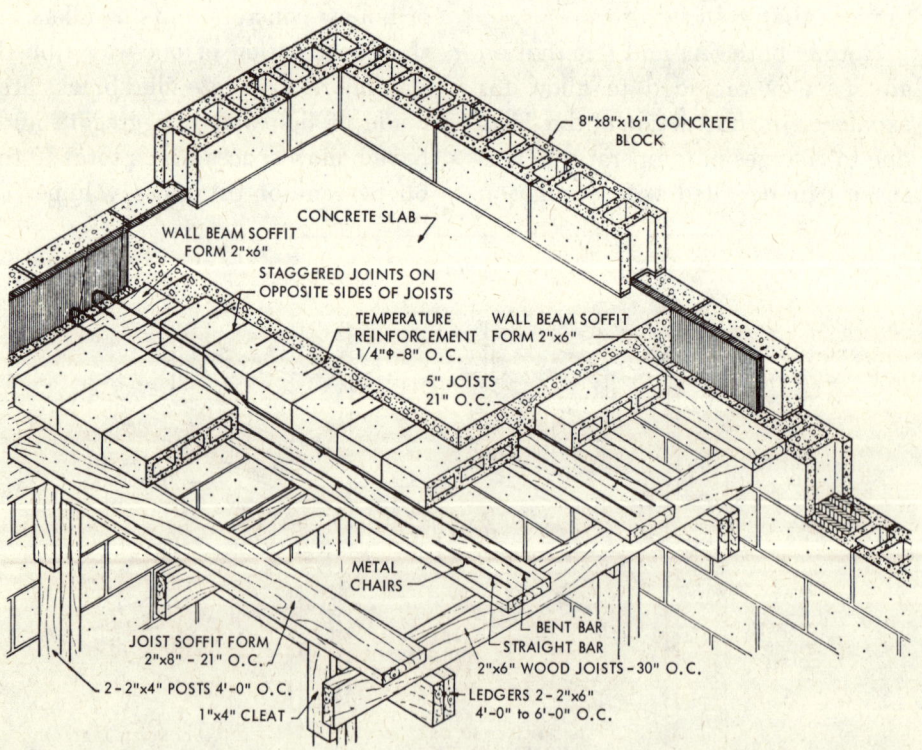

Fig. 8-54. Basic method used in laying a concrete filler block floor. (Portland Cement Association)

Concrete Block Masonry: Units and Building

special construction methods. In addition to cutting down dead load and providing ceiling surfaces which may be plastered directly, there is a marked improvement in the heat insulating qualities of the slab. A minimum of form lumber is required in construction, and the finished floor has excellent fire resistance.

Fig. 8-54 illustrates a basic method used in laying concrete filler block floors. The filler block may be of the size and shape shown in (L) of Fig. 8-3, or they may be the soffit block type shown at (M) of Fig. 8-3. Either block is acceptable but the soffit block presents a more pleasing appearance on the finished ceiling surface. Fig. 8-54 is not intended as a final working drawing, and it is recommended that each job be designed and built under the supervision of a competent architect or structural engineer.

Control Joints. Cracks may occur in masonry walls due to unusual stresses, and increasing use is being made of expansion or control joints to control this problem. The joints are built into the walls at the most favorable location in such a manner as to permit slight wall movement without cracking the masonry. See Fig. 8-55.

Fig. 8-55. Control joints are vertically continuous.

Concrete Block Construction

The spacing and location of these joints depends upon several factors, among them: the length of the wall, architectural details, and especially on the experience records as to the need for control joints in the locality in which the wall is to be erected. Control joints may be placed at junctions of bearing and nonbearing walls, at junctions of walls and columns or pilasters, and in walls weakened by chases and openings. Joints are ordinarily spaced at 20- to 25-ft. intervals in long walls, depending again on local experience and judgment. Control joints should also be used in junctions of walls in L, T, and U-shaped buildings.

Control joints must have a certain amount of "give" in order to relieve the horizontal stresses resulting from moisture and temperature movement. For this reason mortar is not used in the joints. In order to maintain watertightness, the open joints are partly filled from the outside with an elastic calking compound which is usually applied with a calking gun. The two main types of control joints are built-in and manufactured.

Built-in control joints may be made using either some of the common regular types of units or especially designed units made specifically for control joints. Fig. 8-56 shows a simple control joint using regular stretcher units of full and half lengths. Fig. 8-57 shows a similar joint employing jamb blocks.

While the purpose of control joints is to provide flexibility for horizontal stress, lateral stability must be maintained. In such joints as shown in Fig. 8-56 and 8-57, this is provided by the use of Z shaped metal tiebars.

Fig. 8-58 shows the use of specially designed control joint blocks. Lateral strength in this joint is provided by the tongue and groove design.

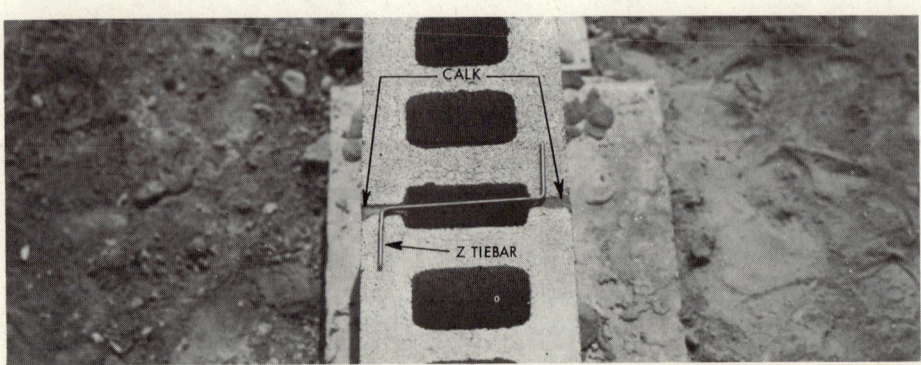

Fig. 8-56. Simple control joint using "Z" tiebars.

Concrete Block Masonry: Units and Building

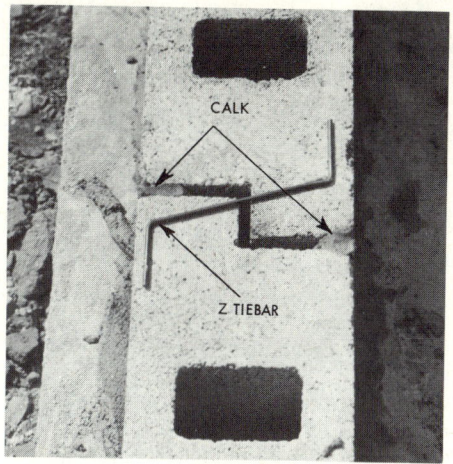

Fig. 8-57. Control joint using jamb blocks.

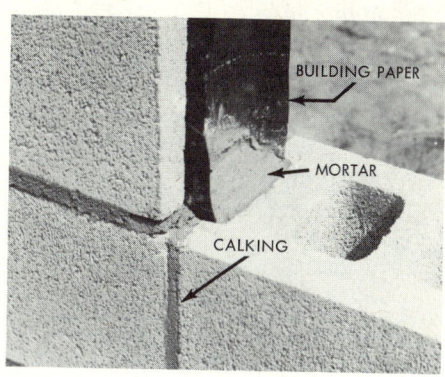

Fig. 8-59. Control joint using building paper to break bond.

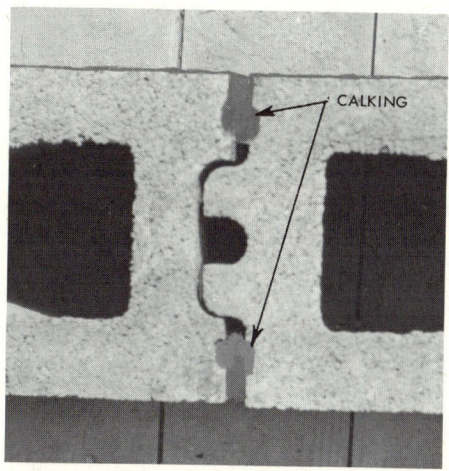

Fig. 8-58. Special control joint blocks.

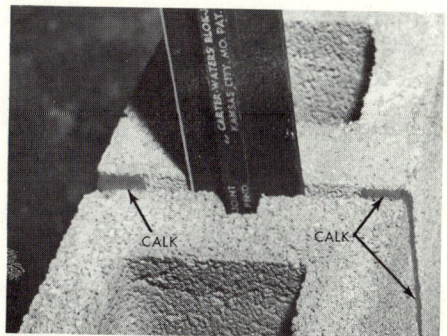

Fig. 8-60. Manufactured control joint.

Fig. 8-59 shows a control joint constructed with building paper inserted in the end core of a regular stretcher block. The core is filled with mortar for lateral strength. Again, the outsides of the joint are calked. Roofing felt may be used in place of paper for this type of joint.

Fig. 8-60 shows a modern manufactured control joint. The unit shown in the illustration is standardized and readily available under several brand names. It is made of rubber or other synthetic resilient materials. Its dimensions are such as to fit into standard block units pre-notched for metal sash windows.

175

Concrete Block Construction

The advantages of this type of control joint are that it is quickly and easily installed and that the unit itself provides both horizontal flexibility and lateral stability.

Concrete Block Wall Intersections. One method of building the intersection when two concrete bearing walls meet at right angles is shown in Fig. 8-61(A). This method

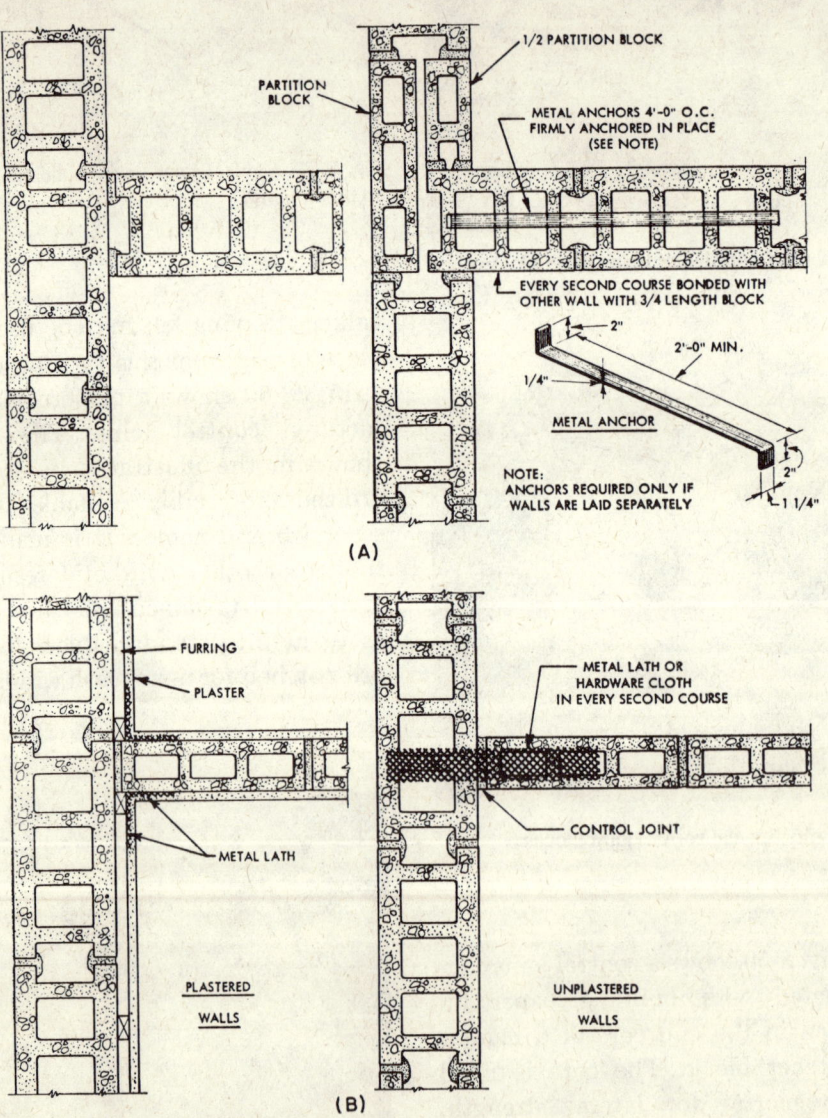

Fig. 8-61. Concrete block wall intersections.

makes no alteration in the exterior appearance of the wall because the partition block used in the alternate courses has the same face dimensions as standard stretcher blocks. The alternate courses shown indicate the method of obtaining a good bond at the intersection. Anchors are required only if the walls are laid up separately.

Proper bonding at the intersection of a bearing and nonbearing wall is much more easily accomplished. As may be seen in Fig. 8-61(B), plastered walls of this type need only metal lath fastened to both wall surfaces. In the case of unplastered walls, metal lath or hardware cloth is inserted in every second course. A control joint is then made at the point of intersection.

Note: Intersecting load-bearing walls should not be tied together in masonry bond except at corners. One wall should terminate at the face of the other wall with a control joint at that point. For lateral support, bearing walls are tied together mechanically as shown in Fig. 8-61(B).

Window Opening Details. The location and size of windows in concrete block walls require careful consideration in order to avoid the cutting of block. Note the window opening shown in Fig. 8-62. It can be seen that the opening width C, the height B, and the height of the bottom of the opening above the foundation, A, are all in terms of an exact number of blocks horizontally and vertically. This is the ideal situation and should be carefully planned for any window opening in a block wall.

To accomplish ideal window planning in block walls, the size of windows must be selected to accommodate the blocks both horizontally and vertically with accommodations made for masonry sills. Any deviation from this rule results in unsightly walls, occasionally poor bond between various blocks, and always increased labor costs. The location and size of doors in concrete block walls require the same considerations necessary for windows.

The masonry work on concrete block walls should never be started until the mason doing the work has carefully checked all of these items. The time thus spent will be of much value and will save a great deal of extra labor, expense, and disappointment.

There are many varieties of windows from the standpoint of the size, shape, and assembly of their various parts, such as casings, stools, aprons, stops, etc. However, all varieties are nearly enough alike that a few typical examples will amply illustrate the general details.

As far as the mason is concerned, when laying a concrete block wall, a window has three principal parts, namely, the *head, jambs,* and *sill.* The head, as the name implies, is the

Concrete Block Construction

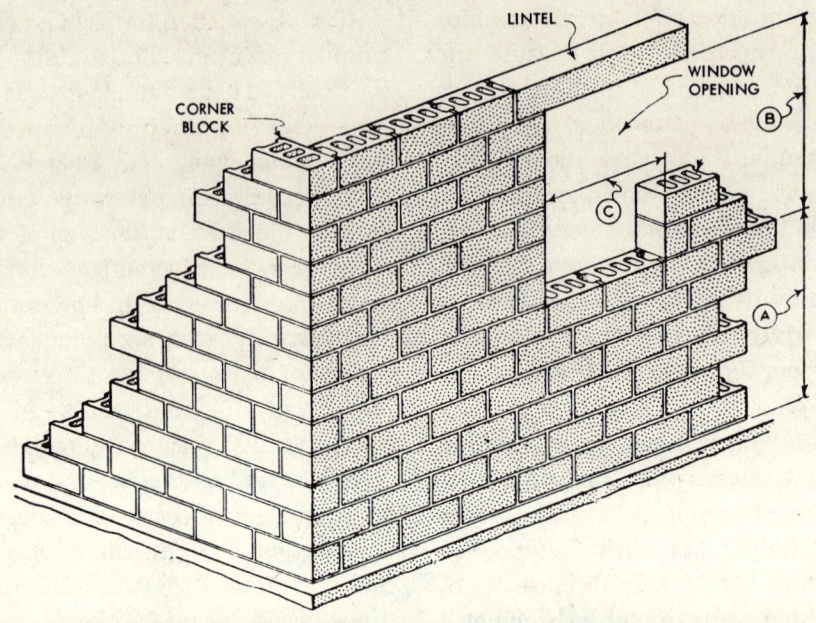

Fig. 8-62. Locations of window openings must be planned.

horizontal top of the window, the jambs are the vertical sides, and the sill is the horizontal bottom.

Although carpenters are usually responsible for installing window frames in masonry walls, it is necessary for the mason to know the basic installation procedures in order to provide properly located and sized openings. The following is the procedure for setting the frame in place and laying blocks around it for a simple window in a regular 8 inch concrete block wall.

You must first determine from the plans commonly provided for construction work, the position of the window in terms of the number of courses under the sill and the number of block on either side of it. Then the wall should be laid up to and including the course under the sill. Thus wall AB would be laid up to and including the course marked A in Fig. 8-63.

Next apply mortar to the blocks which will be directly under the sill. In Fig. 8-63, these block are shown as C and D and the method of mortar application is shown in the mortar detail for the sill. The width and depth of the mortar should be the same as previously described. Then set the sill gently in place and press it down until the mortar joint is the same as for the other hori-

Concrete Block Masonry: Units and Building

zontal joints. Remove excess mortar and smooth the joint surfaces on both sides of the wall. Check the level of the sill by placing the level on the sill in the position of the dotted line, X. If the sill is not level, press or force it downward at either end as required. If leveling cannot be accomplished in this manner, remove the sill, apply more mortar, and try resetting.

When the sill has been properly laid and checked, the next step is to place the window frame on the sill. The frame can be held in place by pieces of 2 x 4 or 1 x 4 or by any other available wood pieces lightly nailed to the frame at one of their ends and supported or held in place at their other ends by flooring, stakes, etc. Carpenters generally put such frames in place for the masons. In any event, the frames must stand vertically plumb and square with the wall.

The sill shown in Fig. 8-63 is a slip sill. When lug sills are laid, mortar should be applied near the ends of the sills only, until such time as the wall has been completed. Then mortar can be forced under the sill and the joint completed.

Many masons prefer to lay the blocks around window frames following the method outlined in laying a block wall. In other words, after the sill is laid, they stretch the line for each course and lay the blocks course by course, including those around the frames. This is perhaps the best method because it assures all courses being laid in proper alignment. Regardless of the method used special care must be taken to keep all blocks level, plumb, and in alignment. Unless you keep all the

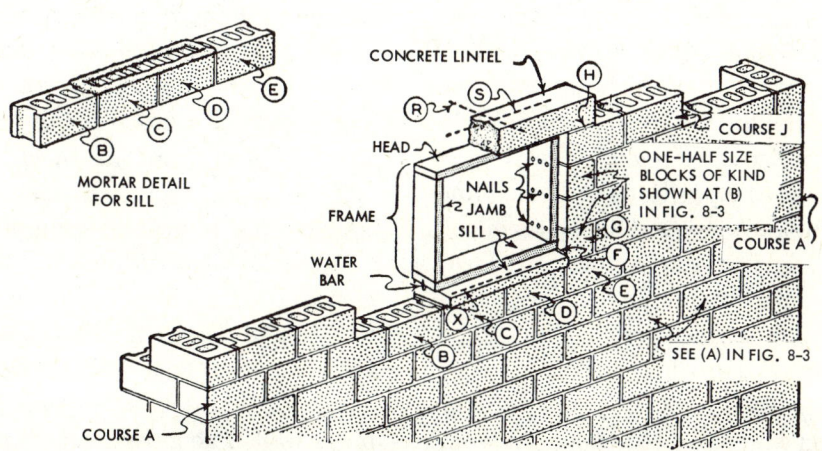

Fig. 8-63. Part of a concrete block window frame, sill and lintel.

blocks exactly one above the other you will not have a vertical wall.

Note the joint F between the sill and the block G in Fig. 8-63. This joint must be well filled in order to avoid a moisture leak.

Before block G is laid, the end of the sill should have mortar applied to it so that joint F contains mortar and is the same thickness as other vertical points.

When the blocks around the window frame have been laid, including the course at J on both sides of the frame, the concrete lintel can be placed. If the window opening is wide and the lintel, therefore, long and heavy, some time should be allowed for the mortar in the courses below to harden before the lintel is set.

To set the lintel, apply mortar to the blocks (see H) on either side of the frame. Then set the lintel gently down into proper position and adjust until the mortar joint is the same thickness as other horizontal joints. Special care should be taken to see that the lintel is perfectly level. This can be accomplished by setting the level in the positions of dotted lines R and S. Above the lintel, the blocks are laid as in the balance of the wall. The lintel should have at least an 8" bearing surface on each end as shown at H in Fig. 8-63.

Fig. 8-64 shows details of a finished window of the type that would be used in the preceding construc-

Fig. 8-65 shows section views of the head, jamb, and sill for a common kind of a metal sash window. The head sections consist of steel (angle) lintels used in conjunction with precast concrete units plus nailing strips, the metal sash fittings, etc. The jamb section consists of a metal sash block plus the metal sash fittings, nailing strip, and plaster. The *slip sill* shown in the sill section is not *let in* to the wall like the lug sill. The metal fittings are anchored to the concrete sill by bolts set into the sill.

Openings for more complex windows, such as double hung, casement, sliding, etc., are planned and executed in the same manner as for the simple window. When the level is reached, the window unit is mounted, leveled and braced in place. In most modern construction, the window units are factory assembled to the designer's specified dimensions. Some windows have built-in sills and are mounted either directly on the top of the concrete block units or a wood nailing block may be placed on the block. Fig. 8-66 shows a typical double hung window in a concrete masonry wall.

Door Details. Fig. 8-67 shows part of a wall for which a door is indicated. The details for this door are quite simple. Fig. 8-67 shows the frame for that door in the partly laid block wall. The purpose of this illustration is to show the positions of

Concrete Block Masonry: Units and Building

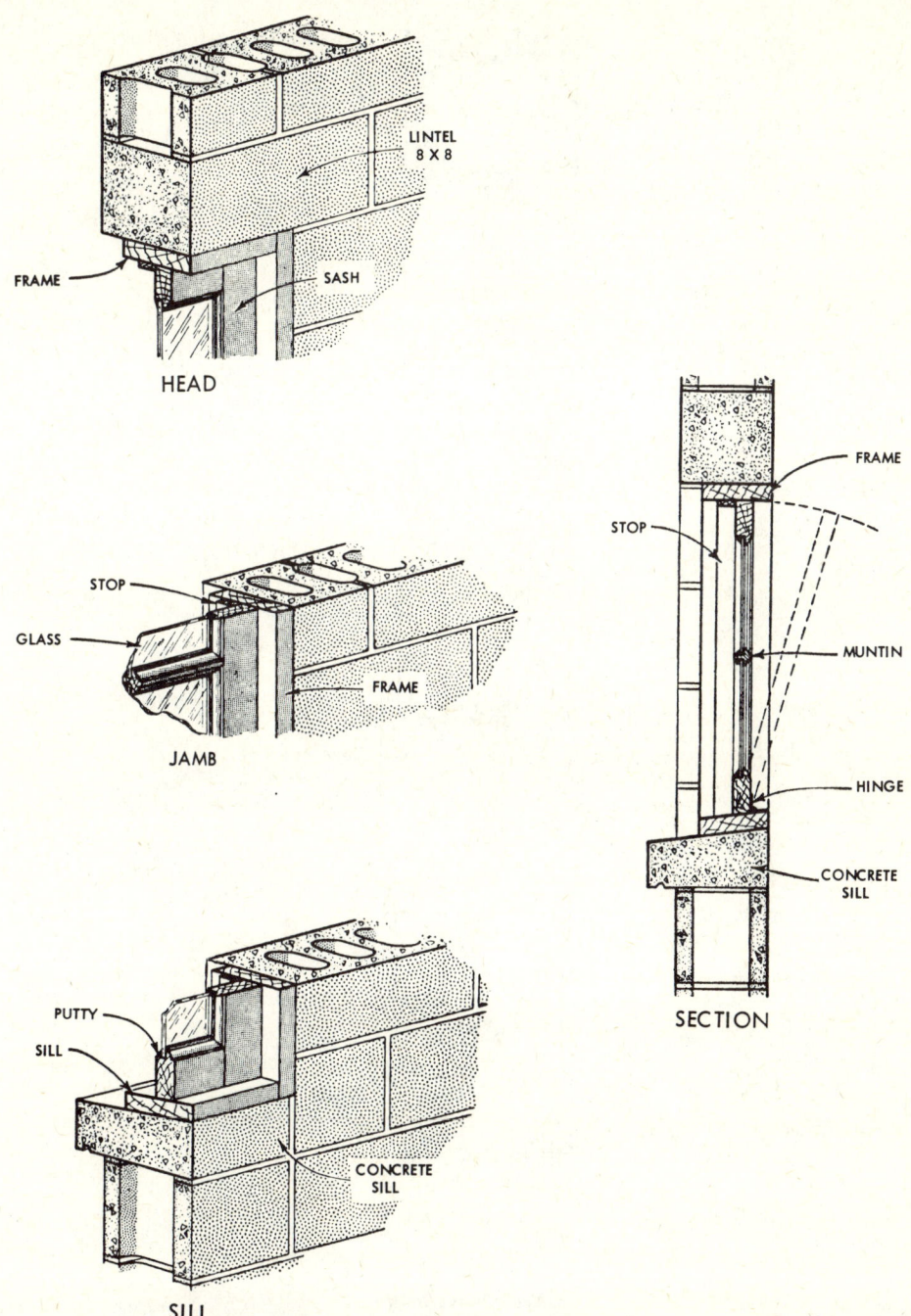

Fig. 8-64. Typical details for a simple window in a concrete block wall.

Concrete Block Construction

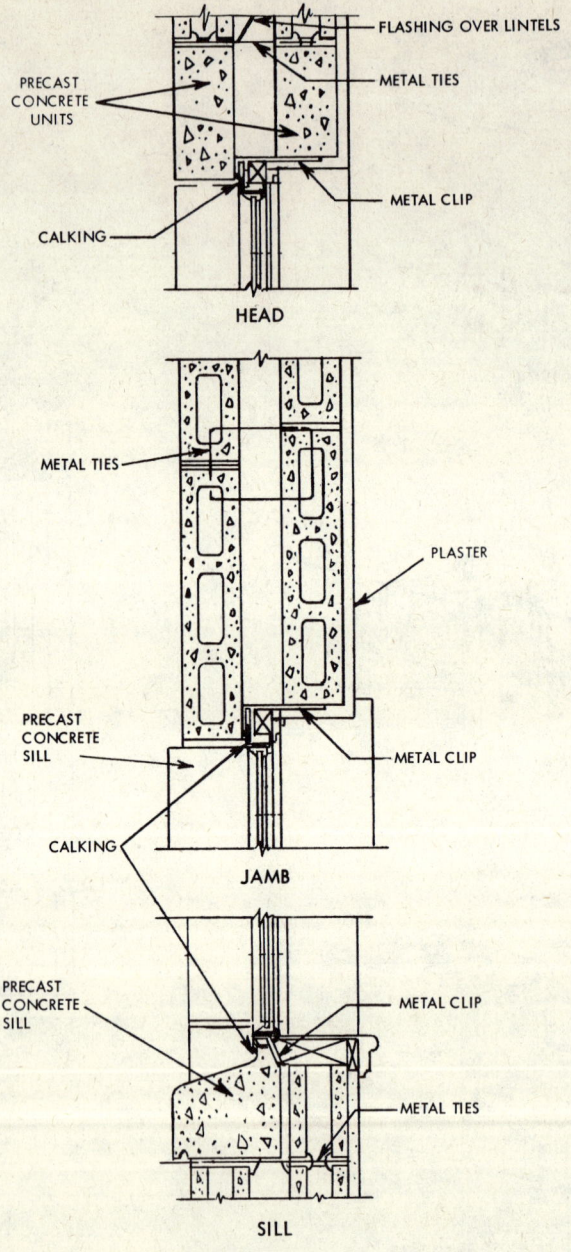

Fig. 8-65. Metal sash casement window in a concrete block wall.

Concrete Block Masonry: Units and Building

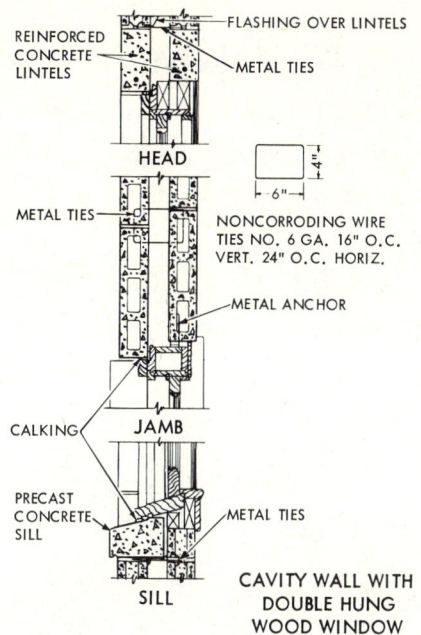

Fig. 8-66. Details of a double-hung window in a concrete block wall.

the frame for the jamb and head in a wall. The procedure for laying blocks around door frames is the same as that given for windows.

For the most part, door details are greatly similar to window details as far as concrete block walls are concerned. In most cases, the mason is guided by the doors and frames purchased for each job, in that the type of frame determines the type of lintels and jamb blocks to be used.

There are various types of door frames available, just as there are a variety of window frames. For residential or store and office construction, doors having details similar to those shown in Fig. 8-68 can be used to advantage. In the head

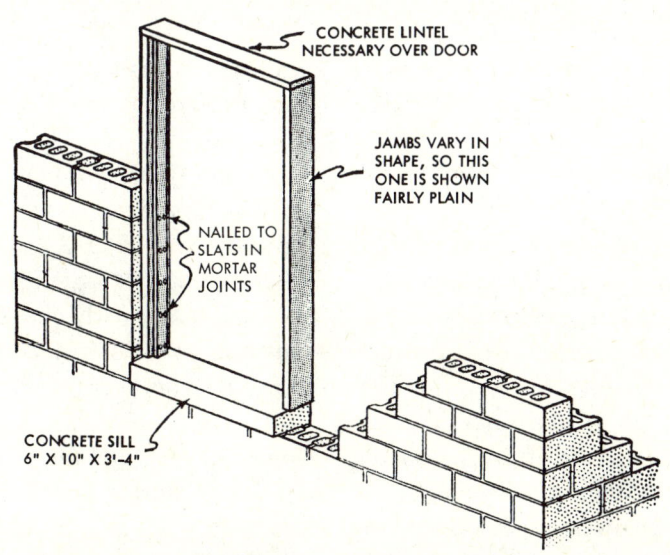

Fig. 8-67. Part of a simple wall showing door frame in place.

183

Concrete Block Construction

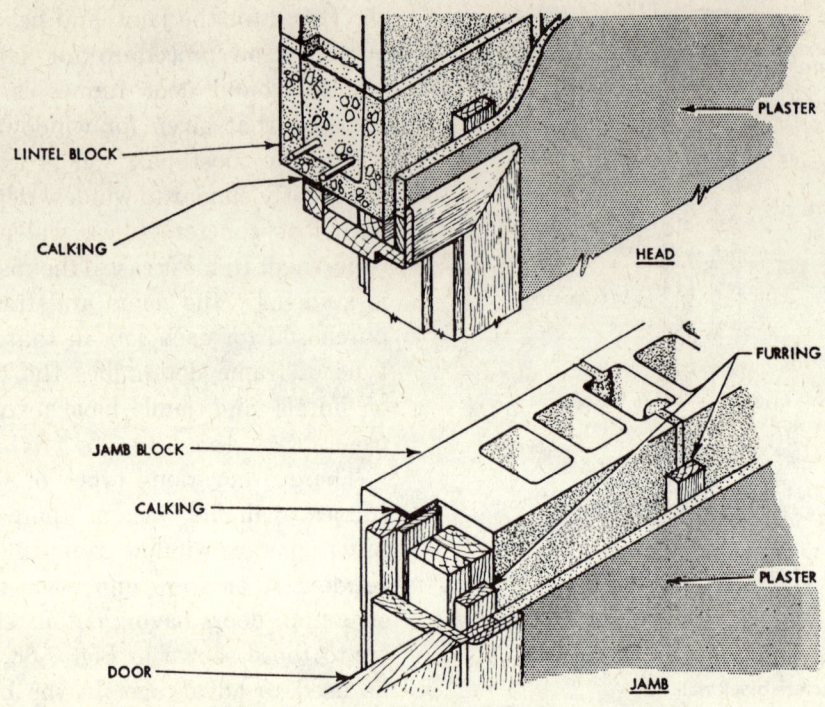

Fig. 8-68. Details for a finished door in residential construction.

section of this particular door it should be noted that lintel block has been employed. This type of lintel is constructed on-the-job by forming a channel with the lintel block. Reinforcing bars are then placed in the channel, and the channel is filled with concrete. Such lintels provide a surface texture which matches the rest of the concrete masonry wall. If the lintel is built in place, it must be firmly supported during construction. In other respects, construction details for the door in Fig. 8-68 are very similar to the details for windows. Jamb blocks are used for the vertical sides of the opening and a precast concrete sill is employed.

Laying Concrete Block Chimneys. When chimney blocks of the general kind shown at Fig. 8-69(A) are laid, the procedure is as follows:

First mark with chalk the exact position for the first course on the footing. The position can be ascertained from the blueprints of the building the chimney is to be in.

Apply mortar to the footing so that it will be under the areas marked X in Fig. 8-69 wide enough to cover the areas and about 1"

Concrete Block Masonry: Units and Building

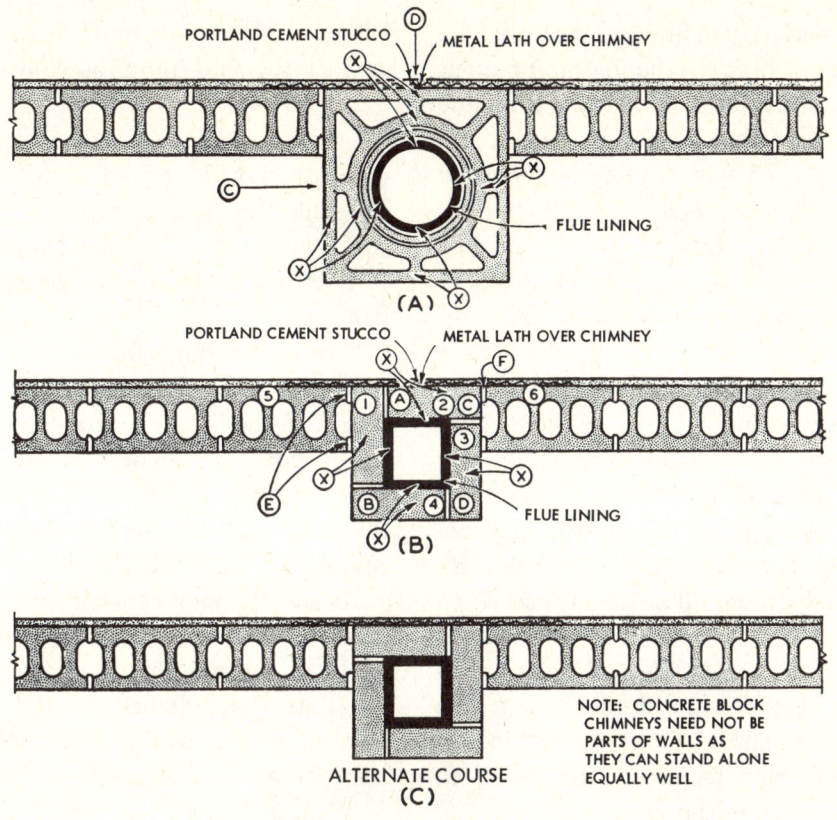

Fig. 8-69. Chimney details.

deep. Note that this includes the flue lining which is part of each block. Care must be taken to have mortar all the way around under the areas marked X. Place the first block and press it gently down into the mortar to make a joint of the same thickness as used for walls. Then remove excess mortar. Check the level of this block by placing the plumb rule across the block in the direction of the arrows at C and D. Make any adjustments necessary relative to leveling. This block must be *absolutely* level.

Apply mortar to the first block at all areas marked X all the way around the block. Then place the second block gently in position. Press it down to form proper thickness of joint, remove excess mortar and smooth the joint, and check its level, as for the first block. Also, place the plumb rule in a vertical position, up against the four sides of the chimney to make sure the sides

Concrete Block Construction

are perfectly in line and vertical. The mortar joint for the flue lining must be smooth and should not protrude between the surface of the lining. Each such joint must be smoothed as each block is laid.

Place succeeding blocks in like manner, being sure to watch every detail explained for the first two blocks.

When chimney block of the kind shown at Fig. 8-69(B) are being laid, the procedure is as follows:

The exact position of the chimney should be marked on the footing. Then place mortar so that it is completely under all areas marked X. In other words, each block must have a full mortar bedding. Also place mortar at the ends of block 5 at the points marked E. Chimney block 1 should then be pressed into position, making sure the joints at E and the joint between the block and the footing are of the proper thickness. Make sure that the end of the block lines up with the face of block 5. Check the level of block 1. Next apply mortar to block 2 at the end where it touches block 1 (joint A) and on block 6 at the point F. Press this block into position as for block 1, making sure it lines up with the face of block 6. Place blocks 3 and 4 in the same manner, taking care to make joints C, D, and B carefully.

Most masons prefer to set the first length of flue lining in place before more courses of blocks are laid. Blocks 1, 2, 3, and 4 must fit tightly against the flue lining as shown at Fig. 8-69(B).

For the second course of blocks, apply mortar all around, completely covering the first course. For this course, place the blocks as shown at (C). This is necessary to create good bond.

Place succeeding courses alternating them as explained. As each length of flue lining is added, a careful mortar joint must be made between lengths. Special care must be taken that all flue lining joints are smooth on the inside of the flues.

As the chimney construction progresses, frequent checks by the use of the plumb rule should be made to see that the chimney is perfectly vertical. All excess mortar should be removed and the joints smoothed.

Note, in Fig. 8-69 that metal lath should be applied to the exterior wall surface at and on either side of the chimney if and before stucco is applied. The lath can be secured to the wall by the use of nails driven into the blocks if they are the lightweight kind or into the joints if heavyweight blocks are used. The metal lath tends to avoid wall cracks near the chimney at times when the chimney sways slightly due to wind, etc.

Cornice Details. Fig. 8-70 illustrates cornice details for two types of roof. Note that in both cases the top two blocks have their cores filled

Concrete Block Masonry: Units and Building

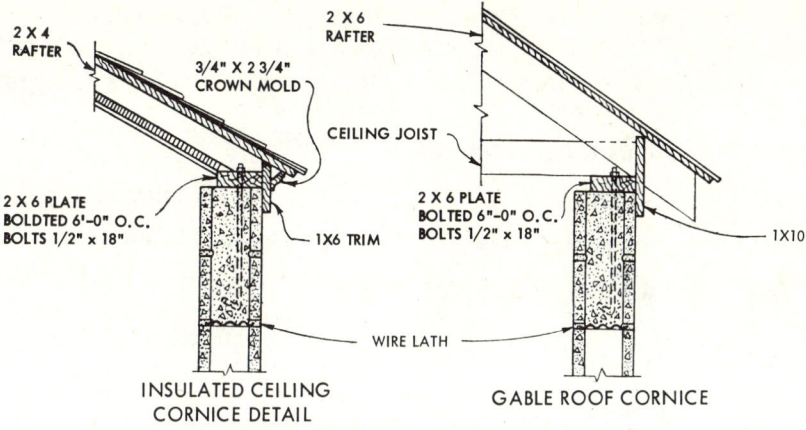

Fig. 8-70. Cornice details in concrete block walls.

with concrete. This practice tends to better distribute the weight coming from rafters and ceiling joists. Some masons make it a practice to fill only those cores where the anchor bolts occur. Either method is acceptable.

The cores are filled by laying wire or metal lath under the top two courses of blocks, as indicated. This serves to keep the concrete in place while it is drying. If metal lath is not available, wads of paper can be shoved into the cores below the top

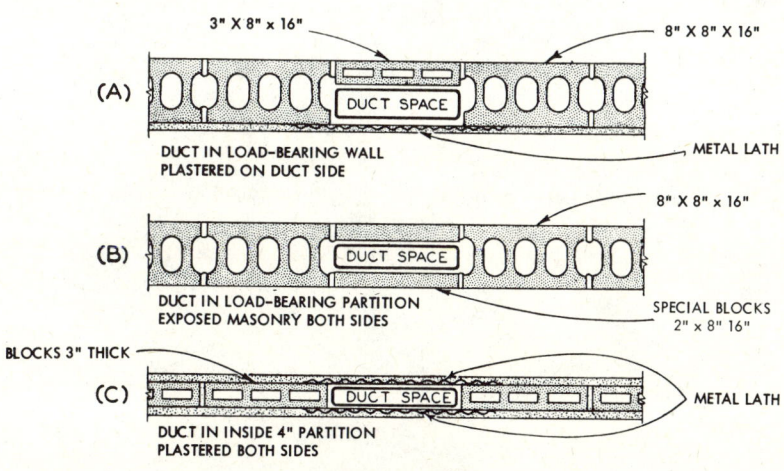

Fig. 8-71. Duct details.

Concrete Block Construction

two courses to keep the wet concrete in place.

Duct Details. The ducts used in connection with heating and air conditioning systems for residences, stores, etc., are generally from $3\frac{1}{2}$" to $3\frac{5}{8}$" thick. They can be built into block walls easily, as indicated in Fig. 8-71.

Waterproofing Concrete Block Foundations

There are many methods of waterproofing which may be used successfully. Those discussed here are typical and are recommended by average building codes, the Portland Cement Association, and by the National Concrete Masonry Association.

Perhaps the simplest form of waterproofing for foundations built in soil which is just damp, is to apply hot tar or asphaltum (asphalt) to the outside surfaces. These materials are moistureproof and constitute satisfactory waterproofing. This is shown in (A) of Fig. 8-72.

Where excessive dampness or severe conditions of water in the soil occur, the exterior surfaces of the foundation can be satisfactorily waterproofed as shown in (B) of Fig. 8-72. Two or more plies or lay-

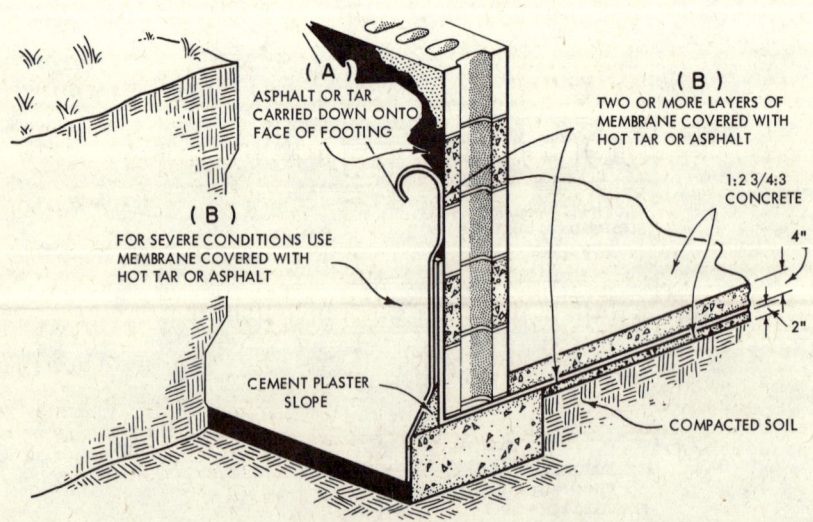

Fig. 8-72. Method of waterproofing a foundation against severe groundwater pressure.

ers of membrane (felt, for example) coated with tar or asphaltum are used. Note in Fig. 8-72 that for extraordinary conditions the waterproofing is applied at the joint between the footing and the foundation and that the floor is built in two layers with the waterproofing placed between the layers. In addition, note that a mix of 1:2¾:3 concrete can be used as a means of further retarding the flow of water through the foundation. Such concrete becomes dense in setting and, because of this characteristic, tends to prevent the flow or seepage of water through it. The slope at the point where the foundation meets the footing also helps to make that joint waterproof.

Fig. 8-73 shows a slightly different treatment of the membrane and tar or asphaltum treatment.

Another waterproofing method frequently used where there is excessive water in the soil is shown in Fig. 8-74. The clay or concrete tile is laid around all sides of the footing with a gravel or cinder fill covering it to the depth shown. The fill material allows the water to flow directly to the tile where it collects and drains off to some point away from the basement where it cannot

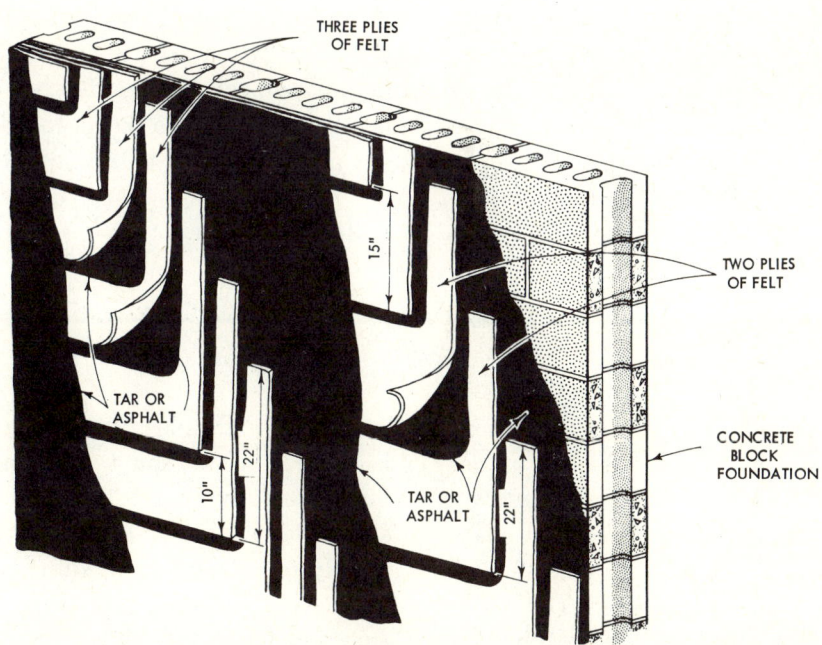

Fig. 8-73. Method of lapping three and two layers of felt waterproofing for a foundation.

Concrete Block Construction

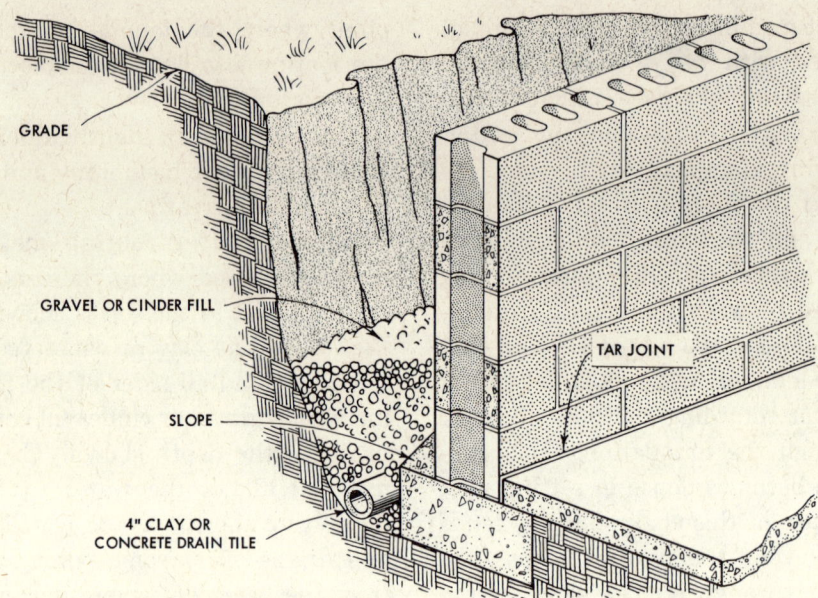

Fig. 8-74. Footing drains for use with all kinds of foundations.

do any harm. Occasionally, the water drains into a sump from which it is pumped to the regular sewer. When soil water conditions are really severe, drain tile are used in conjunction with the waterproofing methods explained in Fig. 8-73.

Note the tar joint between the floor and foundation in Fig. 8-74. This method of calking is effective and helps materially to keep moisture out of the basement in cases where no waterproofing materials were built into the floor.

Stone Masonry

Natural stone, such as limestone, granite, or marble, has been used in masonry for centuries. Stone is available in wide varieties of size, shape, color, and texture, allowing for any number of wall patterns. Due to the different sizes and uneven surfaces of individual units, stone masonry is slower and more difficult than brick or block masonry and, therefore, more expensive. The use of stone at the present time is limited mostly to veneers on building walls and decorative facings on such structures as barbecues, fireplaces, and garden walls. Garden walls may also

Concrete Block Masonry: Units and Building

be constructed of solid stone. The following figures illustrate some of the more common wall bond patterns.

The type of wall shown in Fig. 8-75 is called a random rubble wall. This type of wall employs stones of many sizes and shapes, such as are found in fields and stream beds. Although there is little or no coursing in random rubble, note that the bed joints are made as horizontal as possible.

Fig. 8-76. Coursed rubble stone masonry.

Fig. 8-75. Random rubble stone masonry.

Fig. 8-76 shows another kind of rubble masonry employing stones that are roughly squared. These stones are laid in such a way as to produce approximately continuous horizontal bed joints. This is called coursed rubble masonry.

A solid, freestanding rubble stone wall must be *bonded* for strength and stability just as a brick or block wall. That is, at intervals, there must be a unit which passes all the way through the wall. This is called a bond stone. See Fig. 8-77. Bond stones should be placed as frequently as possible; at least in every 6 to 10 square feet of wall.

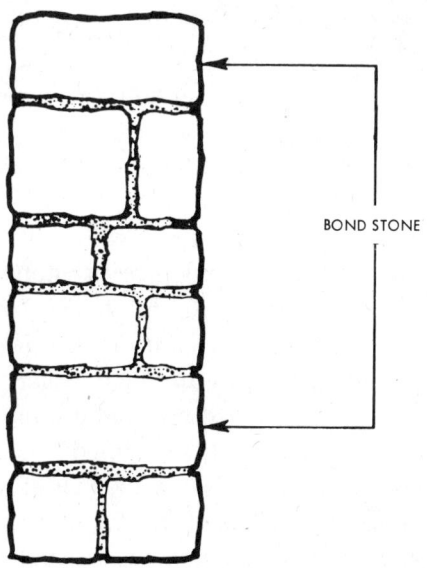

Fig. 8-77. Rubble stone masonry showing bond stone.

191

Concrete Block Construction

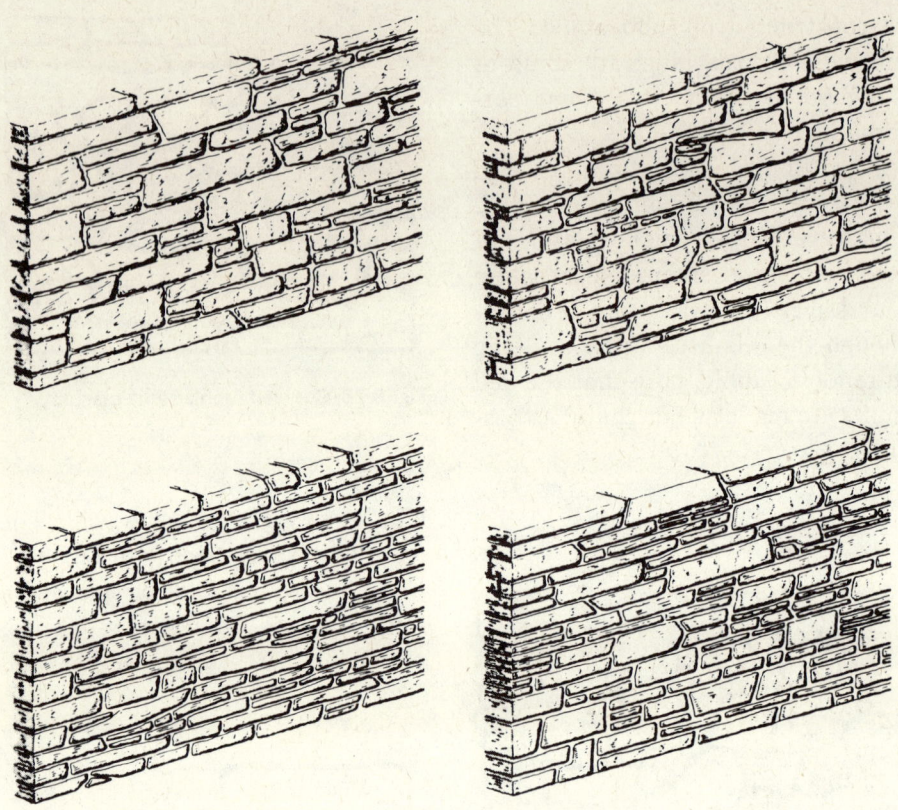

Fig. 8-78. Various patterns using precut stone.

Fig. 8-78 shows a few of the patterns possible using precut stone. The roughly rectangular shapes are laid in the same manner as brick and are commonly used as veneer.

As in all masonry, each joint should be completely filled with mortar. Mortar for stone masonry is usually specified to be 1 part cement, 1 part lime, and 6 parts sand. This formula has been found to be quite strong while still supplying the workability necessary for laying random size stone.

Again, as in all masonry, stonework construction is begun at the ends or corners of the wall. If the wall is to be coursed, the mason's level is used to level the top of each course.

In order to accent the natural rugged beauty of stone, the mortar joints are raked out about $\frac{1}{4}$ to $\frac{1}{2}$ inch. This may be done with regular

Concrete Block Masonry: Units and Building

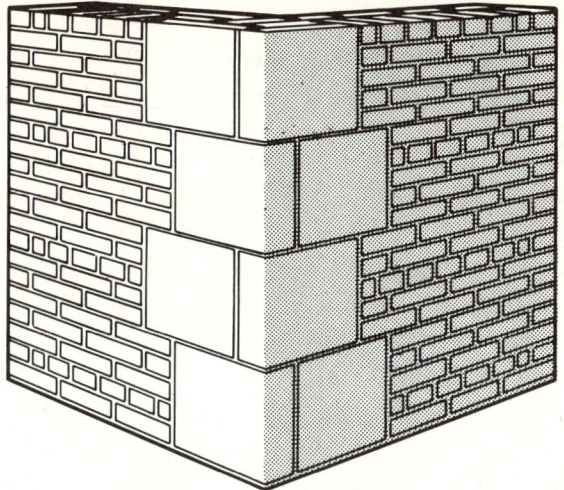

Fig. 8-79. Quoins may be used in corners and around openings in masonry walls.

jointing tools, pointing trowels, or calking trowels.

Another use of stone in masonry is as *quoins*. Quoins are stones used in corners and around openings in walls for contrast with the masonry units in the rest of the wall. See Fig. 8-79.

Maintenance

Concrete block construction, when properly built, requires little or no maintenance. As mentioned, if mortar is accidentally dropped on the face of a block, the burrs may be removed after they are dry by using a trowel or wire brush. If joints must be patched, use good fresh mortar.

Painting Concrete Block

Mixtures of portland cement with water as a vehicle to which waterproofing agents, colored mineral oxides, and other ingredients have been added can be used readily to waterproof concrete block walls as well as to add to their beauty. It is recommended that portland cement paint ready to use be purchased rather than to attempt to make it on the job. Practically all building material dealers sell such products.

If block walls are to be painted for waterproofing, or weather resistance, two coats, called the *seal* and *finish* coats, should be used. Wall surfaces should be dampened just prior to the application of the seal coat. The seal coat should be *scrubbed* into the wall surface as this practice avoids pin holes in the paint. Ordinary scrub brushes with stiff fiber bristles have been found to be the most satisfactory because they force the paint into the pores of the blocks. Use ample amounts of the paint in the brush and completely cover the wall surfaces, including the joints.

The finish coat can be applied within 48 hours after the seal coat has been put on. Enough paint should be applied over the seal coat to cover it completely. The finish coat should be sprayed on, providing ordinary paint spraying equipment is available. When spraying, the nozzle of the spray should be manipulated so that the spray hits every point of the wall surface from four or five angles. If the work must be done by hand, a six-inch brush will be found to be most practical.

Seal and finish coats should be kept in a moist condition for a period of at least 48 hours following application. This can be accomplished by spraying with water at intervals after the paint has set.

If the wall is constructed of dense block and good joints and is to be painted for color only, one coat is sufficient. Interior walls should receive only one coat to preserve sound absorption qualities.

Note: Care should be taken to protect hands in using portland cement paint as prolonged contact may irritate tender or sensitive skin.

Besides portland cement paint, there are several other types of paint suitable for painting concrete block. The main types are oil-base, varnish base, lacquer base, and water-thinned or latex.

Although all types have been found suitable for exterior, above grade use, oil base paints provide a more effective barrier against penetration of rainwater. Varnish base paints are particularly suitable for interior walls. They provide a smoother surface and dry more rapidly than oil base paints. They are available in gloss ranges from flat to full gloss. Lacquer base paints are highly resistant to alkalis and can be applied on damp surfaces. Water-thinned, or *latex*, paints have the widest range of use. They have been found to be suitable for above grade exteriors and interiors and

Concrete Block Masonry: Units and Building

are particularly suitable for interior basement walls because of their alkali resistance and ability to "breathe"; that is, to contain moisture behind the paint film without blistering.

All of these paints may be applied without any special coat although two or three coats are generally required for the desired results. The surface should be thoroughly cleaned before applying. These paints may be applied successfully by brush, roller, or spray, providing good workmanship is employed. As with any commercial product, the manufacturer's directions on the container must be carefully read and followed.

Checking On Your Knowledge

The following questions give you the opportunity to check up on yourself. If you have read the chapter carefully, you should be able to answer the questions. If you have any difficulty, read the chapter over once more so that you have the information well in mind before you go on with your reading.

DO YOU KNOW

1. What type of concrete blocks are generally used in buildings in which the exterior is surfaced with stucco?
2. What type of 8″ x 8″ x 16″ concrete blocks are generally used around window openings?
3. What type of concrete masonry sill actually extends into the walls?
4. What maximum mortar thickness should be used in building a concrete masonry wall?
5. What is meant by the term "modular coordination"?
6. What special processing must be given to the blocks in a wall directly under the point where a beam end is supported by the wall?
7. What can be done to strengthen a block wall under a beam bearing area?
8. What size joists can be used to the best advantage in connection with block walls?
9. What minimum amount of bearing should be allowed for beams in block walls?
10. What the preferred methods for fastening wooden members to concrete masonry walls are?
11. What the function of the cavity in a cavity wall is?
12. What the two methods of reducing shrinkage and expansion of concrete masonry units that are laid into a wall are?
13. If it is necessary to purchase special flue liners for one-piece chimney blocks?
14. How anchor bolts secured in concrete block walls are?
15. What the purpose of allowing a certain amount of air space between the floor joists and a concrete masonry wall is?
16. What tool should be used for tooling horizontal joints?
17. The different types of paint for concrete block?

195

Chapter 9: Panel Construction

In the past few years there has been a great deal of development in masonry panel construction, using both brick and concrete block. Prefabricated panel construction, however, does not replace conventional masonry construction and accounts for only a small fraction of the masonry construction volume. Nevertheless, it is essential that the mason have some introduction to panel construction systems so he may know what to expect when he encounters this type of construction in the field.

In concrete block panel construction, wall panels are constructed on the ground and then hoisted into position in the building and set in place by masons. Both load bearing and non-load bearing panels, including curtain walls, are constructed. They may be designed for built-in openings, such as doors and windows. Both conventional and special mortars are used to bond the masonry units together in the panel.

Masonry panels are used in commercial, industrial and residential (mostly high-rise) construction. Some individual homes are being erected using, in part, several masonry panels.

Panel Construction

Panel Manufacture

Panels are assembled either in a manufacturing plant or on the job site in a specially constructed enclosure. One type of in-plant panel production is shown in Fig. 9-1. In this case panels as large as 10 feet high and 20 feet long can be produced using assembly machines. In-plant panels are also assembled by skilled masons working on an assembly line. After curing, panels are transported by truck to the job site. See Fig. 9-2. Usually panels are not shipped more than 200 miles from the manufacturing plant to the job site.

Fig. 9-1. In-plant concrete block panel construction. (National Concrete Masonry Association)

Fig. 9-2. Cured concrete panels loaded for transportation to the job site. (National Concrete Masonry Association)

Concrete Block Construction

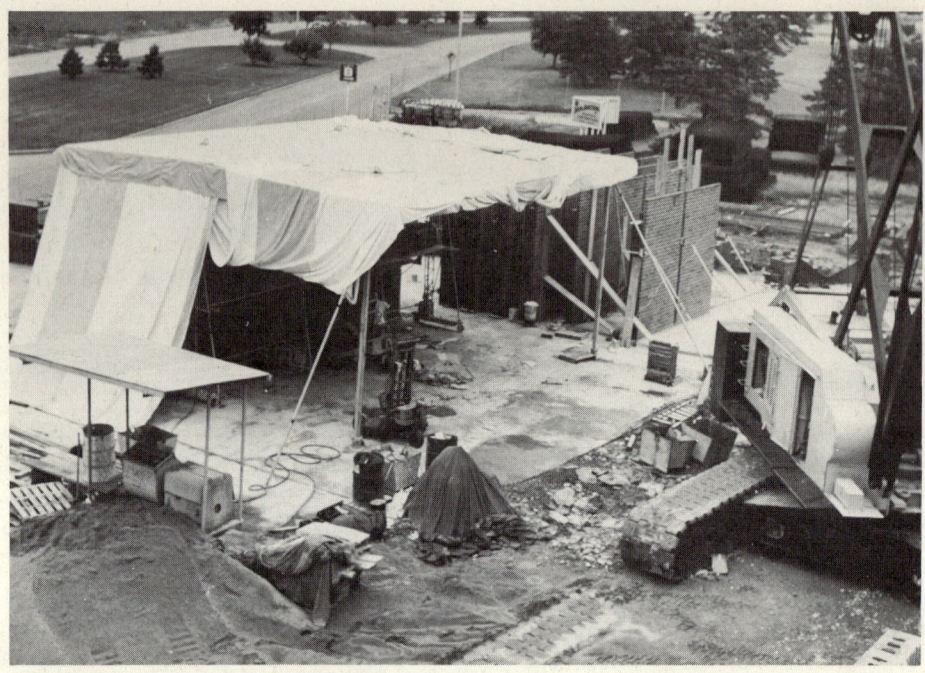

Fig. 9-3. On-site panel construction. (Professional Builder)

Fig. 9-3 shows on-site panel construction. Skilled masons lay the masonry units on a special metal frame structure. They are protected from the wind and the elements by the canvas enclosure. Heaters can be used during cold weather. After curing, the panels are lifted and installed on the building. Both of these methods allow the mason to obtain more man hours of work because he is fabricating the panels under cover, and he can also work the year round without any lost time.

Skilled masons do the actual erection of the panels at the site. A four to seven man crew normally handles the hoisting (with a crane) and placement of the panels. A typical crew could consist of a crane operator, a man on the ground, and a mason and two helpers on the floor.

The structure shown in Fig. 9-4 illustrates panel construction. This 18 story concrete block structure used an epoxy adhesive mortar rather than conventional mortar. Mortar of this kind is often applied with a caulking gun rather than a trowel. A mason applies the epoxy adhesive. Because of the thinness of the epoxy adhesive there are no ex-

Panel Construction

Fig. 9-4. An 18-story TraveLodge motel near Disney World, Buena Vista, Florida, was built using concrete block panels. (Amspec Inc.)

posed mortar joints (see Figs. 9-5 to 9-7). Reinforcing bars run through the walls for additional strength. Also, the blocks in the lower stories, up to the seventh floor, have their cores grouted. Above the seventh floor, a half to only one fourth of the cores are grouted. This structure was raised at the rate of one floor per week and is designed to withstand hurricane winds up to 120 miles per hour.

Figs. 9-5, 9-6 and 9-7 show the panels being hoisted and put in place in a multi-story structure. Often, when the panels are delivered to the site they are marked as to the floor level and wall location.

In the future, we can expect additional panel systems to be tested and introduced to the trade. Whatever the particular techniques involved, however, the basic principles as outlined here should remain the same. Understanding these general principles should prepare the mason for whatever particular techniques he will encounter in the field.

Concrete Block Construction

Fig. 9-5. Prefabricated panel of concrete block joined with epoxy adhesive mortar is lifted to upper stories of an apartment project. This panel will be an interior parti-wall. (Amspec Inc.)

Fig. 9-6. A leveling course of conventional mortar is laid on the concrete slab floor. (Amspec Inc.)

Panel Construction

Fig. 9-7. The prefabricated block panel is lowered carefully into place, guided by masons to meet the leveling course of mortar. The panel itself is dimensionally true as laid. The levelling course of mortar compensates for any irregularities in the concrete floor. (Amspec Inc.)

Checking On Your Knowledge

The following questions give you the opportunity to check up on yourself. If you have read the chapter carefully, you should be able to answer the questions. If you have any difficulty, read the chapter over once more so that you have the information well in mind before you go on with your reading.

DO YOU KNOW

1. What types of panels may be constructed by prefabrication systems?
2. In what types of buildings are prefabricated panels used?
3. Two places where panels may be constructed?
4. Some of the advantages of panel systems construction to the bricklayer?
5. The make-up of a typical panel installation crew?
6. What particular tradesman does the actual construction and installation of panel systems?

Appendix **A**

Math for the Mason

This review can be used by masons and apprentices for quickly finding information to compute areas and volumes, develop geometric shapes, and make practical estimates of materials. For a more detailed study of mathematical problems and formulas, mathematics books should be consulted. Only basic information and items which have general use in the trade can be listed within the scope of this text, which includes:

Operations with Fractions and Decimals

Changing Fractions to Decimals and Decimals to Fractions

Metric-to-English and English-to-Metric Conversions

Elementary Geometry

Estimating Areas, Volumes, and Materials

It is assumed that all readers understand the fundamental processes of adding, subtracting, multiplying and dividing whole numbers and are familiar with common units of measurement such as feet, yards, pounds, gallons, etc.

Operations With Fractions
Addition

To add fractions with the same *denominator* (lower part), such as $1/8 + 2/8$, add the *numerators* (upper parts) and place this sum over the *common denominator* (bottom number). Thus, $1/8 + 2/8 = 3/8$. When the sum

Math for the Mason

of numerators is larger than the common denominator, such as $9/8$, divide this new numerator (top) by the denominator (bottom), giving a *mixed number* (whole number with fractional remainder). Thus, $9/8 = 1\tfrac{1}{8}$.

To add fractions with different denominators, multiply both numerator and denominator of each fraction by a number that will make the denominators equal. Any multiplier may be used without changing the quantity of the fraction. For example, $1/4 = 2/8 = 4/16 = 8/32$, etc. Similarly, $1/4 = 3/12 = 9/36$, etc.

After all fractions to be added have been changed so as to have a common denominator, add the new numerators (top numbers) and place this sum over the common denominator (the bottom number). If the new fraction is larger than 1, it can be changed to a mixed number, as already explained. For example, if $1/2$, $3/8$ and $2/3$ were to be added, the common denominator (the bottom number) would be 24. Thus $1/2$ would become $12/24$, $3/8$ would become $9/24$ and $2/3$ would become $16/24$. To add: $12/24 + 9/24 + 16/24 = 37/24 = 1$ and $13/24$. (Note that $37/24$ breaks down into $24/24 + 13/24$, thus, since $24/24 = 1$, we get 1 and $13/24$, or $1\tfrac{13}{24}$.)

In some cases the various fractions to be added can be changed to have a common denominator by dividing instead of multiplying both numerators and denominators by the same number. Again, the quantities would not be changed. For example, $8/32 = 4/16 = 2/8 = 1/4$.

Although both numerator and denominator of *each individual fraction* must be multiplied or divided by the same number, it is not necessary that the same multiplier or divisor be used for *all fractions* to be added. Thus, to add $1/5 + 2/3$, the first fraction could be multiplied by $3/3$ giving $1/5 = 3/15$. The second fraction could be multiplied by $5/5$, giving $2/3 = 10/15$. The addition would then be $3/15 + 10/15 = 13/15$.

Subtraction

Change the fractions to have a common denominator as in the case of addition. Subtract the smaller of the new numerators from the larger and place this subtracted number over the common denominator. (It is assumed that no negative fractions will be used, such as $-3/8$ or "minus three-eighths", in masonry applications.)

Multiplication

To multiply fractions there is no need to change them first so as to have a common denominator. Simply multiply all the numerators to obtain a new numerator and multiply all denominators to obtain a new denominator. Thus, $2/3 \times 1/8 \times 3/5 = 6/120$. (For the numerator: $2 \times 1 \times 3 = 6$; for the denominator: $3 \times 8 \times 5 = 120$.) This can be simplified to $1/20$ by dividing both numerator and denominator by 6.

203

Another method to simplify calculations is called *cancellation*. In multiplying a series of fractions with no intervening subtractions or additions, it often happens that the same digit appears in a numerator and a denominator. In such cases both numerator and denominator can be cancelled. Thus, in the above case, the digit 3 appears as the denominator in $2/3$ and as the numerator in $3/5$. These 3's cancel each other and disappear in the multiplication. Thus, $2/3 \times 1/8 \times 3/5 = 2/40$. This is readily simplified by dividing both numerator and denominator by 2, giving $1/20$ as the answer, exactly as before.

Division

Division of fractions is very simple but is best understood by example. Consider the problem $1/2 \div 2/3 = ?$ Here the *dividend* (number to be divided) is $1/2$ and the *divisor* (number that divides it) is $2/3$. To do this operation, re-write the dividend without change, change the division sign $\div$ to a multiplication sign $\times$, invert numerator and denominator of the divisor $2/3$ to read $3/2$, and proceed to multiply as the sign directs. Thus $1/2 \div 2/3 = 1/2 \times 3/2 = 3/4$.

It comes as a surprise to some people unused to calculations with fractions that generally the quantities decrease when they are multiplied and increase when they are divided. In common speech, when a person speaks of "half an apple" he is multiplying $1/2 \times 1$ apple, and thus decreasing the quantity.

Operations With Decimals

Decimal numbers, unlike ordinary fractions, have only numerators. Denominators are implied by the place of the last digit to the right of the decimal point. Thus, $0.1 = 1/10$, $0.01 = 1/100$, $0.001 = 1/1000$, etc.

Any number of zeros may follow the significant digits in the decimal number without increasing the quantity. Thus, $0.68 = 0.680 = 0.680000000000$. Zeros to the left of the significant digits and immediately following the decimal point are another matter; the quantity decreases by a factor of 10 for each zero preceding these digits. Thus, $0.75 = 75/100$, $0.075 = 75/1000$, and $0.0075 = 75/10000$.

(Note: It is generally considered good practice to place a zero before the decimal point where no whole number is included with the decimal remainder.)

Operations with decimals differ in no way from those used with whole numbers except in placement of the

Math for the Mason

important decimal point. Because United States money is based on the decimal system, these operations are already familiar to nearly everyone.

Addition

Line up decimal numbers to be added so that the decimal points are directly under each other. Add as with whole numbers and place the decimal point in the sum in exactly the same location as in the numbers added. This is a case where neatness counts.

For example, add 3.236, 0.75, and 107.205. Arrange as:

    3.236
    0.750—Adding zero
 107.205   to right

Adding gives 111.191

This is read as "one hundred eleven and one hundred ninety-one thousandths."

Subtraction

As with addition, arrange the decimal numbers with the decimal points directly underneath each other. Subtract as with whole numbers, and place the decimal point directly under those of the listed numbers.

For example, subtract 0.9 from 2.356. Arrange as:

         2.356
Subtracting −0.900—Add 2 zeros
   gives   1.456   to right

Multiplication

Multiplication of decimal numbers differs from that of whole numbers only in placement of the decimal point in the product. Multiply the numbers. Then place the decimal point as many places to the left of the significant digits as the sum of such places in the numbers multiplied.

For example, multiply 0.9 × 0.3 × 0.5. The digits in the product will be 135. Since there are three places to the right of the decimal point in the numbers multiplied, the answer is pointed off as 0.135. Here the zero to the left of the decimal point has no meaning other than to assure that there is no whole number. The answer is read as "one hundred thirty-five thousandths."

Division

Division of decimal numbers differs from that of whole numbers only in placement of the decimal point in the *quotient* (the number resulting from the division). Consider the problem 7.835 ÷ 0.5 = ? Here 7.835 is the dividend and has three places of decimals to the right of the decimal point. The divisor, 0.5, has one place to the right of the decimal point. In this particular case the dividend has *two more places* of decimals than the divisor. This difference will determine the placement of the decimal point in the quotient. Dividing gives the digits 1567, the quotient, which is pointed off *two places* as 15.67, read as "fifteen and sixty-seven hundredths".

Changing Fractions to Decimals

A common fraction, such as 1/8, is an instruction to perform an operation. It says "divide 1 by 8". Doing this operation, as shown, converts it to a decimal number.

Set down and divide:

```
     0.125
    _____
8 ) 1.000
    8
    __
     20
     16
     __
     40
     40
     __
```

The quotient, 0.125 (read as one hundred twenty-five thousandths), is the conversion. Similarly, 3/8 is an instruction to divide 3 by 8:

```
     0.375
    _____
8 ) 3.000
    2 4
    ___
     60
     56
     __
     40
     40
     __
```

Thus, 3/8 = 0.375 (three hundred seventy-five thousandths).

Conversions of this type are required so frequently that tables such as the one shown in Table 1 have been compiled for quick reference.

TABLE 1 DECIMAL EQUIVALENTS OF COMMON FRACTIONS OF AN INCH

Common Fractions	Decimal Equivalents	Common Fractions	Decimal Equivalents	Common Fractions	Decimal Equivalents	Common Fractions	Decimal Equivalents
1/64	.015625	17/64	.265625	33/64	.515625	49/64	.765625
1/32	.03125	9/32	.28125	17/32	.53125	25/32	.78125
3/64	.046875	19/64	.296875	35/64	.546875	51/64	.796875
1/16	.0625	5/16	.3125	9/16	.5625	13/16	.8125
5/64	.078125	21/64	.328125	37/64	.578125	53/64	.828125
3/32	.09375	11/32	.34375	19/32	.59375	27/32	.84375
7/64	.109375	23/64	.359375	39/64	.609375	55/64	.859375
1/8	.125	3/8	.375	5/8	.625	7/8	.875
9/64	.140625	25/64	.390625	41/64	.640625	57/64	.890625
5/32	.15625	13/32	.40625	21/32	.65625	29/32	.90625
11/64	.171875	27/64	.421875	43/64	.671875	59/64	.921875
3/16	.1875	7/16	.4375	11/16	.6875	15/16	.9375
13/64	.203125	29/64	.453125	45/64	.703125	61/64	.953125
7/32	.21875	15/32	.46875	23/32	.71875	31/32	.96875
15/64	.234375	31/64	.484375	47/64	.734375	63/64	.984375
1/4	.25	1/2	.50	3/4	.75		

Math for the Mason

Not all conversions are as neat as the ones illustrated. For instance, $1/12 = 0.083333333333333\ldots$ (approx.) As many significant figures are retained in the conversion as practicality requires. For most applications 0.083 would be acceptable.

Changing Decimals to Fractions

Translate the decimal number to fractional form, then reduce this fraction to its simplest form by dividing both numerator and denominator by the same number. For example, $0.84 = 84/100$. This can be reduced to $42/50$ (dividing by 2), and again to $21/25$. No number can evenly divide both 21 and 25, so $21/25$ is the simplest form and the fractional conversion.

Metric-to-English and English-to-Metric Conversions

Rapid expansion of trade and industry on an international basis in the past two decades has increased the need for understanding of both the *metric* or CGS (Centimeter-Gram-Second) system used by nearly all countries of the world and the *English* or FPS (Foot-Pound-Second) system used by the United States and some other English-speaking countries.

If the co-existence of two systems seems inconvenient, as it is, remember that in respect to worldwide agreement we are the exception. In view of the increasing need for a universal system to measure lengths, areas, volumes, weights, temperatures, etc., it now seems likely that the CGS system will ultimately replace the FPS system despite immense costs and problems that will be involved in making the changeover.

Table 2 lists factors for converting units from metric to English, while Table 3 lists factors for converting from English to metric units.

To convert a quantity from *metric* to *English* units:

1. Multiply by the factor shown in Table 2.
2. Use the resulting quantity "rounded off" to the number of decimal digits needed for practical application.
3. Wherever practical in semiprecision measurements, convert the decimal part of the number to the nearest common fraction.

207

Concrete Block Construction

TABLE 2 CONVERSION OF METRIC TO ENGLISH UNITS

LENGTHS:		WEIGHTS:	
1 MILLIMETER (MM)	= 0.03937 IN.	1 GRAM (G)	= 0.03527 OZ (AVDP)
1 CENTIMETER (CM)	= 0.3937 IN.	1 KILOGRAM (KG)	= 2.205 LBS
1 METER (M)	= 3.281 FT OR 1.0937 YDS	1 METRIC TON	= 2205 LBS
1 KILOMETER (KM)	= 0.6214 MILES	LIQUID MEASUREMENTS:	
AREAS:		1 CU CENTIMETER (CC)	= 0.06102 CU IN.
1 SQ MILLIMETER	= 0.00155 SQ IN.	1 LITER (= 1000 CC)	= 1.057 QUARTS OR 2.113 PINTS OR 61.02 CU INS.
1 SQ CENTIMETER	= 0.155 SQ IN.	POWER MEASUREMENTS:	
1 SQ METER	= 10.76 SQ FT OR 1.196 SQ YDS	1 KILOWATT (KW)	= 1.341 HORSEPOWER
VOLUMES:		TEMPERATURE MEASUREMENTS:	
1 CU CENTIMETER	= 0.06102 CU IN.	TO CONVERT DEGREES CENTIGRADE TO DEGREES FARENHEIT, USE THE FOLLOWING FORMULA: DEG F = (DEG C X 9/5) + 32	
1 CU METER	= 35.31 CU FT OR 1.308 CU YDS		

SOME IMPORTANT FEATURES OF THE CGS SYSTEM ARE:
1 CC OF PURE WATER = 1 GRAM. PURE WATER FREEZES AT 0 DEGREES C AND BOILS AT 100 DEGREES C.

TABLE 3 CONVERSION OF ENGLISH TO METRIC UNITS

LENGTHS:		WEIGHTS:	
1 INCH	= 2.540 CENTIMETERS	1 OUNCE (AVDP)	= 28.35 GRAMS
1 FOOT	= 30.48 CENTIMETERS	1 POUND	= 453.6 GRAMS OR 0.4536 KILOGRAM
1 YARD	= 91.44 CENTIMETERS OR 0.9144 METERS	1 (SHORT) TON	= 907.2 KILOGRAMS
1 MILE	= 1.609 KILOMETERS	LIQUID MEASUREMENTS:	
AREAS:		1 (FLUID) OUNCE	= 0.02957 LITER OR 28.35 GRAMS
1 SQ IN.	= 6.452 SQ CENTIMETERS	1 PINT	= 473.2 CU CENTIMETERS
1 SQ FT	= 929.0 SQ CENTIMETERS OR 0.0929 SQ METER	1 QUART	= 0.9463 LITER
1 SQ YD	= 0.8361 SQ METER	1 (US) GALLON	= 3785 CU CENTIMETERS OR 3.785 LITERS
VOLUMES:		POWER MEASUREMENTS:	
1 CU IN.	= 16.39 CU CENTIMETERS	1 HORSEPOWER	= 0.7457 KILOWATT
1 CU FT	= 0.02832 CU METER	TEMPERATURE MEASUREMENTS:	
1 CU YD	= 0.7646 CU METER	TO CONVERT DEGREES FARENHEIT TO DEGREES CENTIGRADE, USE THE FOLLOWING FORMULA: DEG C = (DEG F X 5/9) -32	

To convert a quantity from *English* to *metric* units:

1. If the English measurement is expressed in fractional form, change this to an equivalent decimal form.

2. Multiply this quantity by the factor shown in Table 3.
3. Round off the result to the precision required.

Relatively small measurements, such as 17.3 cm, are generally expressed in equivalent millimeter form. In this example the measurement would be read as 173 mm.

Elementary Geometry

Much of the study of geometry from an academic standpoint has to do with theorems and proofs. From a trade standpoint, however, the properties of lines, figures, etc., are of greater concern.

Lines

The *horizontal line* is a level line. It is the opposite of a vertical line. (Fig. 1.)

A *perpendicular line* is a line at right angles to another line. (Fig. 1.)

A *level line* and a *plumb line* produce a square and are perpendicular to each other. (Fig. 1.)

The *diagonal line* is one joining two opposite angles. (Fig. 1.)

Parallel lines are those having the same direction and are an equal distance from each other at all points. (Fig. 1.)

The Circle

The *circle* is drawn from the center and is a continuous curved line, being of an equal distance from the center at all points. (Fig. 2.)

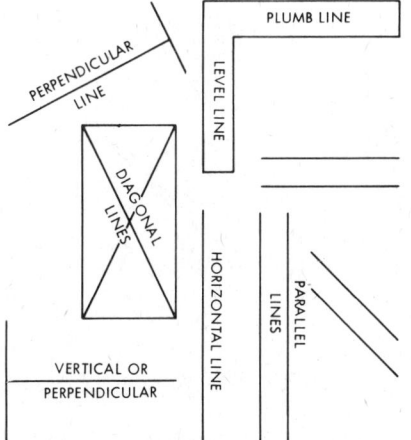

Fig. 1. Straight lines that differ because of their placement.

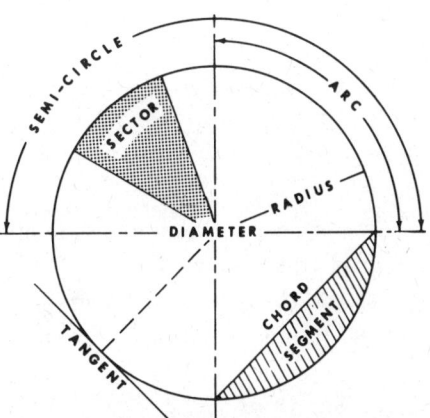

Fig. 2. A circle and its parts.

Concrete Block Construction

An *arc* of a circle is any part of its circumference. (Fig. 2.)

The *chord* is a straight line joining two points of the circumference. (Fig. 2.)

The *semi-circle* is one-half of the complete circle. (Fig. 2.)

The *circumference* is the entire distance around the circle.

The *diameter* is the distance across the circle through the center. (Fig. 2.)

The *radius* is half the diameter or the distance from the center to any point of the circumference. (Fig. 2.)

A *sector* is a portion of a circle between two radii and the circumference. (Fig. 2.)

A *segment* is a portion of a circle contained by a straight line and the circumference which it cuts off. (Fig. 2.)

The *tangent* is a straight line which touches a circle or curve but does not cut it and is at right angle to a straight line from the center. (Fig. 2.)

Circle Measurements

Circumference of a circle equals diameter × 3.1416. (3.1416 = Pi or the Greek letter π.)

Area of a circle equals diameter squared (dia.²) × .7854.

Length of arc equals degrees in arc × radius × .01745. *Example:* 45° × 4' radius = 180 × .01745 = 3.141' length of arc.

Degree of arc equals length/radius × .01745. *Example:* 4' radius × .01745 = .0698, 3.141' length ÷ .0698 = 45°.

Radius of arc equals length/degrees × .01745. *Example:* 45° × .01745 = .78525, 3.141' length ÷ .78525 = 4' radius.

To find the *area of a sector* of a circle: 3.1416 × radius squared × degrees of the sector ÷ 360.

To find the *area of a segment* of a circle: Find area of sector and subtract area of included triangle. Fig. 3 illustrates both sector and segment of the circle.

Spherical Measurements

Surface area equals diameter squared × 3.1416. *Example:* dia. 4' sq. = 16' × 3.1416 = 50.26 sq. ft. surface area.

Volume equals diameter cubed × .5236. *Example:* dia. 4' cubed = 64 cu. ft. × .5236 = 33.5104 cu. ft.

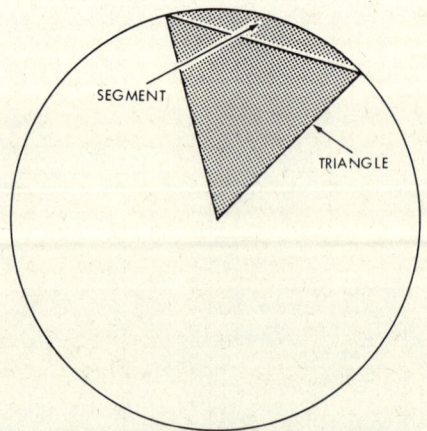

Fig. 3. Area of segment found by subtracting area of triangle from area of sector.

Math for the Mason

Elliptical Measurements

Elliptical *surface area* equals width × height × .7854. *Example:* width 36″ × height 24″ = 864 sq. in. × .7854 = 678.59 sq. in. area.

Triangular Measurements

When two *angles* of a triangle are known, the third can be found by subtracting the sum of the two known angles from 180°. (The sum of the angles of a triangle equals 180°.)

The square of the *hypotenuse* (longest side) of a right triangle is equal to the sum of the squares of the other two sides.

Area of a triangle equals ½ height × base.

Pyramid Measurements

Area equals ½ perimeter of base × slant height + area of base.

Volume equals area of base × ⅓ height or altitude.

Trapezoid Measurements

Area equals height × ½ the sum of its parallel sides.

Rectangular Measurements

Volume = width × length × height. For volume in gallons, divide cubic content *in inches* by 231; for cubic content *in feet* divide by 7.48.

Measurements of Regular Polygons

Regular polygons, also called equi-

TABLE 4 REGULAR POLYGONS: NAME, AREA AND RADIUS OF INCLOSING CIRCLE

NAME OF FIGURE	NUMBER OF SIDES	AREA EQUALS:	RADIUS OF CIRCLE EQUALS:
EQUILATERAL TRIANGLE	3	0.433 X 1 SIDE SQUARED	0.577 X LENGTH OF 1 SIDE
SQUARE	4	1.000 X 1 SIDE SQUARED	0.707 X LENGTH OF 1 SIDE
PENTAGON	5	1.720 X 1 SIDE SQUARED	0.851 X LENGTH OF 1 SIDE
HEXAGON	6	2.598 X 1 SIDE SQUARED	1.000 X LENGTH OF 1 SIDE
HEPTAGON	7	3.634 X 1 SIDE SQUARED	1.152 X LENGTH OF 1 SIDE
OCTAGON	8	4.828 X 1 SIDE SQUARED	1.307 X LENGTH OF 1 SIDE
NONAGON	9	6.182 X 1 SIDE SQUARED	1.462 X LENGTH OF 1 SIDE
DECAGON	10	7.694 X 1 SIDE SQUARED	1.618 X LENGTH OF 1 SIDE
UNDECAGON	11	9.365 X 1 SIDE SQUARED	1.775 X LENGTH OF 1 SIDE
DODECAGON	12	11.196 X 1 SIDE SQUARED	1.932 X LENGTH OF 1 SIDE

lateral polygons, are those having equal sides. All can be inscribed in circles so that all vertices (corners) exactly touch the circle's circumference. It follows that all angles of a regular polygon as well as its sides are equal.

Table 4 lists the more common regular polygons and formulas for calculating their areas.

Estimating Areas, Volumes, and Materials

The most common practical application of the preceding basic math rules is in estimating the amount of materials needed for a given job. Most job estimating is done by professional estimators who are experts in several areas, such as time-labor cost, hardware costs, waste allowances, etc. However, a few examples will indicate to the mason how the estimator arrives at the amount of materials needed for a particular job.

For instance, in estimating for a block wall, the estimator will study the house plans (working drawings) to determine the *dimensions* (length and height) of the wall. By multiplying the length by the height, he finds the total *area* of the wall. He then calculates the area of openings for doors, windows, etc. and subtracts it from the total area, which gives him the actual area to be laid in block.

The standard manufactured concrete block for modular construction is a block $7\frac{5}{8}'' \times 7\frac{5}{8}'' \times 15\frac{5}{8}''$—a size deliberately chosen to allow for $\frac{3}{8}''$ joints between blocks. For practical purposes the blocks can be calculated as $8'' \times 8'' \times 16''$, which can be simplified to $\frac{3}{4}' \times \frac{3}{4}' \times \frac{4}{3}'$. One *course*, in masonry terms, means a single row of blocks. The number of courses used to build a wall will depend on the height. Disregarding openings, calculations are very simple.

First consider the length of the wall.

$N = L \times \frac{3}{4}$, where:

N = number of blocks for 1 course
L = length of wall in feet

Example: How many blocks will be required for 1 course if the wall required is 36' in length?

$N = 36' \times \frac{3}{4} = 27$. This is 27 blocks.

Next consider the height of the wall.

$C = H \times \frac{4}{3}$, where:

C = number of courses for height
H = height of wall in feet.

Example: The same wall (36' in length) is 12' in height.

$N = 12 \times \frac{4}{3} = 16$. This is 16 courses.

The total number of blocks required, is the number of blocks per

Math for the Mason

course times the number of courses, that is:

$T = N \times C$, where:
$T =$ total number of block for all courses
$T = 27 \times 16 = 432$ blocks.

In estimating the amount of concrete required for footings and foundations, the estimator, again working from the house plans, takes the vertical surface area (length × height) of each part of the footing or foundation and multiplies it by its horizontal thickness. This gives the estimator the *volume* of the part. If the thickness is less than a foot, it is multiplied as either a fraction of a foot or as its decimal equivalent. If, for instance, the foundation is to be 6″ thick, the thickness would be either ½′ or 0.5′. The total volume for the complete foundation is determined by adding the volumes of all the parts.

Dimensions in working drawings are given in feet and inches. Thus, at this point, the estimator has the volume in cubic feet. As concrete is usually ordered by the cubic yard, he divides the number of cubic feet by 27, which gives him the number of cubic yards to order.

In estimating for concrete flatwork, the estimator determines the area of the slab by multiplying the length by the width. He then multiplies the area by the thickness in order to determine the volume. If the result is in cubic feet, he again divides by 27 to determine the required number of cubic yards.

Appendix

B | Constructions with Concrete Block

The following illustrations have been included to suggest the sort of constructions which could be built quite easily with concrete blocks. Blueprints and specifications have not been given, since the purpose of these illustrations aims more to encourage the attempts of the builder and to suggest the sort of work he could do, than to provide him with a set of particular and measured diagrams. Guidance on the principles of construction has been amply explained in the preceding chapters of this book, and constant reference to the text should eliminate any of the errors due to your inexperience.

A few brief and explanatory comments have been added to the illustrations for the sake of the novice, but fuller plans and details could be obtained, if necessary, from the local block dealer.

The cheapness and simplicity of construction with concrete blocks has been repeated once or twice to reassure the hesitant layman that the projects illustrated are not so difficult as they might appear. Careful planning and a cautious following of the principles of construction will prove to the builder, quite forcefully, how durable and worthwhile his efforts can be.

Constructions with Concrete Block

Patios and Terraces

Concrete blocks and other masonry units can be used very simply and inexpensively in the laying out of patios, garden terraces, or play areas. The varieties of pattern and design offered by these blocks can be judged from the illustrations on pages 139 to 148 and from Figs. 1 and 2.

Laying the Blocks

Patio blocks sized 15⅝″ × 7⅝″ × 2¼″ are recommended for use in laying flooring. Thicker or thinner blocks may be preferred though for their appearance or for their color. If a strong and even surface is required, the blocks may be embedded in mortar, but the more

Fig. 1. Garden patio with planter boxes, flooring and wall constructed with varying sizes of masonry blocks.

Concrete Block Construction

popular and simple method is to base them on builder's sand. There should be no trouble in the latter case if the sand is levelled smoothly and if the blocks are packed tightly on top of it.

The boundaries of the patio should first be marked with stakes and string, and the soil excavated to a depth sufficient to hold both the 2" of sand and the blocks on top. After providing for a drainage slope, the soil should be graded and the layer of sand added. A perimeter stepping stone or patio block should be entrenched between the string-joined stakes, though wooden slats could be similarly used. (Redwood is recommended for its resistance to rotting.) Then the blocks may be laid out. Previous planning of the design on paper will save a great deal of time, and working with the blocks from the corners into the middle will ensure a tighter fit. Any error in the block's height may be corrected by scooping out or sprinkling in more sand with a trowel. Attention must be paid constantly to the straight alignment of the course. A final sweeping of sand over the fitted blocks will fill any cracks, and the surplus may be cleaned away afterwards with a hose.

Fig. 2. Patio, walls and pool constructed with concrete block.

Constructions with Concrete Block

Barbecue Fireplace Unit

The location of the fireplace should be planned with careful reference to the position of work and play areas, and for possible shelter from the weather. A patio or garden terrace would certainly provide the most appropriate setting.

The base should first be marked out, to the size desired, with stakes and string. In Fig. 3 the economical size of 70" × 33" has been measured for the base, with a projection 17" deep and 21" wide. A footing should be made by removing sod and digging to a depth below the frost level (which can be ascertained locally from the block dealer.) A sub-base of mixed sand and gravel must be firmly tamped and levelled at about 6" below the top of form. This should be covered with a layer of several inches of mixed concrete, and topped with a heavy wire fencing or other reinforcement. A smooth surface level of concrete can then fill the top of form and it should be allowed to cure under the cover of a wet burlap for two or three days.

Seven 17" × 21" chimney blocks will be required, including the base joint. The six center blocks should

Fig. 3. A simple, economical barbeque fireplace.

Concrete Block Construction

be laid on their sides, and flanked by two more courses of blocks at each side (with alternated vertical joints). A maximum width of 19" should be maintained in the center section. A smoke inlet of 5" square may be cut with hammer and cold chisel into the chimney blocks, and it should open into the flue close under the top of the metal fireplace unit.

Concrete caps for the fireplace may be cast in wooden forms at the same time that the footing is placed.

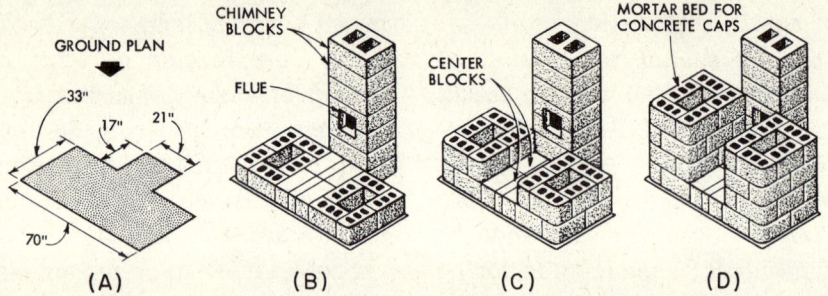

Fig. 4 . Successive stages in construction of the barbecue fireplace.

Fig. 5. An open hearth and barbecue fireplace flanked by a concrete block retaining wall and patio paved with concrete blocks.

Constructions with Concrete Block

They should be set in a firm bed of mortar after the metal fireplace unit has been installed. In Fig. 4 they have been measured at 1″ × 25″ × 32½″. The other 36 corner and bull nose blocks measured 8″ × 8″ × 16″.

Fig. 5 illustrates a barbecue fireplace, patio, and retaining wall, all constructed with concrete block.

Garden Walls and Walks

Concrete masonry can be used in a vast variety of ways in the landscaping of grounds and gardens. Lawns may be separated into terraces at different levels by the construction of retaining walls, and a flight of steps could be added for greater dignity. The ornamental designs effected with geometric or wandering paths could easily remodel the appearance of a garden, and shallow pools or raised flower boxes could decorate the less attractive corners. The varieties of design possible, either with wall and box structures or with concrete walls, allow for considerable improvisations and experiment. See Figs. 6, 7, 8 and 9.

Reference should be made to the

Fig. 6. Descending path constructed of concrete blocks.

Concrete Block Construction

Fig. 7. An attractive garden wall constructed of split block and ornamental designs in the balustrade.

Fig. 8. A boundary wall built with concrete blocks.

Fig. 9. A patio wall which provides privacy as well as sunlight.

Constructions with Concrete Block

diagrams and principles of waterproofing on pages 188 to 190 when the retaining or terrace walls are being built. Foundations can be seriously affected by excessive dampness, and provisions for drainage must be planned carefully if undermining is to be avoided. The construction of concrete paths should present few problems, since they can be laid out like the patio blocks.

The use of vitrified blocks in the design of planter boxes and terrace steps will lend a note of color which could be blended aptly to the setting in which they are placed. In this way, the house, its patio, and its garden can be harmonized into one landscape.

Garages and Carports

Many features may be incorporated in the design of a fairly inexpensive garage. Apart from protecting the cars from the effects of snow and rain, or from the sun, shelter can also be provided for garden implements and sports equipment. The accommodation of a work-bench and tool-rack could be arranged quite simply, and storage closets might be fitted as well.

The appearance of the garage should be planned to blend with the garden or house to which it belongs.

Fig. 10. A single car garage with a concrete block patio.

Concrete Block Construction

Fig. 11. A simple carport attached to the side of a house.

An adequate driveway must be laid out for a two-car garage, and overhead doors should be installed if the entrance space is cramped. Concrete footings will be needed for the garage walls to gain a wider bearing area of soil and to prevent settling. Stucco or concrete masonry will look quite decorative for the garage walls, and a gabled roof might add to the attraction of the garage's setting. Fig. 10 shows one of several possible designs for a concrete block garage.

The carport could accommodate nearly as many features as the garage and at a much lower cost. Built against the side of a house, it could afford spacious room for these other items or for more than one car. The overhanging roof may be raked at any angle, or might even be flat. Fig. 11 shows a typical carport.

Interior Fireplaces

An attractive fireplace can be built into the interior of a bungalow very simply and inexpensively. The position of the chimney stack must be determined in relation to the rafters and supports of the roof. Thought must also be given to the heating requirements and the drafts of the room in which the fire is placed. Nearly all possibility of danger will be removed by using fire-treated masonry, and additional blocks may be added to a large open hearth in which logs are burned. The hearth, in all cases, must be lined with firebrick wherever it is exposed to an open flame.

Index

Numerals in **bold type** refer to illustrations.

A

Accelerants, 44, 45
Admixtures,
    concrete, 66
    mortar, 44
Aggregate, concrete, 52-57, **52, 54, 56**
Aggregate, concrete block, 134
Aggregate, mortar, 41-44, 43
Aggregate proportions for concrete, 59, 60
Air entraining cement, 39
Air entrainment, concrete, 65
American Society for Testing and Materials (ASTM), 39
Anchor bolts, 128, **128**
Anti-freeze admixtures,
Apprentice, 1-7
Apprenticeship standards, 7, **8,** 9
Architect, 6
Ashlar masonry, **188, 189**
Asphaltum, 188, 189,
Asphaltum board, 91
Autoclaves, 135, 136, **136**

B

Backing, concrete block, 159, 160, **160**

Bars, steel reinforcing, 161-166, **163-165**
Beam block, **140,** 141
Beam support, 168-170, **169, 170**
Bearing, joist, 166-168, **167**
Block classification, 137, 138
Block planning, 150-153, **152**
Block sizes, actual and nominal, 140, **141**
Blueprints and specifications, 9-11, **10**
Bolts, anchor, 128, **128**
Bond stone, 191, **191**
Brick and block wall, 159, 160
Building enclosure, 25, 26, 27
Built-in-place formwork, 74-79, **75**
Built-up scaffolds, 20, **23, 24**
Bulking in sand, 60
Bullnose block, 139, **140**

C

Calcium chloride, 66
Cavity walls, 160-163, **162-164**
Cement
    damaged, 58
    distribution, 58

paste, 51
    storage, 58
Chemicals, safety
    practices, 20
Chimneys, 184-186, **185**
Circle measurements, 210, **210**
Classification, block units, 137, 138
Clothing, safety factors, 17
Coarse aggregate for concrete, 54-56, **56**
Cold weather practices,
Colorimetric test, 42, **42**
Columns, footing for, 105-110, **105, 106, 108, 109**
Compacting concrete, 88, **88**
Composite Walls, 159, 160, **160**
Concrete, materials and mixing, 51-69
    admixtures, 66
    aggregate proportions, 59
    aggregates, 52
    air entrainment, 65
    blast furnace slag, 56
    bulking in sand, 60
    cement, 57
    cement distribution, 58
    cement storage, 58
    coarse aggregate for concrete, 56
    coarse aggregates, 52, 54

223

correcting trial mixture, 64
crushed stone, 54
damaged cement, 58
fine aggregate for concrete, 54
fine aggregates, 52
fine and coarse aggregates, **52**
grading, aggregates, 53
grading gravel, 55
gravel, 55
hand mixing, 68
job site mixing, 67, **67**
lightweight aggregates, 57
moisture in sand, 60, **60**
proportioning concrete mixtures, 58
ready mixed concrete, 66, **67**
rubble, 56
slump, 61
trial proportions, 62
water, 57
water-cement ratio, 59
Concrete block
  dimensions, **140,** 141, 149, **149**
  grades, 137, 138
  hollow load-bearing, 138, 149, 150, **149**
  manufacture, 134-137, **136, 137**
  materials for, 134
  painting, 193-195
  sizes and shapes, 139-142, 140
  special, 142-148, **142-148**
  three-cored, 149, **149**
  two-cored, 149, **149**
  types (ASTM), 137, 138
  unit classification (ASTM), 137, 138
Concrete block

construction
  beam support, 168-170, **169, 170**
  block planning, 150-153, **152**
  bond beams, **165**
  brick and block walls, 159, 160, **160**
  cavity walls, 160, 161, **162**
  chimneys, 184-186, **185**
  concrete floor support, 171, **171**
  control joints, 173-176, **173-175**
  cornice details, 186-188, **187**
  details, 159-188
  duct details, **187,** 188
  joint finishing, 158, 159, **158, 159**
  joist floors, 171-173, **172**
  joist support, 166-168, **167**
  laying a concrete block wall, 150-159, **152-159**
  layout, 153, **153**
  lintels, **165,** 179, **180,** 180
  pilasters and columns, 168, **169**
  preparation of materials, 150
  steel bar reinforcing, 101-106, **163-165**
  wall intersections, 176, 177, **176**
  waterproofing foundations, 188-190, **188-190**
Concrete bricks, 138, **140**
Concrete chimney footings, 110, **110**
Concrete column footings, 105-109, **105, 106, 108, 109**

Concrete floor support, 171-173, **171, 172**
Concrete formwork, 71-93
  anchor bolts in concrete foundation, 89, **89**
  basic formwork, 71
  building forms for low walls, 79
  built-in-place forming, 75, **75**
  compacting concrete, 88, **88**
  concrete as a material, 71
  concrete foundation forming systems, 74
  concrete steps and platform, 84, **86**
  concrete walls, 89
  excavation for basement, 71
  float finishing, 89, **89**
  footings used in warm climates, 92, **93**
  forming for foundation, **72,** 73
  forms for footings, 73, **73**
  forms for low walls, 80, **81**
  forms for steps, 81
  form ties, 79
  formwork for basement steps, 84, **85**
  foundations for homes with slab-at-grade, 91, **91**
  grade beam and pier construction, 92, **93**
  manufactured panels, **78,** 79
  panel forms used with "T" footing, 80, **82**
  patented form ties and holders, **78,** 79
  perimeter support, 92, **92**

Index

pre-installed door frame, 81, **83**
reinforcing steel for a concrete column, 87, **87**
removal of forms, 90
rough buck, 81, **84**
rough form for metal framed basement window, 81, **83**
sectional view through formwork, 75, **76**
sectional view through foundation form, 80, **82**
self-supporting steps, 84, **86**
snap ties, 79, **80**
starter wall forms, 73, **74**
steel reinforcement, 87
steel reinforcing in concrete footing, 87, **87**
steps for changes in elevation of sidewalks, 84, **85**
"T" type footing, 73
wire ties, 79, **79**
Concrete foundation footings, 100-103, **100-102**
Concrete foundation forming systems, 74
Concrete foundations, 121-131, **121-124, 131**
Concrete masonry, defined, 133
Concrete pilaster footings, 111, **111**
Concrete pilasters, 125, **125**
Concrete porch and stair footings, 111, **112**, 113
Concrete steps and platform, 84, **86**
Concrete walls, 89
Construction details, 159-188
beam supports, 168, 170, **170**
brick and block walls, 159, **160**
cavity walls, 160-164, **162, 163**
concrete block wall intersections, 176, **176**
concrete floor support, 171-173, **171, 172**
control joints, 173-176, **173-175**
cornice details, 186, 187, **187**
door details, 180, 183, 184, **183, 184**
duct details, **187**, 188
joist support, 166, **167**, 168
laying concrete block chimneys, 184-186, **185**
pilasters and columns, 168, **169**
steel bar reinforcing, 164-168, **164, 166, 167**
wall details, 159
window opening details, 177-183, **178, 179, 182, 183**
Construction Specifications Institute (CSI) Format, 11
Curing, concrete block, 135, 136, **136**

D

Damaged cement, 58
Decimals, 204-207
Decimals, changing to fractions, 207
Deformed steel bars,
Department of labor, 7
Dimensions, concrete block, **140,** 141, 149, **149**
Doors in concrete block wall, 180-184, **183,** 184
Double corner or pier block, 139
Double pole wood scaffold, 23, **23**
Dry press molding method,
Duct details, 187, 188

E

Electricity, safety practices, 19, 20
Electric saw, 18, **19**
Elementary geometry, 209-211
Elliptical measurements, 211
Enclosure, building, 25, 26, **27**
English to metric conversions, 208, 209
Epoxy mortar, 198, 199, **199**
Estimating, 2, 5
Estimating areas, volumes and materials, 212, 213
Estimator, 2
Excavation for basement, 71
Extruded mortar, 147, **148**

F

Face or glazed block, 142, **143**
Fine aggregate, concrete, 53

225

Fine aggregate, mortar, 52-54, **54**
Fire cut, 166, 167, **167**
First aid, 15-17
Float finishing foundation, 89, **89**
Floor block, **129**, 130
Flue linings, 185, 186, **185**
Footings, design and construction, 95-114
  chimney, 110, **110**
  column, 105-110, **105, 106, 108, 109**
  foundation, 100-105, **100-103**
  pilaster, 111, **111**
  porch and stair, 111-113, **112**
  reinforced, 113, 114, **113**
Foreman, 2
Formwork, concrete, 70-94
  footing, 73, 74, **72, 73**
  foundation, 74-79, **75-79**
  low walls, 79, 80, **81**
  placing reinforcement, 87, **87**
  steps, 81, 85, **85,** 86
  ties, 79
  wall openings, 80, 81, **83, 84**
Foundations, design and construction, 115-132
  concrete, 121-125, 130, **121-124**
  concrete block, 125-129, 130, 131, **127-129**
  pilasters in, 125, **125,** 129, **129**
  formwork, 74-79, **75-79**
Fractions, 202-207
  changing to decimals, 206

G

Geometry, elementary, 209-211

Glazed block, 142, 143
Grade beam and pier construction, 92, **93**
Grading aggregate
  crushed stone, 55
  gravel, 55
  sand, 43, 53
Gravel, grading, 55

H

Hanging and swing stage scaffolds, 21, 24
Head joints, buttering,
Header block, 139, **142**
High early strength cement, 39
Hollow load bearing block, 138
Housekeeping, 28
Hydrated lime, 41
Hydration, 38

I

Indenture, 1, 2, **4, 5**
Insurance, 5, 6
Intersections, block walls, 176, 177, **176**

J

Jamb blocks, 139, **140,** 174, **175**
Joint Apprenticeship Committee, 2, 7, 8, 9
Joint finishing, 158, 159, **158, 159**
Jointers, 29, 30, **30**
Joints
  bed, 153, **153**
  closure, 157, **158**
  concave, 158, **158**
  control, 173-176, **173-175**
  head, 153, **154**
  thickness, 151, 152

V tooled, 158, **158**
Joist support, 166, **167,** 168
Journeyman, 2

K

Keys in footings, 73, 74, **74**

L

Labor, Department of, 7
Layout, concrete block, 153-159, **153-159**
Levels, 31, **31**
Lien laws, 5
Lightweight aggregate, 134
Lime, 39-41
Line, mason's, 31, 32, **32**
Lintel block, 140, **141**
Lintels, **165,** 179, 180, **180**
Lug sill, 179

M

Maintenance, concrete block, 193
Masonry, structure of the trade, 1-24
Metal sash block, 141
Metal scaffolds, 25, **25**
Metal ties, 161, **162**
Metric to English conversions, 207
Mineral oxide pigments, 190
Moisture in sand, 60, **60**
Mortar, 36-50
  admixtures, 44, 45
  colors, 45
  durability, 45, 46
  ingredients, 36-45
  lime for, 39-41
  measurements, 48
  mixing, 48, 49

strength, 45, 46
water for, 44
water rentivity, 46
workability, 46
Mortar, extruded, 147, **148**
Mortar joints, 151, 152, 158, **158**
Mortar types, 45, 46

N

Nominal dimensions, concrete block, **140**, 141, 149, **149**
Normal weight aggregate, 134

O

Organic matter in sand, 41, 42

P

Painting concrete block, 193-195
Panels, prefabricated concrete block, 196-201, **197-201**
Panel foundation forms, 77, **77**
Pier block, 139, **140**
Pigments, mineral oxide, 190
Pilasters and columns, 168, **169**
Plinth, concrete, 105, 106, **106**
Plumb rule, 31, **31**
Portland cement
  history of, 36, 37
  ingredients of, 37, 38
  types for concrete, 57, 58
  types for mortar, 39
Power saws, 18, **19**
Power tools and

equipment, 33, 34, **34**
Prefabricated concrete block panels, 196-201, **197-201**
Proportioning concrete mixtures, 58

Q

Quicklime, 41
Quoins, 193, **193**

R

Random rubble masonry, 191, **191**
Ready mixed concrete, 66, 67
Reinforcing steel bars, block walls, 161-166, **163-165**
  concrete footings,
Reinforcement, horizontal, 162, 163, **162, 163**
Retardants, 44, 45
Rotary kilns, **40**
Rough buck, 81, **84**
Rubble concrete, 55
Rubble stone masonry
  coursed, 191, **191**
  random, 191, **191**
Rules, measuring, 33

S

Safety, 13-28
  building enclosure, 25, 27
  chemicals, 20
  clothing, 17
  electricity, 19, 20
  scaffolds, 20-25, **21, 23-25**
  tools and equipment, 17-19, **18, 19**
Salamanders, 25

Sand
  cleanness of, 41
  grading, 43, 44, **43**
  organic matter in, 41, 42
  sieve analysis, 44
  silt content, 41, 42
Sash windows, metal, 180, **182**
Sash windows, wood, **183**
Scaffolds, 20-25
  built-up scaffolds, 20
  double pole wood scaffold, 23
  hanging and swing stage scaffolds, 24
  hanging scaffolds, 21
  heavy trade, double pole scaffold, **24**
  metal frames and diagonal braces, **25**
  rolling scaffolds, 20, 23
  steel scaffolds, 22
  swing stage scaffold, 21, **21**
  trestle scaffolds, 20
  wooden scaffolds, 21
Scored block, 142, **142**
Shadow block, 147, **147**
Shapes and sizes of concrete masonry units, 139-142
  actual and nominal sizes, 140, **141**
  beam or lintel block, 141
  bullnose block, 139
  corner block, 139
  double corner or pier block, 139
  four-inch or six-inch partition block, 141
  header block, 139, **142**
  metal sash block, 141
  solid top block, 139
  stretcher block, 139
  wood sash jamb block, 139

227

Sieve analysis, sand, 44
Sill, lug, 179
Sill, slip, 179, **179**
Silt content in sand, 41, 42
Slab at grade floors, 91-93, **91-93**
Sled runner, **30**
Slip sill, 179, **179**
Slump, 61, **61**
Slump block, 142, **144**
Snap ties, 79, **80**
Sodium hydroxide, 42
Special concrete blocks, 142, 144
  color, 144
  face or glazed block, 142, **143**
  scored block, 142, **142**
  slump block, 142, **144**
  split block, 142, 144, **144**
  textured block, 142, **143**
Specifications, 9-11, **10**
Split block, 142, 144, **144**
Starter wall forms, 73, **74**
Steel bar reinforcing, 164, 166-168, **164-167**
Steel scaffolds, 22
Steel square, 31, **32**

Steps, concrete, 81, 84, 87, **85-87**
Stone masonry, 190-193, **191-193**
Story pole, 155, **160**
Stretcher block, 139
Sulfate attack, 57, 58
Superintendent, 2
Swing stage scaffold, 21, **21**

T

Test, colorimetric, 42, **42**
Test, silt content, 41, 42, **42**
Textured block, 142, **143**
Tools for block masonry, 28-33
Trade unions, 6
Trial proportions for concrete, 62-65
Trowels, 29, **29**
T type footings, 73

U

U.S. Department of Labor, 7

V

V joint, 158, **158**
Vapor barrier, 91, **91**

W

Wales, 76, **78,** 79, **80**
  Wall details, 159-188
Wall intersections, 176, 177, **176**
Wall patterns, 144-148, **144-148**
Water
  for concrete, 57
  for mortar, 44
Water-cement ratio, 59
Water retentivity, 46
Waterproofing concrete block foundations, 188-190, **188-190**
Window details, 177-180, **178, 181-183**
Wire ties, 79, **79**
Wood sash jamb block, 128, 129
Wood scaffolds, 21, **23, 24**
Workability, mortar, 46

Z

Z tie bars, 174, **174**